STUDIES IN
MODERN HEBREW LITERATURE

GENERAL EDITOR
DAVID PATTERSON

ISAAC LAMDAN

ISAAC LAMDAN

*A Study
in Twentieth-Century Hebrew Poetry*

BY LEON I. YUDKIN

EAST AND WEST LIBRARY

CORNELL UNIVERSITY PRESS
ITHACA · NEW YORK

To M.

First published 1971

International Standard Book Number 0–8014–0597–1
Library of Congress Catalog Card Number 72–127781

PRINTED IN GREAT BRITAIN

Contents

PART ONE: LAMDAN AND HIS POETRY

Preface

The aim of this work is to introduce the great twentieth-century Hebrew poet, Isaac Lamdan, to the English reader. Lamdan is a poet insufficiently known even in Israel (except for his MASADA), so the need for such a book is well established. Lamdan offers a single-minded, literary penetration of the great problems that face the modern Jew – problems that he encapsulates brilliantly and profoundly. This volume seeks to understand his work through a close reading of his poetry (some of which is given in literal translation) and through an examination of his poetic technique and the literary sources and influences open to him, both against the backdrop of world events and the literature (Hebrew and European) of the period.

Lamdan's importance lies in his treatment of a single obsession, viz. the dramatic role of the Jew in History and, in particularly intensified form, on the stage of world events in the twentieth century. As an expression of this preoccupation the revival of Jewish nationhood in Israel takes its place at the centre of the stage. The rebirth of Jewish nationalism was, for the poet, a challenge to Fate.

For Lamdan, the myth of the 'chosen' people had a very special meaning. And through his eyes, we can see Jewish existence in another light.

Acknowledgments

IN THE PREPARATION of this monograph, I owe a debt of gratitude:

To Dr Meir Gertner, who was my tutor for two years at the School of Oriental and African Studies, and who first introduced me to the poetry of Isaac Lamdan.

To Mrs A. Lamdan, for her very kind permission to publish a translation of a hitherto unpublished poem (also reproduced here in photostat) and for use of her photograph.

To the Hebrew Writers' Association, for assistance on many points of information.

To Mr Michael Ray, for reading the manuscript, and for his valuable suggestions.

To Mrs J. Slesenger and Mr C. R. Bates for their assistance with the proofs.

To Professor Yigael Yadin, for his permission to use the photograph of Masada.

To my wife, Mickey, for preparing the index.

And to Dr David Patterson, for his encouragement and advice throughout this project.

L.I.J.

LAMDAN AND HIS POETRY

Chapter 1

LIFE AND BACKGROUND

The First World War

THE EVENTS of the First World War brought about the disintegration of European Jewry and the shift of the Jewish centre of gravity from the Russian Empire to Palestine. The great Jewish centres of the Russian Empire, such as Vilna, Odessa, and Warsaw, fell into decline, and soon after the war Russian Jewry ceased to function as a vital organ. In the chaos that followed, the pogroms continued as of old, and the Jews bore the full brunt of the rampaging civil war: 'When Petlura's army [Petlura was commander of the army in the Ukraine, and governor of the country] moved into Kiev for a single day, August 31, 1919, his cossacks found nothing more important to do than cruelly torture and kill thirty young Jews who had been assigned by the municipality to protect the Jewish quarter.'[1] These Jewish centres in the Russian Empire were not only numerically the strongest in the world; they were also the seats of the most vital Jewish creativity of the day, where the Hebrew revival was in progress, and the Zionist movement was at its most powerful. And it was the Russian Empire that provided the main source of strength to the emergent Palestine. One epoch had come to an end, and a new one was beginning. Palestine rose out of the ruins of Eastern Europe, whose population, at this time, was in a frightful state of wretchedness, and deplorably lacking in cohesion.[2]

The war, indeed, had a most deleterious effect on Palestine, and the Jewish population there was drastically reduced by its ravages. The oppressions and persecutions by the Turkish government, together with sickness and famine, reduced the

1. I. Elbogen: *A Century of Jewish Life* (Philadelphia, 1946), p. 498. 2. *Ibid.*, p. 515.

number of the settlers by half. Economic positions tottered, and sometimes completely collapsed.[3] A number of factors combined to produce this severe reduction. Apart from the war itself, the population suffered from the natural phenomena of locusts and famine,[4] as well as from the privations caused by the reactionary Ottoman government until its fall at the end of the war. It was only after the war that Palestine became the object of immigration on a large scale.[5]

The Russian Revolution

The Russian Revolution exerted an enormous influence on European and World History. Under the Bolshevik government, Russia retired from the war, leaving Europe to its own devices, and embarking on the creation of a vast Socialist monolith, marked by a greater uniformity of culture and character than Russia had ever previous known. But the Revolution also had specific relevance for the Jewish population. At first, it seemed that the Revolution was entirely beneficial. For the first time in Russian history, Jews acquired full civil rights[6] in a decree issued by Kerensky's provisional government in March 1917, which annulled all restrictions imposed on any class of Russian citizens on account of their religion or nationality.[7] This unprecedented fortune might have been expected to reduce Zionist ardour, and increase support for the local revolution, which had proved so beneficial. But, in the event, the Zionist movement gained enormous support. The number of enrolled Zionists, previously about 36,000, rose almost immediately after the Revolution to some 140,000.[8] It seemed that Zionism was not merely a negative reaction to the restrictive

3. M. Schmueli: *Ha-ẓiyyonut u-tenuʻat ha-ʻavodah* (Tel-Aviv, 1949), Vol. 2, p. 331.

4. *Ibid.*, pp. 331–55

5. See *The Jews* (ed. Finklestein, Philadelphia, 1949), Vol. 4, Article 'Jewish migrations (1840–1946)',

p. 1198, by Jacob Lestschinsky.

6. Michael T. Florinsky: *Russia: a History and an Interpretation* (New York, 1958), Vol. 2, p. 1392.

7. Leonard Stein: *The Balfour Declaration* (London, 1961), p. 339.

8. *Ibid.*, p. 339.

policy of the Czar, for it flourished even more when the disabilities had been removed. The Zionist leader Chaim Weizmann concluded from this phenomenon that the sufferings of Russian Jewry were not the cause of Zionism, but that the real cause of Zionism was the ineradicable national striving of Jewry to have a home of its own.[9] A number of Jews did, however, choose to support the local revolution, and pledge themselves to the Communist cause. Many clung to Communism as the only way to save themselves from disintegration and complete psychological destruction.[10] Communism appeared to others as a final, apocalyptic solution of the world's problems;[11] it could satisfy a disappointed longing for the Messianic end, with its promise of a perfect future. But it seems that not many Jews were active Bolsheviks, while those who were, were not closely linked with the Jewish masses.[12] Even the Socialist 'Bundists' were Mensheviks.[13] In fact, it was the function of the Jewish section of the Russian Communist Party, the so-called *Yevsektsiya*, to liquidate Jewish institutions and organisations,[14] thus setting itself up against the Jewish population. It also attempted to suppress Zionist activity, branding it both as anti-democratic and as barrenly romantic.[15] And since the *Yevsektsiya* was an official branch of the Communist Party, the militantly anti-Zionist tendency of the Government was reflected in its activities.

Disillusionment with the new regime was not long in

9. Chaim Weizmann: *Trial and Error* (An autobiography—Bristol, 1949), p. 253.

10. Yehiel Halpern: *Ha-mahapekhah ha-yehudit* (Am oved, 1961), Vol. 1, p. 311.

11. This is represented by Isaac Lamdan in the poem *Masada*, pp. 15, 16. See chapter on *Masada* and translation of the speech of the Communist protagonist, in the first chapter of the poem.

12. L. Stein: *op. cit.*, p. 346.

13. *Ibid.*

14. *Standard Jewish Encyclopaedia* (ed. Roth-Jerusalem, 1958): 'It [the Yevsektsia] was responsible for the liquidation of communal organisations and Jewish institutions, boycotting of synagogues, and activities against Hebrew and Judaism'.

15. Joseph Heller: *The Zionist Idea* (London, 1947), p. 65.

coming. The liberal legislation of the provisional Menshevik government was rapidly reversed by the Bolsheviks. The voice of Russian Jewry was soon silenced and the Communists forcibly brought to an end all Zionist activity.[16] Anything tainted with the 'alien' culture of Zionism was banned. As the persecution of Zionism, teaching of Hebrew and the publication of Hebrew books grew more intense, tens of thousands of Zionists were imprisoned and exiled, and at the end even *He-Ḥalutz*[17] and its training activities and the Communist Po'ale Zion party were banned. With this, the gates to the outside world were closed completely. The Russian block was a monolith, and would tolerate no foreign bodies within it; everything had to be absorbed, even if forcibly. Certainly, allegiance to an alien power was to be stamped out. Judaism might be tolerated as a local loyalty, in so far as it was consistent with Russification, but Zionism was to be uprooted. Zionism was considered dangerous because of its international ramifications, so Russian Jewry had to be cut off from World Jewry, and assimilated into the body politic of Russia.[18] Part of this policy was carried out with success, for from the time of the Stalin regime the Jews of Russia played almost no role in the creation of Jewish Palestine, which had become the focus of World Jewry. The seizure of power by the Bolsheviks meant that the Russian Jews were eventually to be sealed off from the rest of the Jewish world, and the Russian Zionists rendered powerless. In other circumstances they would have played an even more important part in building up the Jewish national home.[19]

The Balfour Declaration

Thus far the negative aspects of the radical process of reconstruction expressed by the major part of Jewry early in this

16. L. Hazan, Y. Palar: *Divre yemei ha-ẓiyyonut* (Jerusalem, 1951), p. 185.

17. Training organisation of *ḥalut-* zim led by Trumpeldor. See below.

18. Y. Halpern: *op. cit.*, p. 301.

19. L. Stein: *op. cit.*, p. 348.

century have been discussed. Jewish organisations in the Russian Empire disintegrated during the First World War, and with the triumph of the Bolshevik Revolution, Russian Jewry was cut off from World Jewry, and so rendered irrelevant in the major tides of Jewish history later. These two connected events mark the eclipse of one centre; now, attention must be focused on the new centre, namely, Palestine.

On November 2, 1917, in a letter sent from the Foreign Office to Lord Rothschild, the British Government issued what is known as the Balfour Declaration, saying that: 'His Majesty's Government view with favour the establishment in Palestine of a National Home for the Jewish people, and will use their best endeavours to facilitate the achievement of this object.'[20] At the time of issue, the war was not yet over, and Palestine was still in the hands of the Turks. But Ottoman power was crumbling, and the Entente powers were soon to bring the war to a successful conclusion. Britain and France agreed between themselves that Palestine should come under the protection of Britain in the event of victory.[21] This was facilitated by the retirement of Russia from the war, and the consequent surrender of its claims. The League of Nations later confirmed Britain as the mandatory power, and the 'Balfour Declaration' was embodied in the new constitution. There had been extensive Jewish settlement in Palestine even prior to this time, but it was the Declaration that gave the immigrants a respectable legal status in the country, and allowed them to arrive with the backing of the government. While the first and second waves of immigration or *aliyot* came to Turkish Palestine on sufferance, the third *aliya*, which started soon after the end of the First World War, came by the right granted in an instrument of international law.[22] This distinction between the status of Jews in Palestine after the Declaration and before it was

20. See the Facsimile of the Balfour Declaration at the frontispiece of L. Stein's *The Balfour Declaration*.

21. This agreement discussed by

Leonard Stein: *op. cit.*, pp. 228 and 240–69.

22. Raphael Patai: *Israel between East and West* (Philadelphia, 1955), p. 61.

emphasised by Winston Churchill, as Secretary of State for Colonies, in 1922, in a speech to the House of Commons: 'It is essential that it [the Jewish Community] should know that it is in Palestine as of right and not on sufferance.'[23] The Declaration was the legal embodiment of the transference of the Jewish centre from Eastern Europe to Palestine, and marked the beginning of the growth of that country as a Jewish Commonwealth.

The Third *Aliya*

The third *aliya*[24] refers to the large wave of immigration to Palestine in the four or five years following the First World War. A fourth wave followed in the late twenties, and these two waves together more than trebled the Jewish population of the country.[25] The bulk of the immigration came initially from the Russian Empire, where the war and revolution had the effect that we have seen, and later from Poland. The way was prepared both from without, where Zionist education and aspirations combined with local pressures to encourage the pioneers to leave for Palestine, and from within, when Britain assumed the Palestine Mandate in consequence of the Balfour Declaration.

The immigration began immediately on the conclusion of the war,[26] although the country was not officially open to newcomers until 1920. The material situation was very precarious. There was a lack of food and other necessities, while the institutions of education and health had declined, and could not exist without outside help.[27] Weizmann, who led a committee

23. I. Elbogen: *op. cit.*, pp. 597, 598.
24. *Aliya*—a wave of immigration to Palestine. Lit. 'an ascent', from the Hebrew root *alah*—to go up, ascend. Immigration to Palestine was considered as ascent by Zionists.
25. By 1931 (the end of the fourth

aliya), the Jewish population was about 174,610; see R. Patai, *op. cut.*, p. 61.
26. Alex Bein: *The Return to the Soil* (Trans. Israel Schen, Jerusalem, 1952), p. 233. L. Hazan, Y. Palar: *op. cit.*, p. 197.
27. L. Hazan, Y. Palar: *op. cit.*, p. 190.

of delegates immediately after the war to prepare for the immigration, wrote of the situation: 'But what I saw chiefly was that we had no plan for their reception, because we had no budget'.[28]

This immigration was faced with apparently insurmountable difficulties. The 'fugitives' from Russia of course arrived penniless, save for a small proportion.[29] They had also, in many instances, been victims of pogroms or the violent effects of the war and revolution, and came to the new country in a state of bewilderment, not knowing what to expect from Palestine, or what Palestine expected from them.[30] This immigration had escaped a tragic holocaust: 'The men of the third *aliya*, and particularly those from Russia, brought with them to Palestine the lessons of the pogroms and mass murders perpetuated during the revolutions and the civil war, that ruined the lives of tens of thousands of Jews, and destroyed hundreds of communities. They experienced the preliminary moves in the extermination of European Jewry, and felt that they were really fugitives from terror, and pioneers in the deliverance of the masses of the people.'[31]

The third *aliya* was better organised than the previous waves of immigration, whose members had arrived as individuals.[32] Joseph Trumpeldor[33] had urged that training for the pioneering task in Palestine be undertaken in the country of origin first, and there was created an organisation responsible for this, known as *He-Halutz* (The Pioneer). In Palestine, a labour group (Heb. *gedud ha-avodah*) was created, again under the inspiration of Trumpeldor,[34] and this devoted itself to primary pioneering tasks like road-building. The members of this third *aliya* continued the pioneering tradition of the second, which had

28. C. Weizmann, *op. cit.*, p. 314.
29. A. Bein: *op. cit.*, p. 234.
30. *Ibid.*
31. Y. Halpern: *op. cit.*, Vol. 2, p. 491.
32. *Op. cit.*, p. 466, about the second *aliya*.
33. For information on Trumpeldor see chapter on *Masada*, Section 'Gordon, Brenner and Trumpeldor'.
34. L. Hazan, Y. Palar: *op. cit.*, p. 219.

developed the idea and practice of co-operative living and co-operative work. They shared the ideal of self-labour, and were opposed to exploiting the labour of others in order to make their own personal lives more comfortable.[35] Both the second *aliya* and the third *aliya* supported the pioneering programme. The men of the third *aliya* brought with them a longing to build the land on new social foundations, and to prepare it for the absorption of masses of Jews.[36]

Lamdan the Man—A Brief Biography

Isaac Lamdan, the Hebrew poet, was a product of these historical events and movements. His background was East European. He was born in the townlet (*shtetl*) of Malinov in the district of Wohlin in the Ukraine on the 7th of November, 1899 (5th Kislev, according to the Jewish calendar). His father, Judah Aryeh, was a merchant of Rabbinic family. As a lad, he received both a traditional Jewish education at home, and later, a general and Hebrew education. But in the war years, he and his brother were separated from their family when the fighting reached their native town. In the course of his wanderings throughout the Ukraine and Russia, the young Isaac witnessed riots and pogroms, in one of which his brother was struck down. The poem *Masada* contains reference to that tragic event, which made a deep impression on his young mind. Swayed by the initial emancipation of Russian Jewry, he later volunteered for the Red Army; but following a wave of savagery in the Ukrainian cities, from which he only escaped by a miracle, he made his way somewhat circuitously to Palestine, where he arrived in 1920 with the third *aliya*. Once there, he found work in road-building and in agriculture in various parts of the country, including the village of Ben-Shemen. At the time he served on the cultural council of the Workers' union. From the second half of the twenties, however, he abandoned manual labour for full-time literary employment.

35. R. Patai: *op. cit.*, p. 59.   36. L. Hazan, Y. Palar: *op. cit.*, pp. 235, 236.

But he was always very politically and socially involved in the life of the young country, and his writing reflected this involvement.

He was early interested in literature, and published poems from the age of twelve for the children's Hebrew press (*Ha-peraḥim, Ha-yarden*), while at the age of eighteen, one of his poems was accepted for the important literary journal *Ha-shi-loaḥ*. In Palestine, he was first connected with the periodical *Hedim* (Echoes), edited by A. Barash and J. Rabinowitz, to which he contributed, and which brought out his *Masada*, which has since appeared in no less than ten editions. This poem has hitherto been most responsible for Lamdan's fame, and is often thought of as the most perfect poetic expression of the physical and spiritual struggle of the pioneering movement of the time. His other activities included founding the *Brit 'Ivrit Olamit* (World Hebrew Union) when he was later based for a while in Berlin, and he lectured on Hebrew for that organisation in Lithuania.

In 1934, Lamdan founded and edited the literary monthly *Gilyonot*, which was intended to be independent politically and socially, and to seek a new path in Hebrew literature, though respecting the tradition of Hebrew journalism. It was continued until his death (its last appearance constituted a memorial issue to him) in spite of the fact that it was supported neither by political party nor state institution.

He also collected, edited, and was responsible for an anthology of Hebrew stories *Sippurim 'Ivriyyim* (1947). He translated works by Max Brod, Jack London, Joseph Conrad and others, as well as a number of books of short stories. A large collection of his letters was produced by the Israeli writers' archives—'Genazim A'.

His original work comprises—*Masada* (a long poem, 1927), *Ba-ritmah ha-meshuleshet* ('In the threefold harness', poems, pub. Steybel, 1930), *Mi-sefer ha-yamim* ('From the book of days', pub. *Gilyonot*, 1940, and later incorporated in his collection *Bema'aleh 'aqrabbim* which words mean 'On the scorpions' ascent'—reference to the roughness of the path travelled),

Maḥanayim ('Two camps', an extract from an unfinished play, *Akiba*, pub. *Gilyonot*, 1946) and *Bemaʿaleh ʿaqrabbim* (poems, pub. Dvir Mossad Bialik, 1946), for which he received the Brenner prize.)

Lamdan was awarded the prize for literature from the municipality of Ramat Gan, where he lived in 1951. He died at the age of 55 on the 16th November, 1954.*

Lamdan the Journalist

Although Lamdan is known mainly as a poet, it should be remembered that he was important too as a journalist, as editor of the literary monthly *Gilyonot*, from 1934 until his death. Through editorial comments, under his pseudonym Y. Mitbonen (the 'Observer') and under his own name, he provided a commentary on the situation of the Jews in general, on the development of the Jewish settlement in Palestine and the State of Israel, on spiritual developments within the country, and on its literature. His prose work, too, often echoes his poetry and casts light on it, and we could not do full justice to his poetry without mentioning, if briefly, some aspects of his journalistic work through the issues of *Gilyonot*.

From the very outset, Lamdan, as editor of the journal, established that *Gilyonot* would be a non-party periodical. It would not belong to any particular group, not be financed by any party, and not be necessarily identified with any particular sectional interest. In this object *Gilyonot* was embarking on a course different from that of other Hebrew journals of the time. But Lamdan was highly critical of what he saw as the over-politicisation of the country. Such a tendency was dangerously stretching already limited resources, and so he justified his policy on these grounds if on no other.

From the pages of his journal, sometimes editorially, Lamdan held forth on the most important issues of the day. On the

---

* This information has been drawn from the literary archives of the Hebrew Writers' Union in Tel- Aviv (Genazim), and from the memorial volume of *Gilyonot* to I. Lamdan on his death.

continent of Europe, racism and Nazism were beginning to assume a more violent aspect than ever before. But to one inured to anti-Semitism, this was just one more manifestation of an ancient sickness (vol. XXX). However well established this condition, the Jewish people did not seem to have learned from its history. Lamdan expressed his alarm at the ideology of assimilationism as propagated, for example, by the German Jewish writer, Leon Feuchtwanger. Cosmopolitanism, for Lamdan, could not be a new Judaism, but simply an escape and an illusion. And another sort of illusion was the Jewish Leftist faith in the U.S.S.R. even when that country had abandoned all semblance of legality with its notorious 'Moscow trials', and had outlawed Zionism and the teaching of Hebrew. As a stout advocate of Hebrew nationalism, Lamdan could bear no opposition under the cloak of supranationalism. Zionism had a clear right to exist in the modern world, and had to establish itself strongly. Thus, 'Hebrew labour', a concept also under attack from the left, was a necessity for the creation of a genuine Jewish homeland.

Lamdan's journalistic concerns were not limited to Jewish Palestine. On the wider Jewish front, he was perturbed that the Hebrew schools in Poland were allowed to close. For him, Jewish education and culture were an insurance policy for the Jewish people, and were necessary to guarantee its future. Lamdan always demanded from the Jews an awareness of their history and their potentiality. Such momentous times had to bring about an appropriate response. History and the Jewish Fate had to find their echo in action as in literature. Lamdan's writing is an attempt to provide a substantial response, mainly in poetry, but supported by his prose. In his journalism, there is the rhetoric of his poetry, and its sense of doom. He sees a recurring pattern in Jewish history. There has, for example, constantly been a possibility of assimilation. But it has always been resisted by some apparent accident of history. Perhaps this proves that what looks like a series of historical accidents is an inevitable process, that each 'accident' is obeying a rule: 'If so, the regularity of these events rather proves that these events are not casual but causal, fixed, constant, fateful, and that the cultural and historical unity of the Jewish people is not an accident at all' (vol. VIII).

Zionism was, of course, Lamdan's central creed, and he worked at its very hub; within labour Zionism, political Zionism, cultural Zionism. Dearer to him than anything were the land and the people of Israel. Going to Israel was, he stressed, an *aliya*, a spiritual ascent, and not merely an emigration from one country to another. Such emigration, if merely careerism, deeply distressed him. If conditions were appropriate these people would come, but if conditions were to change, they would leave again. Lamdan was devoted to the notion of imbuing a new generation with genuine Hebrew and Zionist idealism, and even suggested the creation of a new organisation to be called 'the Hebrew Guard' (*Ha-mishmar ha-'ivri*) (vol. X).

Lamdan was a writer as well as an editor of a primarily literary journal. So his views as a literary commentator and critic are of great interest. He also had a particular attachment to Hebrew language and literature as the spiritual and intellectual expression of the Jewish people.

As will emerge later, Lamdan had a great affinity with the most famous Hebrew poet of his time, H. N. Bialik, and the latter's death moved him deeply. Lamdan wrote, on Bialik's death: 'It is not a branch that has dropped—a powerful, leafy tree has fallen mightily, and our heads are suddenly stripped of the shade of the great shelter, and are abandoned to the furnace of mournful days; it is not a brick that has fallen from the building—a wall has collapsed, a bolstered-up protective wall, and we have been set, undefended before a vacuum' (vol. VII).

This was in immediate reaction to Bialik's death. But this kind of literary impressionism characterises much of Lamdan's writing about literature. He was impressionistic rather than analytical, though his impressionism could often convey the salient character of the literature under discussion. One of Lamdan's favourite contemporary Hebrew writers was M. J. Berdichevsky, of whom he said (on the occasion of his seventieth birthday):

'He was a discovering saw, sinking into our depths and calling from them. He was the great asker in our literature, the awakener stirring us to ask, to observe, to test ourselves and our ways, who has poured into the veins of modern Hebrew thought some of his natural disquiet' (vol. XVI). Berdichevsky is praised for his honesty, his frankness, his ability to appreciate a rival, his fearlessness, his creative imagination that could bring a story to life, and his ability to face a situation.

The poet Zalman Schneur, on the other hand, is praised for different qualities, for being a thinking poet on a large scale: 'The logic in things, the thinking, are the basic background of Schneur's poetry, and they bring about the broad vistas of the poem. He is not a singing poet, but a thinking poet, not an etcher-artist who produces smooth, controlled, miniature etchings but a hewer-artist hewing strongly the rocks of his poetic vision, taking out heavy blocks lined with dust, natural, unformed blocks.'

Here we have a glimpse of Lamdan the enthusiastic, impressionistic critic seeking for signs of Hebrew genius, and warmly acclaiming them when he believes that he has found them. This appreciation is a vital part of his journalism, which is a true echo of his poetry.

Lamdan the Poet

Lamdan was first and foremost a poet. Although his output was small, all his greatest concerns found their most perfect expression in his poetry. Poetry, for him, was the most concentrated form of writing, and even his prose is highly poetic in tone, as it sings and rings with images.

Lamdan wrote poetry throughout his literary career. The work for which he is best known is the long poem *Masada*, written in 1927. *Masada* to a large extent determines the themes and the tone of his later poetry. The imprint of European Expressionism is already discernible, as is the influence of the vanguard of the younger Hebrew poets, most of them arriving in Palestine with the third *aliya*. *Masada* is a hymn to this generation, a celebration of its struggles and tribulations, of its rejection by the outside world and its search for a new scale of values, of the disillusionment with popular ideologies, old and new, and its turning in on itself in an attempt to pioneer a Zionist ideology and a viable civilisation. There is despair at history and a limited but possible hope in the future, the hope of a people at the end of its tether. The 'final judgement' is about to come. The apocalyptic atmosphere is in evidence. The language is that of the new Hebrew poetry of the time. Above all looms the God of the Jewish Fate, inexorable and apparently unchangeable. But the new Hebrew man must fight on, because he has no choice.

None of Lamdan's later poetry has yet attained the popularity and renown of *Masada*. But it is characterised by a sharpening and deepening of the thematic material of the first great poem. The title *In the threefold harness (Ba-ritmah ha-meshuleshet)* of his next collection of poems already tells much about the poems therein. The harness restricts the poet to bearing his traditional destiny, to being the poet of his generation and to bearing the weight of the contemporary Jewish drama. The poet has not the freedom of others to select his theme and to write as the mood takes him. He is bound and determined by his history and situation to carrying out a specific function. This tension between what he would like to do and what he is forced to do is never resolved in favour of the former, but it is, nevertheless, a prominent theme in his poetry. Lamdan writes in the spirit of the ancient Hebrew prophet, commanded by God to speak words of truth to his people and allowed no freedom in what he says or, indeed, in whether he says it. But Lamdan's God is the modern Fate, who has operated throughout history, and has selected the Jews for a special role. Lamdan's poetic and literary function is to bear witness to this role. He celebrates the Jewish Fate rather than the traditional Jewish God because God is dead for him, or, at any rate, He is hiding. Lamdan is in the ironic position of having been called by the Great No-one—'I did not hear the word of God out of the tempest'. But he fights on nevertheless, and this cycle of poems closes on the poet's statement of determination to remain in the fight: 'I will draw a circle round me like Honi the Circle-maker, and close it with the explicit word—"here".'

Most of the remainder of Lamdan's poetry was included in the volume *On the scorpions' ascent* (*Bema'aleh 'aqrabbim*) (1946). Thematically, the poems in this collection are similar to his previous poetry. They are dominated by his single-minded obsession with Jewish Fate. Biblical figures are invoked as historical precursors of the Jew throughout the ages, and in the way in which they embody this inevitable tragedy. The modern pioneer continues the function of the Biblical hero trying to escape a manifest destiny, but conspicuously failing. This harsh God, this inaccessible, immovable God, will be neither denied nor thwarted. History is a spokesman of His will, and must repeat itself.

Lamdan's poetry would carry the overtones of Greek tragedy, with its sense of inevitable disaster, were it not for Lamdan's 'nevertheless'. For this 'nevertheless' and 'in spite of everything' are central in Lamdan's works. Disaster is certain and irretrievable, but nevertheless the fight must be fought. This is the paradox of Lamdan's work. You must continue the war against your insuperable Destiny. For this also is your destiny. This and unlimited love for the Jewish people expressed in a twentieth-century Hebrew idiom are the dominant characteristics of Lamdan's poetry.

Chapter 2

THE NEW HEBREW LITERATURE

Changes in Hebrew Literature

IN ORDER to understand Lamdan's work, we must set it against the background of the literature of the period, and appreciate that, both from the point of view of form and of content, the new literature was of a different mould from the classical. In distinguishing between 'classical' and 'new', we are, on the whole, distinguishing between two generations. A. Shlonsky and I. Lamdan, of the new school, were born about a quarter of a century after the classical H. N. Bialik and S. Tscherni-chowsky, and also hailed from the Russian Empire.[1] The typical representatives of the new generation reflected the background of the twentieth century as it affected Russia in general, which suffered the violence of war and revolution, and the Jews there in particular, those who adopted the Zionist experiment and who fought to build a Socialist home for the Jews. These new writers tried to embody the turbulence of the Jewish experience in their literature, to forge a mirror of their lives. And they attacked the classicists for not fulfilling this task.

The expressionist poet and Lamdan's contemporary, U. Z. Greenberg (born 1895) says in a manifesto 'To the ninety-nine' that 'as for them [i.e. the ninety-nine out of a hundred writers], it is not their mode of life that constitutes their psychological content, not bodily desires that tell them what to say, but "nice sentiment", and outward capacity, the capacity of fingers to produce a pretty, gentle form.'[2] Greenberg here

1. Shlonsky (1900–). Lamdan (1899–1954). Bialik (1873–1934). Tschernichowsky (1875–1943), see *Millon ha-sifrut ka-hadashah*

(ed. A. Shaanan, Tel-Aviv, 1954).
2. See U. Z. Greenberg: *Kelapei tish'im ve-tish'ah* (Tel-Aviv, 1928).

attacks fastidious aestheticism, the preoccupation with form. This feeling of dissatisfaction with prevailing literary modes in the light of contemporary conditions was prevalent in European literature of the period in general.[3] It was asserted that literature should not be an isolated limb, but an integral, vital, and relevant expression of the whole, which is contemporary life. Life had changed radically in the twentieth century, particularly in Palestine where a social revolution was taking place, and literature must satisfactorily reflect these changes, So what was good for the past is probably insufficient for the present. New circumstances demand new tools. As Greenberg says in the same pamphlet: 'Yesterday's style is the style for those who are still living the life of yesterday here. But it is completely estranged from the style of the pioneers of today and tomorrow.'[4] Contemporary reality is the only thing that interests Greenberg, and he sees his function as complete absorption in it. He has no other literary ambition: 'Immortality I achieve in the heart of the time in which I live, in whatever physical or psychological state I happen to be. I look with eyes of flesh. In any other sort of immortality I do not believe.'[5]

Shlonsky too stresses the concern of literature with the contemporary situation. Journalism and literature should not be considered as two separate provinces, as territories set off from each other. On the contrary, the literary élite should be actively concerned in journalism, i.e. with the contemporary situation, otherwise journalism becomes debased, as in Nazi Germany, where the Press became the organ of the Nazi State: 'It is possible that this "puzzling" catastrophe that came over the State of Goethe and Kant, "blown up to bursting point with culture" can be partially attributed to this German peculiarity of making a distinction between "eternal questions" and "questions of the moment".'[6] Writers and thinkers should be

3. See section on 'Expressionism' in chapter on *Masada*, and section 'Imagism' in chapter on 'Lamdan's Imagery'.

4. See U. Z. Greenberg, *op. cit.*, p. 10.

5. *Ibid.*, p. 29; A. Shlonsky, *Yalkut Eshel* (Tel-Aviv, 1960).

6. *Ibid.*

active in the Press, and not above it. There was a time when this situation prevailed in Hebrew journalism, according to Shlonsky. But it unfortunately does so no more, and the mark of 'journalist' has become a badge of shame for the writer.[7]

So literature must reflect the consciousness of man in his new environment, the environment of the twentieth century. But so violent and radical have been the changes that have taken place that man himself has become a different creature. In Greenberg's view, man has now become the centre of interest because of the new technological capacity at his command: 'Man has ceased to be the operated passive, and has become causer of causes, and turner of wheels.'[8] Characteristically, Greenberg sees the technological revolution as central to the new world. He would also make man, the operator of the machine, the focal point of poetry. The poet should shift his focus from the distant universe, from the heavens, and rivet it on earth. He need not even be concerned with the natural world; what is of more importance is the new world created by man, the world peculiarly characteristic of the twentieth century. Greenberg's slogan is 'iron, smoke, electricity, and concrete'.[9] In these things, he finds poetry. And in his view, he would thus give expression to the feelings of a generation that has ceased to find poetry in heaven: 'Not for nothing do people rarely look into the heavens, for Divinity has come down to earth.'[10]

The use of technological images is common to modernist poetry in general. Shlonsky, too, is as much concerned with this aspect of the world around him as is Greenberg, and his poetry is brimming with imagery drawn from technology. He is concerned to find a means of expression adequate to what he wants to describe. He regards twentieth-century man as not only a new, but also a very complex being—particularly Hebrew man. Poetry must not lag behind the reality; its tools must be flexible and efficient. The old tools cannot cope; simplicity and poverty of language could not match up to the desired picture.

7. *Ibid.*   9. *Ibid.*
8. U. Z. Greenberg: *op. cit.*, p. 37.   10. *Ibid.*, p. 45.

New language, new forms and images are needed, and the unavoidable result is verse of a complex and difficult nature: 'This miraculous revolution that has taken place in this tiny land is at the foundation of the wondrous vista, at the root of everything Israeli, both particular and general. So it is neither right nor proper to dress it in simplified poverty.'[11] The means must be adequate to the end. A complex situation must be expressed in complex terms, and the new poetry attempts to meet the challenge.

This new Hebrew literature is the literature of the third wave of immigration (*aliya*) to Israel. Almost all the representative writers of the generation arrived in Israel between the years 1920 and 1925.[12] This third *aliya*, like the second, is particularly characterised by the fusion of socialist and nationalist ideals. The immigrants did not set up odd farms individually, as did those of the first *aliya*; they evolved a conscious national ideal, which was to build up a Jewish country on an agricultural basis, and on socialist principles. The writers under discussion were either working pioneers themselves, or they, at any rate, identified themselves with the pioneering ideal, and with the image of the Palestine then in creation. The young literature of the twenties and thirties is a recognisable phenomenon of its own, and it can justly be labelled 'the Literature of the third *aliya*'. As Shlonsky says: 'It [i.e. the new literature], from the point of view of time and quality, is the logical product of the third *aliya* in all its manifestations.'[13] In all its manifestations, for though the main building effort was concentrated on agriculture, and on raising the status of the labourer to that of the élite, urban settlement was also growing.

Tel-Aviv, now Israel's largest city, which was founded in 1909,[14] began to grow at a great pace in the early twenties.[15]

11. A. Shlonsky: *op. cit.*, p. 30.

12. E.g. Lamdan in 1920, Shlonsky in 1921, Greenberg in 1924, and Altermann in 1925; see *Millon ha-sifrut ha-ḥadashah*.

13. See A. Shlonsky, *op. cit.*, pp. 56–7.

14. For details, see Alex Bein: *Toledot ha-hityashevut ha-ẓiyyonit* (Tel Aviv, 1945), pp. 103–6.

15. *Ibid.*, pp. 263–6.

So the reality of Palestine includes the city as well as the agricultural settlement. Greenberg admires growing technological strength, N. Altermann, also a contemporary, sings imagistically[16] of Tel-Aviv, and Shlonsky is mainly devoted to the pioneering effort. But all, in one way or another, attempt to capture the new reality. Altermann searches the exact image to catch a fleeting impression. Greenberg allows the emotion of his subject matter to sway his verse so as not to impose form on it, and Shlonsky writhes in a heap of complex images to give expression to the pain and hope of his age. Greenberg, Shlonsky and Lamdan try to express the extreme agony of their generation. Shlonsky says: 'O night! You have given us great agony, and it constantly scorches our flesh like the trampled sun at your feet'.[17] 'Night' is the dark Fate of the people, the obstacle that they must overcome, without supernatural help; for the people cannot pray: 'How can we pray, when we know no prayer?'[18] Lamdan indeed does pray, as in the section 'The Prayer' in *Masada*, and in the poem 'When a man prays' in the collection of poems *In the threefold harness*. But this prayer is made only at certain moments of stress, and more often, he is conscious that it can have no effect, since his God is dead.[19] Agony is constantly at the heart of all Greenberg's work, though the agony here is more national than personal.

But Greenberg's subjects have also lost God, and have to suffer, without the consolation of faith: 'Their ancestors stretched out their arms to God—and their necks to the sword—on the day of wrath. But these people are bereaved of God and His heaven, and do not stretch out their hands in prayer. But they do stretch out their necks, even if a mere boy flashes his knife in their eyes.'[20] This is Greenberg's attack on

16. For a discussion of Altermann's use of imagery, see second section of the chapter—'His Imagery'.

17. Shlonsky: *Collected Poems* (Tel-Aviv, 1965), Vol. 1, pp. 15, 18.

18. *Ibid.*, p. 15.

19. See *Ba-ritmah ha-meshuleshet*

(Berlin, Tel-Aviv, 1930), p. 89 'I am resident in their congregation, for there was my God burned.'

20. U. Z. Greenberg: *Sefer ha-kitrug ve-ha-emunah* (Tel-Aviv, 1937), p. 14.

what he saw as the pacifism of his people. But even much earlier, he had begun to identify Judaism with pain, as he speaks symbolically of the act of circumcision: 'And on the eighth day [i.e. of his life], they hurt me so in the name of the great Judaism. So the lad grew up, and so did the bush of agony grow. Now, in my rising maturity, I do not know what was the meaning of the exceeding joy that there was in Father's house thirty years ago.'[21] We see that Greenberg here regards Judaism as a yoke imposed on him, for he cannot himself understand why other people should have rejoiced at the ceremony. The idea of Judaism as a yoke to be borne, that makes demands, but gives no comforts, is one that we shall become familiar with in the work of Lamdan. It is the dominant theme of our poet's work.

The consciousness of this young group of writers, then, was born of the strife and violence of the war years, and of the strenuous adaptation to the new country. Since they were a conscious literary group, they demanded their own literary organs. The first organ of this sort was the weekly literary magazine *Ketuvim* (Writings), edited, at first, by E. Steinmann alone, and then later by Steinmann and the poet Shlonsky jointly. This was published weekly between 1926 and 1931. We see that the editors and contributors were conscious of departing on a separate course, and representing a new generation. As the editor, Steinmann, says in answer to a complaint that the older established writers do not write for *Ketuvim*: 'The Hebrew reader has to be taught the basic and simple idea that generations come and go.'[22] The writers of a new generation bring with them a new literature that is not content to imitate the past.

Steinmann himself tells us something of the approach to literature made by the group of writers round him.[23] He apparently felt the need to defend the new movement against

21. U. Z. Greenberg: *Ha-bagrut ha'olah* (Tel-Aviv, 1926), p. 8.
22. *Ketuvim*, issue of 27.11.27. No. 59—editorial.
23. E. Steinmann: *Be-sha'ar ha-vikuah* (Tel-Aviv, 1933—Alexander Moses).

attacks and doubts raised by the Hebrew reading public, of pretentiousness and unintelligibility. The pretentiousness is exemplified by disrespect for the classics and departure from the traditional literary patterns, and the unintelligibility is that of prolixity and innovation. As regards the first charge, Steinmann says that it is in the nature of true criticism to fight tradition: 'The critic is the enemy of tradition, whatever it be, and in whatever sphere—"I do not believe" is his credo.'[24] Classicism is comparable to Religion; they both attempt to obstruct initiative and free thought. But the writer must go his own way: 'I think that everyone has the right to breathe the air of thought,'[25] he says.

In respect to the second charge, Steinmann argues, as does Shlonsky, that complex material demands complex treatment, and that the classical writers, such as Mendele and Ahad Ha'am, were guilty of oversimplifying matters. They did not present complex, modern man. The classicists' view was: 'Give the people land, and they will again be simple and happy as in years gone by. And the class question? And the class war that every man fights with himself? And the complex of urgent problems in the culture of today? And all the metaphysical pains that sap the vitality of modern man? These questions did not concern them. Perhaps they did not even notice them. Metaphysical man, like the metaphysical world, did not exist for them.'[26] Steinmann's counter-accusation is of superficiality. The new writers are not content with such a surface picture of life. Just as they want to paint the reality, so they strive to suggest the depth. And since the ambition is greater, so must the materials used be more intricate. The old pattern is insufficient.

Steinmann, in the same work, touches on a particular aspect of the literary portrayal of the modern consciousness; the aspect of language. One of the outstanding characteristics of the new literature is the attempt to coin new forms of language and new words It was on this point, as much as on any other, that the

24. *Ibid.*, p. 22.   26. *Ibid.*, p. 39.
25. *Ibid.*

innovators were taken to task. But new language for these writers was an integral part of the modernist's equipment. And Steinmann thinks that the writer should be free of the yoke of tradition with respect to language, just as much as in respect to subject. The only justification demanded by the neologism is internal need. Genuine creativity involves newly minted terminology and form: 'The feeling of joy also shies at logical presentation, and needs wild and joyful expression. . . . Neologisms and rearrangement of the order of sentences are mostly the result of strong, new, unclear feeling that can find no satisfaction in logical, traditional order.'[27] And he goes on to say that 'it is only being different that makes the work effective'.[28]

Steinmann regarded the proper function of literature as the attempt to express something of the consciousness of modern man, a consciousness completely out of the range of those writers he was criticising. With the discoveries of psychoanalysis, modern man can have a better sense of these depths than his predecessors. And the language of literature must make some attempt, however superficial or unsuccessful, to plumb these depths. It must go beyond the bounds of logical expression, to be constantly renewed, and even to create its own thought. Language may take its writer beyond the point that the writer intended to go, it may lead him into territory uncharted, and acquire a power of its own. It may stem from the unconscious over which the writer has no rational control, by ascending to the abstractness of music: 'As the musical basis in literature becomes dominant, it stops using words as logical instruments, and turns them into notes.'[29] It is to be expected at this point that literature becomes difficult. It is now acting as the interpreter of the unconscious; thus the apparent 'unintelligibility'. But the difficulty is not artificial, it is the necessary result of his own ambitions. It cannot always be understood in a rational sense. Steinmann asks: 'Why should it [i.e. Art] be understood by others, when it is not understood by itself?'[30]

27. *Ibid.*, p. 114.   29. *Ibid.*, p. 113.
28. *Ibid.*   30. *Ibid.*, p. 130.

Lamdan exemplifies some, though not all, of the characteristics of the new literature in his long poem *Masada*. The work is deeply rooted in the contemporary situation, and the language is heavily imagistic[31] in the modern manner. The poet tries also to plumb the depths of his own (and his people's) soul, and to match his suffering with his verse. Lamdan has tried to suggest the complexity of the third *aliya* pioneer, and the ambiguity and depth of his personality. Both on the personal and on the national level, Lamdan traces the impression of his suffering, distracted age. He does not himself invent words, but he does use them in unusual combinations. His verse is swayed by the moods of the poem, and the metre and language flex to reflect them; it is, on the whole, 'free verse'. The Lamdan of *Masada* fits into the pattern of the new, young literature, that of Shlonsky and Greenberg.

Modernism

It is generally agreed that the first exponent of modernism in Hebrew poetry was Abraham ben Yitzhak (1883–1950): 'The blooms of the new path in the poetry of our time were first seen in eleven small poems that were published in periodicals between the years 1908 and 1930[32] under the signature of Abraham ben Yitzhak, literary name of the poet, Dr Abraham Sonne.'[33] Abraham ben Yitzhak's poetry is impressionistic and idyllic, treats of nature, love and the virtues of 'sowing without reaping'. In all, it is not characterised by the contemporary awareness that is the hallmark of the modernist poetry so far discussed. But that this poetry did introduce a new note into Hebrew literature was recognised by Bialik himself: 'Who were the first [poets] to give me the flavour of the new movement, apart from what their value may be? The first was

31. See chapter on 'His Imagery', Chapter XII, Section: *Masada*.

32. Later published together by

'Tarshish', 1952, with biographical introduction.

33. See Aharon Ben-Or: *Toledot hasifrut ha'ivrit bedorenu* (Tel-Aviv, 1954), Vol. I, p. 51.

Abraham ben Yitzhak, who wrote in all some half-dozen or, perhaps, a dozen poems. . . . I think that I was the first to offer them to the public.'[34] Bialik does not specify what he means by the 'new movement', and it would be difficult to isolate poetic devices used by Sonne that Bialik himself did not know. For Bialik himself was not entirely, or even predominantly, a national poet, but was egocentric, i.e. the poet's own personality was at the centre of his poetry,[35] a characteristic peculiar to modern poetry.

Until the time of Bialik, national poetry had been the mode. Now Ben Yitzhak also took a symbolic view of nature, i.e. he described the world around him, not merely to record impressions, but to transmit its essence. The portrayal of nature is idiosyncratic: 'As for the mountains gathered round my city,/The secret is hidden away in their wooden flanks/ With the stirring restless tree-sea above it,/And the secret lying hidden in their mantling shade.'[36] (trans. Lask). The poet was preoccupied with purity. 'Whiteness' is a word that occurs often in his verse as a symbol of the innocence that he tried to attain. Rhythmically, his verse is free, but is adaptable to the mood of his subject: 'Their [the poems'] "free metre" is free only to transmit the movement, but it is bound to the internal music of the matter.'[37]

Abraham ben Yitzhak gave to the new poetry the elements of flexible, free verse (i.e. an unfixed verse that is suppliant to the mood of the poet), subjectivism in description of nature, and a private symbolism. These elements are characteristic of modern verse in general, in that it puts the poet at the centre of the universe, and sees his subjectivity as the principal in the

34. H. N. Bialik: *Devarim she-be'al peh* (Tel-Aviv), Vol. 2, p. 220.
35. According to Kurzweil, Bialik was the first Hebrew poet to approach the objective realities of the world and tradition with complete subjectivity. See B. Kurzweil: *Bialik ve-Tschernich-owsky* (Shocken, Tel-Aviv, 1961), p. 3.
36. Abraham ben Yitzhak: *Poems* (Jerusalem, 1957), with translations by I. M. Lask, p. 11.
37. Leah Goldberg: *Pegishah im meshorer* (Sifriyat Poalim, Tel-Aviv, 1952), p. 69.

composition. David Vogel (1891–1943) writes along the lines laid out by Sonne. With him also, colour symbolism is predominant: 'A black melody accompanies the dance of death.'[38] Night is despair, the hopelessness from which there is no escape: 'How we have spilled our sparkling life all along the way as we hurried along. And at dusk, we move along slowly, leaning on night, for we are tired—and our vessels are all completely empty. And fear mounts in the eye, whether we look behind or ahead.'[39]

Vogel's symbols express his pessimism, a pessimism more unambiguous than Sonne's, that was later to characterise what we call 'expressionist' Hebrew poetry. Even Vogel himself is spoken of as an expressionist, in the *Dictionary of Hebrew Literature*.[40] Like Ben Yitzhak, Vogel's metre is free, governed only by the internal need of the poem; like him, for example, he often has lines consisting of a single word. But since the poet is so economical, more meaning has to be concentrated in the existing material. This is the peculiar virtue of the symbol, that in one word it can conjure up a whole range of emotions that the experienced reader can understand when he learns to interpret the poet's symbolism. The psychology of depth has to be suggested to fulfil the ambitions outlined by Steinmann. Where the scientist uses a host of technical terms that the mind may grasp inadequately, the poet uses the symbol, whose significance he appreciates from the emotional reverberation stirred in his soul.

The colour symbolism of Vogel can be understood simply because the scale is common to literature in general. He tries to aspire to the white, the pure, from the black, the impure, i.e. himself: 'Before your gates, O white of dress, do I stand confused. Before the purple, golden soul of a Summer morning. From the dark deep do I rise, and your restful laughter hovers towards me. How could I come to your bright rooms,

38. Quoted in *Millon ha-sifrut ha-ḥadashah*, p. 586.

39. From a poem published in *Gilyonot* (1934, third issue).

40. See *Millon ha-sifrut ha-ḥadashah*, p. 586.

when my clothes are black?'[41] The contrast between dark and bright is the key to Vogel's poetry. The soul in despair is not the specifically Hebrew soul, but that of the modern European consciousness, that has been called, in this respect, decadent. Modern man feels sorrow, and he knows not the cause. The roots cannot be traced; only the effects can be recorded, and even these not in the simple terms that Steinmann accuses the classicists of demanding. We see that the first shoots of the new poetry attempt to get to grips with the complexity of the modern mind.

Although the new trend in poetry was already clearly marked with the appearance of the work of Ben Yitzhak and Vogel, opposition was stimulated for the first time by Shlonsky's verse: 'Abraham ben Yitzhak, David Vogel, Avigdor Hameiri and others, were, as said, the forerunners and guardians of the new trend in our poetry. But their poems lay by the side of the great poetry of the period without disagreement or conflict. The quarrel between the "new and old" broke out only with the appearance of Shlonsky's first poems, formed in the pattern of the new poesy, that in its time seemed strange, surprising, obscure, and, most importantly, inartistic. The Hebrew reading public, reared on the poetry of Bialik and his contemporaries, regarded Shlonsky's poetry negatively.'[42] He embodied the characteristics of modernism to an extent more extreme than any of the other poets of the circle. His metre is usually free, his language is often of his own mint, his images are juxtaposed surprisingly, abstract and concrete and mingled, and his symbolism is obscure.

Shlonsky was born in Russia in 1900, and after spending a short time in Palestine, returned to Russia for the war and revolutionary years there. He was much influenced by the revolutionary spirit, and by the literature of the period. Since then he has carried the banner of 'progressive culture' in Hebrew literature.[43] In the periodical *Ketuvim*, he publishes many translations of revolutionary Russian literature, and constantly cited it as the example to be followed by Hebrew

41. Quoted in Ben-Or: *op. cit.*, Vol.   42. Ben-Or: *op. cit.*, Vol. 1, p. 219.
    1, p. 219.   43. *Ibid.*, p. 220.

literature. The characteristics of his poetry here mentioned are borrowed or imbibed from the Russian Futurist masters. The poet considered revolutionary tools appropriate in the country that was undergoing a revolution of a different sort, i.e. in Palestine, for Hebrew literature. The new literature should adequately represent the new society, and so the temper of his verse is expressionistic, the temper of revolutionary verse. The characteristics of expressionist literature are violence, newness and surprise; contemporary awareness is mingled with the attempt to satisfy the emotional drive of the whole personality in a revolutionary age. Shlonsky's verse is very conscious of its age and of its own newness, and the poet spared no effort to publicise his work, and to justify it. He did this through the agency of his periodicals, round which he gathered a school of like-minded writers. This school soon became dominant in Hebrew literature.

Thematically, there seems to be three main strands in Shlonsky's poetry: the general pessimism of the age, hatred of urban, capitalistic society, and affirmation of the agricultural life, closeness to the soil. It has been said that the Dionysiac (as opposed to the Apollonic) element predominates in his work,[44] It is certainly true of his earlier poetry that it is written in the minor key, and that the negative scale is weightier. In his first series of poems, *Devay* (Sickness), written in the early twenties, he tells of man's disease, and the failure of religion and of all economic administrations to cure him. The poem ends in desolation: 'The drop flows, and the dog howls. And men rot, rot with leprosy.'[45] But even in his early poetry, there is the search for the salvation that can come with the pioneering life, with creative life. The series *Gilboah* is such an invocation to his country to save him: 'Dress me, O excellent mother, with a striped coat for splendour, and bring me at morn to toil.'[46] That the pioneering work of building seems to have this religious power of salvation can be seen from Shlonsky's ecstatic

44. See *Moznayim*, Vol. 5, p. 661—1937—article by Israel Cohen: *Le-shirato shel Shlonsky*.

45. Shlonsky: *Collected Poems*, Vol. I, p. 110.

46. *Ibid.*, p. 165.

language, and from the associations of language and phraseology: 'My country is wrapped in light like a prayer shawl. Houses stand erect like totems. And like phylactery straps do roads, that palms erected, glide down.'[47] Building is seen as creative work of the highest order. The builder is associated with God, the creator: 'So does the lovely city pray a morning prayer to her creator. And amongst the creators is your son Abraham,[48] a builder poet in Israel.'[49]

The two poles of pessimism and optimism are not each concentrated in any one period of the poet's creative activity, but they stand on parallel lines throughout the poet's work. His series, *Avne Tohu* (*Stones of Void*) (1935), again plays on the minor key, and violently attacks urban civilisation: 'City beautiful with lies! Both then and now. It seems to be a rising mushroom like the black of a phylactery. I am so confused amongst the vain shouting, in the flashes of the metropolis, cold as the brightness of a pole.'[50] Shlonsky suddenly comes to the realisation that he is in a strange land (in the poem *Montparnasse*), and that he will always be uneasy in it: 'Emptied beakers—like the solutions of secrets. A hailing voice calls out: "Sale finished". And like the name of the station after the dark of fields, there suddenly glimmered the inscription "Foreign land".'[51] The suddenness of the feeling of estrangement here can be compared to Lamdan's similar experience abroad, where he longs for the homeland.[52] The sensitive pole of Shlonsky's verse again comes to the fore in the series *Al millait* (1947), which reads like the text of a fertility rite. In these poems, Shlonsky communicates only with the elements, sometimes using religious language to express his enthusiasm.[53] He has a prayer that

47. *Ibid.*

48. i.e., the poet himself, Abraham Shlonsky. Here, he is addressing the country as his mother.

49. Shlonsky: *op. cit.*, p. 165.

50. Shlonsky: *Poems*, Vol. 2, p. 23.

51. *Ibid.*, p. 26.

52. See Lamdan: *Ba-ritmah ha-meshuleshet*, Section 'Mi-yamim ba-nekhar', p. 52. See also chapter on *Ba-ritmah ha-meshuleshet*.

53. See chapter on 'His Imagery', for discussion of the use of religious terminology in a new, secular context.

the earth sings: 'Have you heard how in the desert, in the country against the sky, each cloud prays "Give us water: water, water, give water! For we are thirsty for water. For we are thirsty. Who will slake our thirst, who will give us water?".'[54]

The accusation made against the new poetry in general, and against Shlonsky in particular, was that it was obscure, unnatural, and untalented. Shlonsky himself dealt with the charges of difficulty and obscurity by saying that he tried to match his theme with his language. His verse is certainly difficult and complex, but not artificially so. We have seen that his colleague Steinmann defended the use of new language by saying that genuine talent needs its own form of expression. If the poet has new things to say, then he will need new ways to say them, and we should not allow conservative instincts to block his path. Shlonsky certainly created a wealth of language, especially in his earlier work, where the innovations are more pronounced. But the poetry is not unduly weighed down by familiar forms, and any loss is more than compensated for by the gain of the invigorating fillip that Shlonsky gave the language and the literature.

His language is also deeply rooted in tradition, in older Hebrew sources: 'From the point of view of its [the poetry's] substance and content it is completely native, its Hebrew language has a pure pedigree. Its expressions and images are steeped in the Bible, Halevy, and Bialik: its sights and smells, depth and height, manner of vision and inclination, are of the source of Israel.'[55] When Shlonsky innovated, he innovated in the spirit of the language, wherever possible using Hebrew roots. Innovation in Hebrew is time-honoured, and the language has been in particular need of revitalisation in the twentieth century, after being unspoken for so long. It had to be adapted to the complex needs of modern times in general, and to the peculiar needs of the poet. Shlonsky did not overstep the boundaries in his ambition to forge a suitable tool in accordance with his demands for Hebrew poetry.

54. Shlonsky: *Poems*, Vol. 2, p. 270, the poem 'Shir ha-mayim'.   55. *Moznayim*, Vol. 5–I. Cohen: *op. cit.*, p. 661.

Uri Zvi Greenberg is of a similar poetic temper to Shlonsky in some respects. As we have already seen from his literary manifesto,[56] Greenberg wanted to make poetry correspond with the reality of life in modern Palestine. Like Shlonsky, he wanted to forge new literary forms, to update poetic technique. We have classed them together in the same school because they were both trying to renovate poetry, because they both wrote expressionistically, and because they were both concerned with contemporary reality, including the political. However, they were on different wings politically, and, because of the nature of their poetry, the political outlook is of great significance. Shlonsky was a Marxist, a sympathiser with the Bolshevik revolution, who drew his literary inspiration from the work of Russian contemporary writers, and was concerned with the world-wide problems of urban corruption and the renovation of man through labour.

Greenberg, on the other hand, although also an enthusiast of the pioneering movement, was almost exclusively concerned, in his poetry, with the national Fate of the Jewish people. He was an extreme nationalist, and his nationalist feeling forms the material content of his work. His mood is agonised. The Jew suffers because his state is so contemptible, and was once so magnificent. As a nationalist, he conjures up a glorious past to be contrasted with the mean actuality of the present. Of his people he writes: 'Rags, not even scrap of the broken kingdom, not one royal robe here where there was the light of kings, where the bush of our kingdom burned from the wadi of Egypt to the river Euphrates.'[57] The poet looks back longingly to the time when the Jewish people had its own territory, and when its boundaries were so extensive. The past was glorious, and its like cannot be achieved now because of the pacific nature of the people.

Socialism is, for Greenberg, a term of contempt: 'The stink of a rotten tribe under the plaster of Socialism. The stink of falsehood perfumed with red piety. Philosophical, clerical,

56. *Kelapei tish'im ve-tish'ah, op. cit.,* discussed at beginning of chapter.   57. Greenberg: *Sefer ha-kitrug ve-ha-emunah,* p. 8.

literary, sick Judaism pouring its watery mixture into the beakers of the people.'[58] The people must fight to restore its past glory, and not sink in a sea of paperwork. Greenberg also pours out his contempt on those who are apparently more concerned with the lives of 'murderous' Arabs than with their own people. This is misplaced, hypocritical sympathy, which also gives off a 'stink': 'The stench of their uprightness that streams hypocritically from their mouths, delivered in merciful letters by the nib of their pen. Those who pity the murderous Arab, but not their brothers' blood shed before their eyes, not far from their homes.'[59]

We see from these examples of Greenberg's verse that the poet introduced matter into his poetry that was traditionally considered unpoetic. Terms from modern technology place the poem well in its modern context; abuse of particular political ideologies is considered suitable material for poetry. As Greenberg advocated in his pamphlet—To the ninety-nine—his poetry is wholly occupied with the contemporary plight of his people. He does not sing of nature or of God nor of the wonder of the universe, but of man as a political animal living in the twentieth century. He says in verse what he was later to formulate in prose: 'Generations sunk in their aching flesh and blood, through lands all over the world, command the grandson: ascend, express us, living man! Sing not of the glory of heaven, talk of living men on earth.'[60] The poet feels it incumbent on himself to fulfil the wish of bygone generations. And this wish he interprets as one to express the suffering generation: 'Life is pain. U. Z. Greenberg mostly enjoys pain, because he is a vital poet.'[61] The poet revels in his pain and wallows in it to attack and rebuke. His subject is unified, and his standpoint is always consistent. His attack is conditioned by his faith.[62]

58. Ibid., p. 15.

59. Ibid.

60. Greenberg: Ha-bagrut ha-'olah (op. cit.), p. 6.

61. See I. Zemorah: Sifrut al para-shat dorot (Tel-Aviv, 1949), Vol. 2, p. 124.

62. Ibid. Zemorah points out that accusation is based on faith: thus the title of Greenberg's Book of Accusation and Faith.

We saw earlier that Greenberg deplored the state into which poetry had fallen, that it was too much concerned with form. Greenberg used words not as ornaments, but as instruments of power. They have an object: 'With him [Greenberg], the main thing about a word is not its beauty but its strength, and speech, it seems, like writing is, according to the need, either a sweet stick or an angry stick, but always a stick.'[63] The poet felt the events of the time too strongly to ignore them in his verse. He had to write in blood: 'The time has poured blood on my eyes, on my hands, on my pen. Letters have flowed together. It is in my poems.'[64] Greenberg is the poet of the bloody twentieth century.

Lamdan's *Masada* is also a full-blooded expression of the twentieth century. The three poets—Shlonsky, Greenberg, and Lamdan—are the most typical representatives of Hebrew expressionist poetry.[65] *Masada*, composed in the early twenties of the century, is written in the light of the violent events experienced by an immigrant from Russia. Like Greenberg's poetry, *Masada* is a highly political poem. The poet imbibed the fury of the World War, the Revolution, and the Zionist struggle. These things constitute the historical background to the poetry of Shlonsky and Greenberg, and to *Masada* too. Lamdan here achieved Greenberg's ideal of contemporaneousness; he too wrote in the blood of his period. *Masada* is not a lyric poem; it is an expression of a generation, exposed and alive to the contemporary cataclysm, which opted for a particular solution. The 'I' of the poem is not so much an individual as the prototype of the third *aliya*. He presents not what is peculiar to himself, but what is common to the group. The roar of battle, the despair, the clash of ideologies, pioneering enthusiasm, disappointment and determination, form the content of the poem. These Lamdan has not experienced alone, but together with all the pioneers.

63. *Ibid.*, p. 129.
64. Greenberg: *Sefer ha-kitrug ve-ha-emunah*, p. 10.
65. That the three were usually considered together as forming a school, see D. Sdan: *Dyokan*, on Lamdan, in *Molad*, 1954, Issue 7, p. 78.

Different points of view are expressed in the poem, and they are put forward here to represent the whole gamut of opinion in *Masada*. Lamdan's main energies are concentrated on the Zionist struggle. From the broad panorama of Jewish existence, *Masada* passes to the treatment of the few select: the pioneers who survive the struggle. Many have dropped by the way. The three 'friends' at the beginning, who are protagonists of different points of view, do not join him in emigration. Here, we receive a picture of the ideological trends amongst the people as a whole. The majority of Russian Jews, of course, did not elect for the Zionist solution; in this poem, Lamdan suggests the currents of thought that might have attracted them. In highly symbolic terminology, unlike Greenberg's, where the ideological terminology is prosaic, the poet sketches the non-Zionist reaction to the Zionist proposal. All three protagonists use religious language, adapted to a secular context, endowing the conflict with an atmosphere of hysterical desperation.

The imagery is on a very large scale; the speakers are apparently conscious of fulfilling historic roles. The revengeful nihilist would shake the world: 'The world has gone off course —let us pour confusion into its blood, that it reel and stagger like a drunkard, and never again find its course.'[66] The old world seemed to be collapsing in blood and turmoil. The Communist would have it that there will be a new world to justify the present suffering: 'This last tribute let us pay to Molech, let us cover this border-duty before we pass on cross-armed with an afflicted and sick world to the atoning kingdom of redemption.'[67] The third protagonist has nothing to offer but despair and resignation. He is tired of pseudo-solutions, and of having his hopes raised only to be again cast down. For the Jews, there is no way out; their fate is constant: 'As there is but one sun in the firmament, so there is but one Fate for Israel, a fixed planet amongst the heavenly bodies whose course cannot be altered.'[68] Three possible solutions are here proposed, and a fourth, the Zionist, which is never explicitly defended, is the

66. *Masada*, p. 13.   68. *Ibid.*, p. 18.
67. *Ibid.*, p. 15.

one accepted. In the face of the revolution, there seemed to be four possible ways of acting—to exploit it for purposes of revenge, to support it, to ignore it, or to escape it. In the four alternatives offered, we have Lamdan's survey of contemporary Jewish ideology. In symbolic language, he presents the history of the period, and rationalises the different trends of thought and action amongst his people.

The bulk of the poem is concerned, however, not with Russian Jewry, but with the pioneers themselves in Palestine. Here again, the poet tries to voice the whole people. He categorises them to give a brief background to their *aliya*, and to observe their reactions to the experience. Again, more drop by the way: 'Did you see? Today in the midst of battle, someone cast himself from the top of the wall into the abyss—too weary to bear, exhausted.'[69] That the poet identifies himself with his people in this poem can be seen from the way he varies the use of the first person singular with the plural. Lamdan is speaking for the whole movement when he says: 'With the termination of tranquillity, with the disappearance of the Sabbaths, we come now to Masada with the *Havdalah* cup[70] in our hands.'[71] The *havdalah* cup is a symbol of the discrimination that the people must exercise in order to make the Zionist experiment a success; the people must learn to distinguish 'the remnant of wine' from 'the poison mixed therein'. The poet here says 'we', for the exertion has to be made together. And this exertion is specifically localised in time and place.

Revaluation of Judaism

We have now considered changes in Hebrew literature, both as regards the spirit of the new literature, and the form of the

69. *Ibid.*, p. 72.
70. *Havdalah* is the traditional Jewish prayer made at the termination of the Sabbath, to 'divide' the holy from the profane, i.e. Sabbath, from the rest of the workaday week. A blessing is made over a cup of wine.

71. *Masada*, p. 79.

poetry. What we have still to consider is its spiritual content, and its revaluation of Jewish existence and the Jewish heritage. Hebrew literature of the period was naturally concerned with Jewish existence, if of a new order, and with the confrontation between the new and the old in a revolutionary context. The age-old values of the religiously enclosed past were questioned and undermined. The major Hebrew literature of the early twentieth century records the revolt of Hebrew writers against Judaism. Judaism could not be ignored, for it played too conspicuous a part in the mental make-up of the writer. The writer comes from an intensely Jewish background, is now participating in the creation of a new order of Jewish existence, and his tool, the Hebrew language, the traditional holy language of prayer, is rich with religious associations; Jewishness is embedded in the consciousness of the Hebrew writer. Yet this same past becomes the object of vituperation on the part of those who cannot yet escape its influence. We thus witness the phenomenon of the Hebrew inheritors who try to return to the sources of the past, to build their ancient land, and to recreate their language, and who yet must reject the past, and the values embodied therein. Our Hebrew writers would build a secular culture with the holy tools of tradition.

The revolt against tradition did not begin in the twentieth century, although it then took on its most fierce aspect. This revolt, as we call it, began when the Jew, entering emancipated into the modern world, started to take his standards from the world around him, rather than from his Jewish sources alone. This characterises the modern period in Jewish history, from the nineteenth century: 'Not only did outward conditions change, and outward possibilities open out, but—and this is the main thing—Judaism began to measure itself in other ways and according to standards other than those of the past.'[72] Judaism, up to this time, had been self-contained; all its standards had been drawn from within its own tradition. But, with their entry into the modern world, the Jews had another standard to

72. See N. Rottenstreich: *Ha-maha-shavah ha-yehudit ba-'et ha-* *hadashah* (Tel-Aviv), Vol. 1, p. 9.

consider—the external, or the European. In other words, the certainty in the complete validity of Jewish sources and authority was undermined.

The acceptance of external standards gives modern Hebrew literature its 'secular' character. 'The distinctive characteristic of our new literature is its secularity.'[73] And this secularity is the loss of traditional religious certainty: 'The secularity of the new Hebrew literature is conditioned by the fact that, almost in its entirety, it springs from a spiritual world emptied of the primordial certainty in a background of sanctity covering all life's phenomena and measuring their value. Our new literature assumes, knowingly or unknowingly—"the breaking of the covenant with the unity of Jewish culture".'[74] Once 'the unity of Jewish culture' is broken, the pieces move further and further apart. The retreat from Jewish values, and from a traditional context within the framework of Jewish tradition, becomes constantly more marked. By the twentieth century, a conscious effort has to be made to reassert the unity of Jewish culture, and its sequence to the present time; but then, the attempt is unconvincing. Twentieth-century Hebrew writers are modern Europeans, who are either tremendously attracted to, or excessively repelled by their Jewish heritage. But the original unity is irrecoverable.

In Bialik's poetry, we have chronicled the experience of the Jew, deeply rooted in his Jewish sources early in life, who is later alienated from them, and finds that he cannot return to them. In the poem, *Before the bookcase*,[75] the poet tries to communicate once more with his past, to find the same succour in his sources as he knew in his youth. These sources had been neglected for other ones; but now, he would return: 'From wandering amongst foreign islands has my soul returned, and, like an errant dove, tired of body, and trembling, does it flap

73. Kurzweil: *Sifruteinu ha-ḥadashah —hemshek o mahapekhah* (Shocken, Tel-Aviv, 1959), p. 13. It is Kurzweil who uses the word 'secular' in the way described here.

74. *Ibid.*, pp.16, 17.

75. Bialik: *Poems* (Tel-Aviv, 1944), p. 211—*Lifne aron ha-sefarim*.

once more on the door of its youth's nest.'[76] Then the poet goes
on to describe the single-minded devotion of his youth, when
he knew nothing outside of his religious environment: 'Did
not my youth know only you [i.e. the parchments, symbol of
the ancient tradition] of all the delights of God on this great
earth?'[77] The youth was faithful to the very end, and himself
witnessed the death of the tradition: 'On my lips did the
ancestral prayer flutter and die, and at a secret corner there by
your bookcase was the everlasting lamp completely extinguished before my eyes.'[78]

The images are taken from traditional Jewish practice. The
prayer has ceased to be meaningful, and there is no longer any
need for the everlasting light in the synagogue. But the poet
clings with all his determination to the last remnants of his
faith, in spite of the 'furious storm' raging outside: 'Before me
on the table, a dim wick still flickered, whilst the oil was being
consumed in the lantern.'[79] The light of tradition is trying to
withstand the furious onslaught of the outside world. But it
cannot. The flame, so weak now, against such forces is not
strong enough. It must die: 'Only the flame of my candle alone
is still dying, wandering, meandering, jumping the jump of its
death. Suddenly a window bursts open, everything goes out.'[80]
The tradition dies, and the youth is left to himself: 'And I, a
tender chick, am cast from the nest into the night and its darkness.'[81] His religion was his light in the world, and now it is
no more. He must grope in the darkness.

It is because of this darkness that the poet tries to find his way
back to his sources. He has, it seems, found no other light in the
interim, and so he is again confronted with the ancient tradition: 'Now with the passing of time, that I am already wrinkle-
browed and wrinkle-souled, the wheel of my life has brought
me back, and placed me once more before you.'[82] But the new
confrontation is a failure: 'Your pages have been widowed, and

76. *Ibid.*

77. *Ibid.*

78. *Ibid.*

79. *Ibid.*, p. 212.

80. *Ibid.*

81. *Ibid.*

82. *Ibid.*

every letter on its own is an orphan.'[83] The poet hoped that the
original validity of his tradition would be restored to him, but
his hope was groundless. The fault may lie in himself, the subject: 'Is my eye dimmed, is my ear thickened?' or in the
object: 'Or are you rotten, even dead, with no more remnant
in the land of the living?'[84] But this question is almost irrelevant. For wherever lies the fault, the result is the same. The
poet is cut off from his source of light, and, most importantly,
there is no way back. It seems that the innocent trust of the
child can never be recovered by one exposed to the 'night' and
'storm' of the twentieth century.

An attempt was made to reconcile historic Judaism with
nineteenth-century rationalism in the Hebrew literature of
Bialik's time. Ahad Ha'am (1856–1927) was the leading representative of this trend. A thoroughgoing rationalist, he believed
that the Jewish people could be true to their past without commitment to religious supernaturalism. He wanted to continue
the historic tradition of Judaism; for to cut off the tradition
would be to cut off its source of life. The past is the root of the
people: 'Can a tree be freed of its roots that are buried deep in
the soil to deprive it of freedom of movement?'[85] he asks.
Although there are apparent differences between the present
and the past with regard to belief, the national culture is still
valid. As he goes on to say in the same essay; just as the
Germans pride themselves on their national culture although
they believe no more in the mythic gods, so can the modern
Jew be a true son of his own culture without the ancient
faith.

At various points in his work, Ahad Ha'am tells us of what
this culture consists, and how it can be assimilated in modern
times. The history of the people and its language must be
known—these requirements are always demanded by nationalist movements. But Ahad Ha'am considered these things
insufficient to guarantee the historic and natural continuity of

83. *Ibid.*, p. 213.

84. *Ibid.*

85. See Ahad Ha'am: *Writings*
(Tel-Aviv, 1947); the essay *Torah
mi-zion*, p. 407.

the Jewish people. Neither was Jewish raciality a sufficient substitute for the religion of the past. These things—language, history, and race—were admitted by all the Hebrew revolutionary writers of the period as constituents of the new Hebrew civilisation. But these writers did not speak of continuity with the past, for they knew and appreciated the revolutionary rupture that was taking place. Ahad Ha'am, who was no more a traditional believer than the revolutionaries, was still unwilling to admit the rupture. He needed yet another link. And this link he found in 'morality'; not morality in general, but 'a special national morality, based on its [the nation's] qualities of spirit, on its historic life in the past, and on its situation and needs in the present'.[86]

This morality peculiar to the Jewish race is never defined, but we are assured that it exists. And though we may not know exactly what it is, we can know something of its nature by what it has produced, i.e. the Jewish religion. According to Ahad Ha'am, the Jewish religion, with all its rules and regulations, and its literature and history, is the visible embodiment of the best of Jewish morality: 'Under the cloak of religion does the best branch of national life hide.'[87] Religion is of secondary importance, merely a means of exemplifying the principal, the morality. Different ages, of course, act differently; so that whilst one age dresses its 'morality' in the form of religion, as did Jews in the past, another age, which has lost faith in religion, like the present one, may embody the same national morality in another form. The principle remains unchanged throughout, only the form changes. Thus does Ahad Ha'am attempt to establish a link between the past and the present, and guarantee historic Judaism.

But this link is clearly unsatisfactory. If there is such a thing as specific Jewish morality, we are never enlightened as to what it is; nor do we know how to act according to it in a specifically Jewish way. The traditional way of life in the past was valid

86. *Ibid.*, essay *Ha-musar ha-leumi*, p. 162, speaking of Israel, he says that it has its own morality. 87. *Ibid.*

because it was commanded of God. The Jews had been a 'peculiar' people with a special morality and specific practices because this was God's wish. Ahad Ha'am would apparently preserve the form of Judaism, but without that which gives the form meaning, i.e. a very specific conception of the Almighty: 'Ahad Ha'am's Judaism is Judaism without the demanding validity of the Torah. It is also Judaism without God.'[88]

Ahad Ha'am seems not to understand the radical departure he has made from the mainstream of Judaism, with his contemporary rationalists. He does not believe in the divine source of the commandments, nor in the divine election of the Jewish people. And yet he would still have the Jewish people constitute a separate unit, though not necessarily all concentrated in Palestine, which would serve as 'spiritual centre'. His justification of the separate existence of the Jewish people was largely a belief in its peculiar morality, a morality neither defined nor clarified. Berdichevsky (see p. 45) was to ask which particular Jewish morality Ahad Ha'am intended, as there are many sources, and they are by no means unanimous, even on major points. We are left in doubt as to Ahad Ha'am's meaning, and can only conclude that he was deluding himself. As extreme a rationalist as anyone in the revolutionary camp, he would not admit that this rationalism constituted a break with the past. But his importance lies in the influence he exerted over his like-minded generation, which, also rationalistically inclined, attempted to stress the link between the past and the present, rather than the break. Although weak philosophically, Ahad Ha'am's work satisfied the psychological need of a generation with no God.

But others were to face the problem with greater integrity. Micah Joseph Berdichevsky (1865–1921), influenced by the German vitalistic philosophy of his surroundings,[89] unambiguously launched an attack on official Judaism, and on the history of its leadership since the days of the prophets: 'The Jews have

88. Kurzweil, *Sifruteinu ha-ḥadashah*, pp. 192, 193.

89. One series of essays he called 'Transvaluation of values', *Shinui 'arakhin*.

been rejected because of Judaism.'[90] Reared in an orthodox environment he, like other Hebrew writers of the period, became alienated from it on contact with the outside world. He began to despise the restricted, stifling atmosphere of the Judaism he knew: 'Then I saw the chasm crouching between the world of grandfather Israel, folded in its books and religious ordinances, and between the great, broad world. I saw—and felt faint.'[91] He could not resist the great European enticement: 'With the coming of enlightenment—all my knowledge and bookish feelings were ruined, my heart became emptied of all its ancestral property . . . became emptied of all ancient words, and full of new knowledge and feelings, that made me drunk with enthusiasm.'[92] He was at first irresistibly drawn to Europe; but he later returned to his own Jewish people, and to their culture. He did not return in any spirit of submission. The tradition had to be overthrown, for it was dead: 'Wherever we turn we see in ourselves signs of death, signs of waste and howling desolation.'[93] The alternatives are clear, as clear as the difference between life and death: 'To be or not to be! Either to be the last Jews, or the first Hebrews.'[94]

If no new civilisation can be created, a Hebrew civilisation, then there will be nothing, for the old will collapse anyway. The people have been and still are buried in their dead books. There has been concern only for the fossilised past, and none for the living people; Berdichevsky's slogan is 'Israel before the Bible'.[95] The past is dead, but the people live, and they can build the present. But destruction must take place before construction: 'The negative precedes the positive, and destruction precedes building.'[96] The bad must be removed before good can replace it. This is where Berdichevsky differs from Ahad Ha'am, who would lean on the past. Berdichevsky takes his starting point from the present: 'Men of all nations and tongues begin their lives from the present, and go back to the past . . .

90. Berdichevsky: *Collected Essays* (Am oved, 1952), p. 30.
91. *Ibid.*, p. 27.
92. *Ibid.*, p. 29.
93. *Ibid.*, p. 28.
94. *Ibid.*, p. 29.
95. *Ibid.*, p. 35.
96. *Ibid.*, p. 36.

but with us, it is in reverse.'[97] Ahad Ha'am would have contemporary Hebrew culture as a link with the past, and as a
continuation of its history. Berdichevsky recognises that this is
impossible, for the old God is dead in the hearts of his generation. But he stresses that even if it were desirable to continue
the chain, it would be impossible along the lines suggested by
Ahad Ha'am. Ahad Ha'am sees a national morality still relevant to the present day. But Berdichevsky points out that there
is no single national morality, but that there are several:
'National morality is an illusory principle, a principle like other
religious principles that come and go.'[98] Judaism has never been
a moral unity; Ahad Ha'am is living in a dream world. The
illusion should be surrendered. We want 'not that abstract
Judaism should be our light, one Judaism or another', for 'we
are Hebrews, and would serve our hearts'.[99] The distinction
made here between 'Jews' and 'Hebrews' is one that has been
taken in general to symbolise the gulf between the ghetto Jew
and the Hebrew or Palestinian worker.

Rebellion against the orthodox tradition is characteristic of
many writers of the period. A character of the novelist Haim
Hazaz (1898–) attacks the whole course of Jewish history since
Biblical days as being a non-history. This attack is made within
the framework of the story—'The Sermon'[100]—where Judka,
the hero, delivers an address to a Zionist meeting. He questions
the function of the land of Israel, and the link between the
Zionist present and the Jewish past. The history of post-Biblical
Jewry is not worthy of the name of history: 'Since we were exiled
from our country, we have been a people without history.'[101]
But this sub-existence in exile has in itself become the object of
worship, to the extent of masochism: 'We not only accept
afflictions; more, we love them'.[102] Martyrdom, the hallmark
of Jewish history; the helplessness of the Jew in the hands of the
gentile, is considered admirable in itself. And the same is true

97. *Ibid.*, p. 37.
98. *Ibid.*, p. 38.
99. *Ibid.*
100. H. Hazaz: *Ha-derashah.* To be
found in the collection *Sippurim nivḥarim* (Dvir, 1952), p. 184.
101. *Ibid.*, p. 189.
102. *Ibid.*

of the exile: 'Exile—ah—how they love it, how they cling to it.'[103] And the belief in the Messiah was very convenient, because it excused passivity: 'The Messiah king will do everything for them and they have nothing to do but to sit and wait till he comes.'[104] But in truth 'they do not want to be redeemed'.[105] The speaker then goes on to contrast this with the reality of the new Jewish Palestine. The traditional Jew does not really want Palestine; he wants to believe in future redemption by a Messiah who will never come. The Zionist starts from the other end. He would destroy Judaism, the Judaism of the dream, and build a reality that is its opposite. The Zionist is the anti-Jew, and Zionism is anti-Judaism: 'Zionism and Judaism are not the same things, but two different things, perhaps even two contradictory things.'[106] The Zionist is the disenchanted Jew: 'When a man cannot be a Jew, he becomes a Zionist.'[107] Zionism is built on the ruins of Judaism, and is not its continuation or fulfilment: 'Zionism is not a continuation, not the cure for a blow. Nonsense! It is uprooting and destruction, the opposite of what went before.'[108]

Another completely negative appraisal of Judaism was made by Joseph Haim Brenner (1881–1921), the great Hebrew novelist, addressed by Lamdan in *Masada* as 'the wallower'.[109] Brenner in writing about Mendele Mocher Seforim,[110] says of Rabbinic literature that it has the uniform colour of the words of a dead God.[111] Brenner also regards the Jewish people as only half alive, contemptible in its passivity and helplessness; and he sees them for the first time objectively portrayed in Mendele's work, particularly in his *Book of Beggars* (*Sefer ha-kabzanim*). Brenner is opposed to Ahad Ha'am's generous appreciation of the past. The Jew is rootless, strange, and helpless: 'He is other, odd, foreign and ridiculous, and never earns

103. *Ibid.*, p. 191.
104. *Ibid.*, p. 193.
105. *Ibid.*, p. 196.
106. *Ibid.*, p. 197.
107. *Ibid.*, p. 198.
108. *Ibid.*, p. 199.

109. *Masada*, p. 65—The Wallower.
110. Brenner: *Collected Works* (Steybel, 1928), Vol. 7, p. 219—*Ha-'arakhat azmenu bi-shloshet ha-kerakhim*.
111. *Ibid.*

any respect for himself. But all this does not matter to him, and anyway, he cannot help himself, push himself, instead of needing a push. He always needs others.'[112] Even for the fact that he is hated, he is contemptible, for he stimulated that hatred: 'Not the fact that gentiles are superstitious should depress us, nor that they are false and absurd. But ourselves, that we give rise to the strange legends by which we are known.'[113] Religion, Brenner sees as an excuse for inactivity, as Judka views the belief in the coming of the Messiah: 'The Jews are not a religious people, but men who cling to religion, many out of hypocrisy and debasement, that religion should support them.'[114] Brenner denies that there is anything of value to be taken over from the Jewish past: 'We have no inheritance. No future generation will add anything. And as for what they did leave—Rabbinic literature—it would have been better had we not inherited it.'[115] Brenner, like Berdichevsky, would start a new national life right from the beginning. What is left of the past is unusable, and must be cast aside: 'Now we are living in non-surroundings, completely in non-surroundings. We must begin everything anew, lay the first stone.'[116] But Brenner's positive proposal for the new life is something not mentioned by Hazaz or Berdichevsky; it is pioneering work, *ḥaluẓiut*. Brenner concludes his essay on a note of hope for the renewal of the Hebrew people, if they move in the right direction: 'Our life longing whispers hope to us: workers' colonies, workers' colonies.'[117] Such a colossal evil as the two-thousand-year sickness that Brenner describes can apparently be removed by such a simple cure as 'work on the soil'. What Brenner is giving voice to here is the faith of the Zionist socialists of the second and third waves of immigration in the efficacy of pioneering Zionism as a cure for the ills peculiar to the Jewish people.

What Berdichevsky, Hazaz and Brenner had in common was that they recognised the revolutionary nature of the new society that was being built, or were prophets of its creation.

112. *Ibid.*, p. 234.
113. *Ibid.*
114. *Ibid.*, p. 250.
115. *Ibid.*, p. 259.
116. *Ibid.*, p. 266.
117. *Ibid.*, p. 267.

Ahad Ha'am, who lived contemporaneously with Brenner and Berdichevsky, did not fully recognise the nature of the crisis. Our poet, Lamdan, did recognise the crisis, and he accepted the Zionist solution as a participant of the third *aliya* to Palestine. We have already seen that from the point of view of form and content, *Masada* is a modern poem, a work of the new literature that can only be understood in the context of the literary revolution of the twentieth century. Likewise, his views of the Jewish past should be understood in the modern context. But, like Ahad Ha'am, he attempts to stress the link between the past and the present, and what is common to both. He often does this by the use of traditional imagery.[118] The enthusiasm of the pioneers he compares to that of his ancestors during religious festivals: 'Thus danced our fathers: one hand on a neighbour's shoulder, the other holding a scroll of the law.'[119] And in the same section, Lamdan says explicitly: 'The chain is still not broken, the chain still continues from father to son.'[120] A leading critic says of Lamdan's verse: 'Generations pass and go, but from a certain angle, divisions of place and time fall, and what is left is the archetype of the nation's fate', and 'Lamdan is characterised by a deep consciousness of an unbreakable link between the people and the personal experience, even the most intimate, of the present'.[121] This was said of Lamdan's Biblical poems, where the poet's consciousness of historical inevitability, and the Jewish Fate, was even stronger. But here, as well as stressing the link with the past, the poet is also conscious of the newness of the experiment. At the end of *Masada* he writes: 'We have no praise for God, creator of the world. As from now, a new book of Genesis is opened on the wall.'[122] With Brenner, Berdichevsky and Hazaz, Lamdan is aware that the 'book' to be opened is a new one, though he has a strong historical consciousness and, in his later verse, was to stress the historical link to the exclusion of all else.

118. See discussion of his use of imagery in chapter 'His Imagery' (Chapter VII).

119. *Masada*, p. 39.   120. *Ibid.*

121. See Kurzweil: *Ha-toda'ah ha-historit be-shirei Yitzhak Lamdan* in *Molad*, Issue 19.

122. *Masada*, p. 82.

Chapter 3

MASADA—A DESCRIPTION

For a translation of the text of *Masada*, see pp. 199ff. below.

The Background

Masada[1] is a part-dramatic, part-epic poem, composed in six sections, that describes the spiritual struggle of the poet in arriving at his decision to 'ascend', i.e. to emigrate to Masada (Palestine), his reactions to the new environment, and his adaptation to the new country. The title *Masada* is taken from the name of the mountain in Judea where the Jews last held out in the war against Rome. This fortress was held by the Zealots until after the fall of Jerusalem.[2] Masada is intended in the poem to symbolise the modern Zionist struggle for Palestine. The poem was written in the years 1923–24 after Lamdan had arrived in Palestine with the third *aliya* in 1920; but the background of the first dramatic section of the poem is revolutionary Russia,[3] and the civil war that followed in the wake of revolution. The chaos of the country fell particularly hard on the Jews,[4] and in this poem, Lamdan outlines a typical experience:

'One Autumn night, on a restless couch far from our ravaged

1. The spelling 'masada' is based on the Hebrew מסדה. The Biblical form of the word is מצדה, meaning 'fortress' or 'mountain fort', see Jud. 6:2. But LXX transliterated the 'צ' by 's' and the English spelling customarily follows, see e.g. G. A. Williamson's paperback translation of Josephus' *The Jewish War* (London, 1959), p. 399.

2. See H. Graetz: *History of the Jews* (Philadelphia, 1891), Vol. 2, p. 316.

3. The October revolution in 1917, after the fall of Kerensky.

4. Compare the stories of the revolution by Haim Hazaz (1898–), e.g. in the volume *Avanim roteḥot* (Tel-Aviv, 1946), p. 195.

home, my mother died; In her eyes a last tear glistened as she whispered me a dying blessing, before I went to distant, foreign battlefields, with my army kit pressing on my shoulder. . . . On Ukrainian paths, dotted with graves, and swollen with pain, my sad-eyed, pure-hearted brother fell dead, to be buried in a heathen grave.'[5]

It is during this period of violence that Lamdan (and this applies to the third *aliya* in general) made his decision to emigrate. After a description of the violence done to his family, Lamdan says of himself:

'Whilst I, still fastening my crumbling soul with the last girders of courage, fled at midnight to the exile ship, to ascend to Masada.'[6]

Masada represented for the poet a challenge, a slap in the face of the traditional Fate of the Jewish people. Masada could re-adjust the balance of History with one final act of defiance:

'I was told: The final banner of rebellion has been unfurled there, and demands from Heaven and Earth, God and Man: "Payments". Stubborn nails grind the gospel of comfort on tablets of rock: Against the hostile Fate of generations, an antagonistic breast is bared with a roar: "Enough! You or I! Here will the battle decide the final judgement!"'[7]

Of course, the commitment to Masada was not easy to arrive at, and it is matter of historical fact that only a small minority elected for the Zionist solution. The other ideologies current at the time are echoed in this first section of the poem. Three separate reactions to the holocaust are expressed here, other than the Zionist. So the poet's affirmation of Masada is not made blindly, without awareness of other possible courses of action. Of the four counsels presented here, two are negative, and two are positive. The two negative counsels are nihilistic, although one would attempt to exploit the situation by shedding as much blood as possible in his worship of the 'God of Revenge', and the other would lie in wait passively for the end to come. Of the two positive counsels, one is Communistic,

5. *Masada* (Dvir, Tel-Aviv, 10th ed.)   6. *Ibid.*
   p. 11.   7. *Ibid.*

i.e. it sees a positive virtue in the chaos of the revolution, which is in the nature of 'a last tribute' to Molech.[8] After the payment of this tribute, there will be a 'new world'. And the second positive counsel is the poet's own. But this also has a negative side to it—the flight from the campaign.

The poet can apparently not find sufficient cause to remain in his homeland, although: 'Like a weary moth, deprived of a day and sunlight am I drawn to its [i.e. this country's] cold, consuming flame'.[9] He would escape from the chaos; not in order to await death, nor to fan the flames of destruction, but in order to build something new. In the first section, it is the negative aspect of the decision that is stressed. The poet must leave because 'over everything [is] chaos, chaos, chaos—no people, no land, no God, and no man'.[10] The poet comes as 'a fugitive';[11] it is twice mentioned that he 'flees' to Masada.[12] So he arrives in the new country as a refugee who has fled from his homeland to find 'refuge'. This seems to be the primary motivation of Lamdan's emigration; but his positive motivation lies in his choice of Masada as a refuge, and his regard for it as a challenge to the miserable Fate of his people.[13] From the moment of his emigration, the poet would commit himself entirely to the country of his choice:

'I pin myself entirely to the bars of your gates. Open them, Masada, and I, the fugitive, shall come.'[14] A negative reaction becomes a positive selection.

Proposed Solutions

In this first chapter, we find three sections which consist of the speeches of certain people who encounter the poet on his flight to Masada. The three, who briefly set out their ideology in relation to the contemporary holocaust, are characterised neutrally as 'friends' (Heb. re'a, re'im). In keeping with the

8. *Ibid.*, p. 15.
9. *Ibid.*, p. 22.
10. *Ibid.*
11. *Ibid.*, p. 22.

12. P. 11.
13. See above, Note 7.
14. *Masada*, p. 23.

character of the poem, not only are these figures given no names, but are also in no way individually characterised. All that exists of them is their ideologies; so we too can regard them as embodied ideologies. These ideologies or anti-ideologies were certainly current at the time of the Russian revolution, and we may consider this section of the poem either as an attempt to characterise the theoretical mood of the period and place, or as a description of the poet's own individual conflict, and the alternatives with which he felt himself confronted. Rather than refer to the speakers as 'friends', we would more accurately designate them 'protagonists' of particular viewpoints.

The first protagonist, who has just heard of the miracle of Masada, where 'the Divine Presence, dropping atonements, has descended on the heads of the warriors',[15] is a nihilist craving revengeful violence. He is willing to believe in no solution at all. Masada, i.e. the Zionist solution, is an illusion, just one more snare: 'Masada is a fiction, a new snare laid by Fate in its scorn for the last remnant.'[16] Fate is dominant, and not benevolent. The course of Jewish existence has been strictly mapped out; no deviation is possible. A curse has been pronounced, and there can be no existence without it: 'Into our blood has the curse been poured, and it is oil to the wick of our existence, without which the wick will not burn, even in Masada.'[17] As long as the Jewish nation exists, the curse will co-exist with it. Only one task remains to be fulfilled, and that is to take revenge; any other course is utopian and cowardly. He reproaches the poet for wanting to escape his duty by leaving: 'How can you leave behind you the tight fists of graves, that, in their fury, have congealed against the extended tongue, whirling about between the furthest horizons?'[18] The only thing that Israel should now find worthy of attention is the propagation of revenge: 'To one God should the eye of Israel be lifted unto extermination—the God of vengeance.'[19]

15. *Ibid.*, p. 12.   18. *Ibid.*
16. *Ibid.*, p. 13.
17. *Ibid.*   19. *Ibid.*

This modern invocation of the God of Vengeance is a per-
version of the Biblical reference. In the Bible, the plea for
God's vengeance to fall on certain people is based on an absolute moral conception of good and evil. In Psalm 94, where the
psalmist invokes this God: 'A God of Vengeance is the Lord.
Appear, O God of Vengeance',[20] he invokes punishment on
people whom he considers to be evil, who 'kill the widow and
the foreigner, and murder orphans.'[21] The psalmist there would
restore the balance of justice, so he calls on an absolute Authority to do that, to punish the bad and reward the good. But in
this nihilist speech, no moral authority of any kind is invoked.
In the Bible, negative judgement is based on positive value; but
here, revenge is considered an end in itself, and not as a means
for establishing a coherent moral order. This protagonist sees
destruction coming upon himself and upon his people, so his
desire is to wreak more destruction in his own fall, that
nothing be left: 'A heavy night has descended on the world—
come let us strangle the sun of the morrow whilst it is yet in
the swaddling clothes of its twilight, that it be not appeased
with fresh mornings!'[22] For the purposes of destruction, any
means at hand may be employed. Since there is a Communist
revolution in progress, it constitutes a useful instrument for his
own purposes. He is prepared to join the revolution; but in
order to shed blood. The red shawl will serve as a protective
veil over the murdering knife: 'Here is spread out a red shawl
—a new, striped coat that the priests and prophets of the world
have fashioned for the festival of its happiness, for the morrow.
Come, let us wrap ourselves in this red shawl, and secrete the
knife of revenge beneath it.'[23] This God of Vengeance should
be worshipped with all the ceremony due to a true God:
'Come, let us set an altar for Him, and act as His priests in the
Temple . . . this is the task of every lad in Judah amongst the
last remnant.'[24]

The second protagonist is a true Communist, and supports

20. Ps. 94:1.   23. *Ibid.*
21. Ps. 94:6.
22. *Masada*, p. 13.   24. *Ibid.*, p. 14.

the revolution for the beneficent results that he thinks will accrue from it. He criticises the poet for fleeing the campaign instead of assisting; Masada is a counsel of despair: 'A lie is Masada, invented by the despairing and confused who have no strength to hold the oars, and to row in the stormy night to the shores of morning that await the ravaged boat of man.'[25] Those who flee from the campaign are cowards, and they are mistaking a difficult period of transition for a complete disaster: 'What darkness? Night has fallen to cover the corpse of the old world.'[26] The protagonist here admits to the ravages, but holds that their importance will be eclipsed by the following millennium: 'and why should you weep for the slaughtered and for Jacob's flock that is much bereaved? This last tribute let us pay to Molech, let us cover this border duty before we pass on, crossed-armed with an afflicted and sick world, to the atoning kingdom of redemption' . . .[27]

Messianic language is used here in a secular sense. To the Communist, the revolution is the key event in world history, the watershed beyond which the course of man must radically alter. Turmoil is naturally to be expected at such a moment: 'See how the red curtain is lowered on to the stage of great events to divide off one campaign from another; Be strong, friend, until the curtain be raised and the storm abate with the appearance of the last campaign that the actors of the future have prepared.'[28] The poet is wasting his humanist idealism on the Zionist idea: 'You have dreamy eyes, and a heart sensitive to human agony, so why do your eyes bear their dream, and your heart is faith, to sow them on the fallowness of Masada, upon rocks of a ruined fortress.'[29] The reference to 'ruined fortress' is aimed at the attempt to sustain the actual fortress of Masada against huge odds, in the war against Rome. The attempt failed then, and it is not likely to succeed now; the odds against success are still tremendous. And when the revolution prevails, all will fall before it, including Masada itself:

25. Ibid., p. 15.

26. Ibid.

27. Ibid.

28. Ibid.

29. Ibid.

'But when the red curtain is raised over the stage of great events—even [Masada] will kneel at the sight of the last campaign, and break off its rusty armour to place it at the feet of the regnant morrow!'[30]

The third protagonist is, like the first, a nihilist, i.e. he believes in the virtue of no constructive solution. But, unlike the first, he is unwilling to take any positive steps in any direction at all. He would just passively await the end, which he is confident will come soon. Solutions are illusory: 'Where is the last redeemer? He is wandering in the dense forests of generations and has delayed until now, until now. . . . Woe to the pathfinders in Israel, to those who seek solutions and conclusions—and know not that we were created to be only a riddle of delight.'[31] Both proponents of solutions, the Communist and the Zionist, tend to use Messianic terminology, and stress the apocalyptic 'last'. Here the nihilist contradicts such trust, and is sceptical of the projected arrival of this 'last' redeemer. As did the first protagonist, this speaker believes in the apparent immutability of the Jewish Fate. Here, it is the Jewish Fate to be 'a riddle of delight', i.e. an exploitable toy for the use and entertainment of other nations. Joseph Trumpeldor,[32] in his letters, speaks of the Jews in similar terms, as an 'insignificant plaything'.[33] But Trumpeldor is vehemently opposed to this concept of the Jew, and would uproot it through the Zionist solution. Although there is agreement on terminology, the approach is different. The protagonist here is resigned, whilst Trumpeldor thinks that the situation is capable of change. Communism is also rejected here; it is seen as 'a new red veil',[34] underneath which remains 'your afflictor of yore'.[35] Ideologies pass like fads, but Israel's Fate remains the same: 'As

30. *Ibid.*, p. 16.

31. *Ibid.*, p. 17, For a discussion of the terminology here, see Chapter 7, 'Lamdan's Imagery', section on *Masada*.

32. See below, section on 'Gordon, Brenner and Trumpeldor'.

33. See *Me-ḥayyei Joseph Trumpeldor*, (Tel-Aviv, 1945, ed. Poznanski), p. 26. The expression he uses there is *Keli mishak kal.*

34. *Masada*, p. 17.

35. *Ibid.*

there is but one sun in the firmament, so there is but one Fate for Israel; a fixed planet amongst the heavenly bodies whose course cannot be altered.'[36]

It is important to note not only what alternatives are considered here, but also what alternatives are not considered. There is, for example, no mention of any possibility of emigration to America, or to other parts of Europe, although this happened to be the choice of large numbers, perhaps the majority, of people, in Lamdan's position. Such a consideration would indeed have been irrelevant for the poet, because his concern was, not with which country offered the best opportunities for prosperity and comfort, but with the question of whether Zionism, the election of Masada, was a viable ideology or not. To this ideology, he placed his counterpoints; the negative assertion that there is no possibility of a true, positive ideology, and the positive assertion that the revolution has to be supported, not for any narrow nationalistic end, but for universal, humanitarian ends. The poet had reached the point where only apocalyptic solutions seemed relevant, so crucial did the general human and particular Jewish situation seem. He is conscious of the whole weight of history leaning in one direction; they must either surrender to the irresistible Force, as do the negative protagonists, or bring to bear vast ideological potential, as do the Communist and the Zionist. Mere everyday questions, such as the particular choice of country for immigration, are of no concern in the large issue here.

The Men of Masada

The second chapter of the poem has its setting in Masada, i.e. in Palestine, after the poet, without theoretical argument, has elected to join the Masada forces. This chapter is concerned with the nature of the human material which has chosen the same path. As in the first chapter, the poet does not endow the

36. *Ibid.*, p. 18.

characters with individual traits, but ascribes to them characteristics which may be appropriate for the collective. So again, the protagonists involved here are types.

The first type has been characteristically exposed to the violence of the epoch; he has just escaped hanging, and asks: 'What shall I do with the end of the rope that still pinches at my neck?'[37] It is possible that this was an attempted suicide, and that the rope still pinching at his neck is the possibility of a further attempt. He has come to Masada out of despair.

The second is a 'tender sacrifice' mourned by his parents. He has come because 'the legend of Masada is so beautiful, and the wondrous wall attracts so'.[38] He has come of his own free will, inspired by the idea that Masada represents.

The third, like the first, has experienced violence, and also comes as a last resort. He was the only one left alive of his family on a day of violence. He thinks there must be some reason for this: perhaps to find 'atonement'. But if to find atonement, where? 'And it happened that whilst I was so pleading, a secret voice answered me: "In Masada." I hearkened to the voice, and came.'[39] But if his hopes be disappointed, then he intends, as hints the first, to kill himself. Masada is, for these people, the last fortress. If it should fall, nothing remains.

A fourth is also in despair, not so much at his personal lot, as at the lot of Israel. For he speaks in the person of Israel: 'They are not my hands!' he says in answer to a question. 'They are the hands of Israel, clutching everything, though everything slips from their grasp.'[40] This is a plaint at the Fate of Israel, which is always grasping at new things, but which never receives the fruit: 'Oh, these hands, the first to raise the flags of every gospel, and the last to receive comfort.'[41] For him too, Masada is the last station, for if Masada as well is not held, then the hands must be cut off: 'I implore you [the hands] to grasp the wall of Masada, to grasp it unceasingly. If not, may these hands from which everything drops, be cut off!'[42]

37. *Ibid.*, p. 27.
38. *Ibid.*, p. 28.
39. *Ibid.*, p. 29.
40. *Ibid.*, p. 30.
41. *Ibid.*
42. *Ibid.*

We have seen that there are two main categories of people in Masada; the idealistic optimist, who comes of his own free will in order to build a new country, and the disillusioned pessimist, who has been driven to Masada by despair, and regards it as a last resort. The poet now sums up the essential qualities of these two groups from the point of view of this contrast. Lamdan tries to capture the difference in tone. The first group brings not first fruits (as they do in *Massekhet Bikkurim* from *Seder Zeraim* in the Mishnah, whose language the passage suggests), but 'handfuls of hearts, [and] the gold of dreams'.[43] Their jugs contain 'singing blood', and their baskets are full of love: 'Everything is an offering for the battle, and a dedication to Masada.'[44] What they offer is the first fruit of their lives and the wells of their youth, i.e. their enthusiasm, idealism and sacrifice.

This optimism is not shared by the second category. They say: 'We, needy and barefoot, ascend to the wall.'[45] This group is naked, because it has already been stripped of its idealism on other occasions before the Masada project: 'On all the poles fixed at the crossroads, we have hung our cloaks as flags announcing freedom. In festive processions, far over there, are the flags waved, and we, naked, are forsaken on the crossroads.'[46] But because they have lost their youthful idealism, it does not mean that they are totally unequipped: 'We still have one treasure: the defiance that follows despair—the jewel of all hopeless, and friend of the oppressed.'[47] What looks like a weakness can be a strength. If they have lost all, there is no fear of losing anything more, so they constitute a purely efficient fighting force, formed by hatred: 'The anguish of hatred shrinks us into one closed fist that is brought down in all its wrath on the skull of our Fate—let either the fist or the accursed skull be dashed to pieces!'[48] Again, there is expressed the notion of Masada as the last hope. It will be either a success, or the final failure.

43. *Ibid.*, p. 31.　　　　　　　　46. *Ibid.*
44. *Ibid.*　　　　　　　　　　　47. *Ibid.*
45. *Ibid.*, p. 32.　　　　　　　　48. *Ibid.*

Character of the Poem

We have already mentioned that the author in the poem identifies himself with the nation.[49] His theme is not his personal suffering and history, but that collectively experienced by the section of society in which he is interested, viz. the third *aliya* to Palestine in the twenties of this century. The poet deals only with those aspects of his individuality which are common to the group. When he says: 'Whilst I, still fastening my crumbling soul with the last girders of courage',[50] he represents a whole generation in their feeling of disintegration over these violent years. The idea of Masada here acts as a sort of glue saving the personality from complete disintegration. Of the two categories of people mentioned in the last section, the childishly idealistic and the despairing defiant, the poet identifies himself more with the latter, as can be seen both from the language he uses when speaking of himself and his 'crumbling soul', and from the fact that of the four separate types he mentions in that chapter, three look on Masada as a last desperate possibility. So the poet is consistently close to this category of immigrant, and the poem embodies in abstract terminology his own background and hope.

Lamdan is concerned with discovering a viable ideology for the Jewish people at this point of history. But no possibility other than the Masada idea, the Zionist solution, is seriously considered. At several points, the poem hovers near nihilism, and a chief characteristic of the poem, that was also to characterise Lamdan's later work, is the vehemence with which the poem attacks popular ideologies. But Communism, the only positive alternative that is heard here, is apparently dismissed without argument. Of course, there is no intellectual consideration of the problems concerned, and the only thing that interests the poet is his own particular solution, considered as a defiance of Fate. Communism is similarly defiant, and to know why the poet rejects it we have to turn not to his persona, but

49. See above chapter on 'The New Hebrew Literature', Chapter 2.

50. *Masada*, p. 11.

to the third protagonist who encounters him on his flight, and who calls the new ideology 'a red veil', and its proponents 'false prophets'. That the narrator in *Masada* was himself sympathetic to this view of Communism, we see in the following section, where in his own persona, he says of the proponents of Communism: 'Says the man donning the red veil'.[51] The veil is a suitable cover, but the face beneath remains the same. Communism is only the latest, most fashionable guise.

Once in Masada, the mood varies and changes, and the view of Masada's possible success, too, varies with the mood of the piece. Also, the poet's description oscillates between first person singular, first person plural and third person. It is sometimes difficult to tell exactly who is speaking. In the optimistic passages, at one time he says: 'At such a time are night bonfires raised on the wall, and round them, the children of Masada go out with flaming dances.'[52] Here, the third person is used, as if the poet is detached from the group. But then later, when they are dancing, the poet chants: 'So let us dance; one hand gripping the circle, the second clutching the load of a generation.'[53] Here the poet identifies himself directly with the group. Often the poet speaks in the first person singular, as when he questions his own and the group's motives in going to Masada: 'Then why did we leave everything to ascend to the wall? Even if I knew, it would be all the same to me. I am too tired. I can no longer stand on the wall facing the battle. I am too tired!'[54] Here the poet seems to be speaking personally, especially when he sentimentally recalls his past: 'I remember scenes of yesterday: on soft carpets of forgetfulness I rolled as a young foal rolls on grass beds in the Spring.'[55] But it is also possible that he is adopting one of the personæ of the other pioneers, as he does in this section.

In the following section 'Bereavement', he may be speaking for himself when he writes: 'I said that my people sent me, and that I bore everything for my sender',[56] because this is the

51. *Ibid.*, p. 19.
52. *Ibid.*, p. 37.
53. *Ibid.*, p. 39.
54. *Ibid.*, p. 60.
55. *Ibid.*
56. *Ibid.*, p. 63.

passage where the 'I' receives the revelation of 'Abtalion', i.e. A. D. Gordon, the theoretical representative of the pioneering third *aliya*, and of 'the wallower', the novelist and publicist, J. H. Brenner. It is after the revelation of these two teachers that the mood of the poem again veers from one of complete despair at the seeming futility of the pioneering effort in the light of the complete indifference with which the rest of the people regard it. After the appearance of these two figures, we have the incident of the prayer, when someone slips away 'out of the camp' to kneel in supplication. Again, the poet reverts to the use of the third person, but we may wonder, since this comes immediately after the comforting revelation of the two 'seers' of Masada to the poet himself, whether the poet does not speak of himself still in these sections, though the only characterisation here is of a 'shadow' rising, and the neutral 'one'.

The prayer is addressed directly to God (Heb. *Elohim*), i.e. to a powerful agent who can intervene in the affairs of man, and shape his destiny. This 'God' may be contrasted with the 'age-old hostile Fate', which is apparently immutable. We heard earlier of 'the final banner of rebellion' that was raised in Masada against this Fate. This banner had been raised by man, i.e. by a natural force, in his fight against blind Forces. This is the first and last time in the poem where God is requested to intervene, or even where the possibility of His powerful existence is admitted. We have heard so far of man's fight, success and failure, and we are to hear later an appeal to man to fight again, and to take what has traditionally been God's realm on his own shoulders—'Be strong, be strong, and we shall be strengthened!'[57] is the demand there made to the people of Masada. We also witness the charge of hope that Joseph Galili, i.e. Trumpeldor, gives to the poet: 'I am also true to that same calling answerer'.[58] The exceptional feature of the prayer is the appeal for the intervention of a supernatural force. Otherwise, in this poem, the only supernatural force that is admitted is the passive one of 'Fate', clearly something not open to supplication. It is impossible to say to what

57. *Ibid.*, p. 82. 58. *Ibid.*, p. 75.

degree the poet was intellectually inclined towards a deistic viewpoint from his poetry alone. There is a possibility that he drew sustenance from the belief of others, or that he was merely assuming the possibility, or that in some moods he did hold this belief. We can only record the divergence of the theoretical assumption of this prayer from the rest of the poem.

It is perhaps best to conclude that the poet in *Masada* speaks in part personally, but in the main nationally. It is impossible, and probably not very fruitful, to try to disentangle the different strands of identification. People can believe many different, and even contradictory things, in different moods. What is important is the degree of sincerity with which emotional impressions are recorded. But it is certainly true to say that *Masada* is a political rather than an existential poem, i.e. that it is open to the influence of great events, the course of history, and the life of the nation, rather than to that of intimate experience. The poet is concerned with public rather than with private life, and with the people and its riddle rather than with the individual.

Gordon, Brenner and Trumpeldor

There are three figures who appear to the poet in the time of his distress, when it seems that his depression has reached a new low. In the fifth chapter, in the section entitled 'Bereavement', terrible disappointment is recorded: 'By the dying camp-fires, heroes stumble, kneel, and murmur their sorrow in the gloom.'[59] The dying campfires are symbolic of the hope which is dying amongst the people. The pioneers have, it seems, failed in their effort. The poet asks himself for what purpose the ascent to the wall was made in the first place, and his tentative answer is: 'I said that my people sent me, and that I bore everything for my sender.'[60] The effort was made not for his own sake personally, but for the sake of the people, who craved salvation. But apparently, the people are not interested in Masada; they come, but only for motives of personal gain:

59. *Ibid.*, p. 57. 60. *Ibid.*, p. 63.

'They are our brothers, they are coming to us. But oh woe, they are pedlars! They have heard that there is a crisis in Masada, that there is a battle, and they have come here as camp followers to store the spoil of the battle.'[61] It seems that the sole justification for the pioneering effort has been nullified: The very people for whom the fight has been fought are unconcerned. The poet begins to doubt the point of the exercise: 'My God, my God, God of Masada, God of the few aspiring men who bear the last prey in the great famine of generations, —should we fight for them? Is it to them that we want to bring the tidings of victory?'[62]

It is at this point that 'Abtalion' appears to the poet. Abtalion is a Rabbinic name,[63] and is here the alias of the spokesman of *ḥaluziut* (pioneering) of the time, A. D. Gordon (1856–1922). The surname may be a compound of two separate words, 'ab' meaning 'father', and 'talia' meaning 'young man', the young old man, i.e. old in body, but young in spirit. This name for Gordon hints at the youthful behaviour and thought of this middle-aged man, who was already forty-eight years old when he came to Palestine to begin his pioneering life.[64] Gordon was considered the spokesman of the pioneering movement, and had already been long established in Palestine,[65] so his advice is of the utmost relevance to Lamdan's question. It was from Gordon that one such as Lamdan drew inspiration and courage. As the poet addresses him: 'You, seer of Masada, who have raised us to battle, and trained our hands to bear the shield and draw the bow.'[66] Gordon's and Lamdan's concern was the same: the redemption of the people, and they chose the same means to fulfil the end: the pioneering, Zionist solution.

61. *Ibid.*, p. 64.
62. *Ibid.*
63. See Mishnah, *Aboth*, 1:10, 11.
64. For biographical details here, see Gordon, *Writings* (Jerusalem, 1952), Vol. 1, ed. Bergmann and Shohet, entitled *Ha-umah ve-ha-'avodah*, pp. 55–72.

65. *Ibid.* He immigrated in 1905, at the time of the second *aliya*. He was, of course, already dead by the time Lamdan wrote *Masada*, as were also Brenner and Trumpeldor.

66. *Masada*, p. 65.

It was Gordon more than anyone else who justified labour as a redemptive force, the labour which is the engine of Zionism. Labour would bring genuine independence in its trail, and would be the salvation of the Jewish people. As he says: 'A great human idea, which has constant and great revitalising power, is the idea of the revival of life through labour and nature. . . . It really does resurrect Judaism, the spirit of true Judaism.'[67] But what if the people are indifferent to the possibility, as they are here? 'Look, pedlars, our flesh and blood, come to Masada, spread out in camps at the foot of the wall, [they would not dream of aspiring to its peak for their fear of battle, and do not even desire victory] as previously they came only as camp followers, and it is all the same to them who the camp belongs to, and where it goes. Is it their head that longs for the crown of redemption? Did you not err, seer of Masada, in your vision?'[68]

The poet here fundamentally challenges 'the seer of Masada', who seems to have made a mistaken estimate of the spiritual material of the people. The poet embodies the seer's answer and advice in one simple sentence: 'Do not ask, and do not enquire, my son. You redeem yourself, and say to your friends: let each man redeem himself in the battle, for you are the vanguard of the people, and your head is its head.'[69] Gordon's advice is that each person should do what is right in his eyes. Thereby, will they constitute together an élite, a vanguard (Heb. *shekhinah*). We find in Gordon's work that he does actually give such advice. In an open letter to Brenner, he writes in answer to a criticism that labour will only redeem 'the few': 'And when you look from this point of view at man's lot in general, you see that the power of the few is not so small . . . and that the power of all of them together to direct the stream of humanity to the chosen place is great.'[70] And he also says of the individual that 'he does not make calculations, or look to the sides',[71] i.e. he does not worry about what others

67. See Gordon, *op. cit.*, pp. 174–5.

68. *Masada*, p. 65.

69. *Ibid.*

70. A. D. Gordon: *op. cit.* Essay,

'Open letter to J. H. Brenner', p. 164.

71. *Ibid.*, p. 160.

do, but concerns himself with his own redemption, through, in this instance, work on the land in particular. This idea is characteristic of the writers of the period. Brenner himself sees workers' colonies as the only possible hope for the people,[72] and the poet David Shimoni (1886–1956) writes: '[The earth] wept, pleaded: redeem me from captivity, save and be saved.'[73]

J. H. Brenner (1881–1921), the novelist and publicist, is the next person to appear to the poet, and to be questioned by him. We have already seen that his estimate of Jewish existence was gloomy in the extreme,[74] yet the novelist did not turn away from this existence; on the contrary, he dwelt on it, probed its indignity, and exposed every sore. For this reason, he is addressed by the poet here as 'the wallower', and is thus approached: 'You, who taught us to lick our wounds in order to cure them, and mercilessly bared every bereavement and our great failure that we might see them and know them as one knows the face of the enemy in the battle.'[75] Brenner is here appreciated because he does not try to escape the sombre reality, to paint a fictional picture. And yet comfort is afforded by the very act of 'licking the wounds', of 'wallowing'.

Brenner strove for a position of commitment on social questions, as he wrote in one of his novels: '. . . We must not stand round life as mere spectators. We must fight, to reform, to grow to exalt. Mere watching is a rejection of the sanctity of life! Cursed be those who merely watch.'[76] This deeply committed honest person opted for the Zionist solution, for the idea of redemption through labour, i.e. for everything implied in commitment to Masada as Lamdan understood it. Surely he, so frank in his estimation of the situation, would be able to offer the poet some counsel. So Lamdan asks. But the answer

72. See above in chapter on 'The New Hebrew Literature.'

73. See Shimoni: *Idylls* (Jerusalem, 1957), p. 43.

74. See above in chapter on 'The New Hebrew Literature', section 'Revelation of Judaism'.

75. *Masada*, p. 66, refers to Brenner's novel *Bereavement and Failure*.

76. *Mi-saviv la-nekudah* (*Selected Works*, 1953; Tel-Aviv), p. 74.

received is negative. The 'wallower' can offer nothing but his wallowing: 'He answered me not a word, but his dumb reply was: "I know that I have not wallowed all my life for nothing. To wallow, to wallow!".'[77] The 'wallower' will apparently offer no constructive advice, but will continue to lick the wounds, and be sure that there is some purpose and point to it.

Joseph Trumpeldor (1880–1920) makes his appearance to the poet through the person of 'Joseph Galili', who is Joseph of Gamala, leader of the last stand in the Jewish war against Rome in the Galilee, in Gamala.[78] Like Joseph of Gamala, Trumpeldor too was killed in battle; in his case, in the defence of Tel-Hai, a fortress in the North of Palestine, against Arabs, in 1920. But incredibly, after the spiritual depths plumbed by the camp, he echoes the psalmic cry of *la menazeah*—'to the victor', a rousing victory cry that will brook no defeat. Trumpeldor once said of himself: 'When I come to taking a course of action, all my doubts melt and disappear.'[79] It is a leader of this calibre that is needed now, with the voice of rebellion, the voice that the poet himself once heard: 'Thus did they sing there when the rebellion was raised, and when flags were unfurled . . . thus sang I too when I ascended to the wall.'[80] This voice calls: 'Ascend, ascend,' and though reluctant and incapable at first, the poet eventually assents: 'I am also true to that same calling answerer.' The Masada project is once again affirmed, though perhaps not intellectually, because the poet is conscious of something else speaking within him: 'I and not I, someone else in me, one bold, obstinate, blind, answers.'[81] It is the practical leader, rather than the theoretician or the writer, who captures and commands the poet's enthusiasm. He is swept off his feet by the action that defies logic and history.

77. *Masada*, p. 66.

78. See Josephus: *The Jewish War* (ed. Williamson, London, 1959), pp. 214–18. Also Graetz: *op. cit.*, Vol. 2, pp. 289–90.

79. See *Me-ḥayyei Joseph Trumpeldor op. cit.*, p. 90.

80. *Masada*, p. 74.

81. *Ibid.*, p. 75.

Adaptation to the New Country

Masada remains a foreign place to Lamdan in the poem. It exists for him more as an abstract ideal than as a concrete home. He still thinks in exilic terms of a solution for the Jews, and is not inured to the Palestinian realities. In this respect, he is more of a Russian Hebrew poet than a Palestinian. By contrast, David Shimoni, a contemporary of Lamdan, is already thoroughly Palestinian in his *Idylls*. Shimoni had had an opportunity to get acclimatised to the new conditions, as he spent a year in Palestine in 1909, as a farm-hand and guard.[82] Shimoni was influenced by Saul Tschernichowsky (1875–1943), the creator of the modern Hebrew idyll. But Tschernichowsky wrote with relish about the old Jew in Russia itself;[83] Shimoni transfers the idyll to the Palestinian scene. His characters are not nostalgic for the past; on the contrary, the present is brilliant by contrast, as sun to the shade: 'He [Berele] walks towards the mountains of Samaria, and sadness squeezes his heart for the fate of a close and miserable people; he feels empty, and the light of his life grows dim. But suddenly the stream is before him. . . . And its murmur [of the cold waves of the stream] passed his soul, and he forgot the close, miserable people, and there was delight for his heart.'[84] Shimoni's imagery is not exilic, and he takes a true, a positive delight in the countryside. His characterers are buoyant; unoppressed by suicidal tendencies and inferiority complexes. *Ḥaluẓiut*, to Shimoni, is not a last desperate plunge into an uncharted and stormy ocean; it is something completely natural. He is exchanging a repulsive way of life for a delightful one, and it is incomprehensible only that more people do not follow his example. Through Katriel in *Maẓevah* (trans. 'memorial stone'), he attacks those Zionists who regard the *ḥaluẓim* worshipfully, as though *ḥaluẓiut* were

82. See Benzion Benshalom: *Hebrew Literature between Two World Wars* (Jerusalem, 1953), p. 98.

83. E.g. Tschernichowsky's description of a circumcision celebra-

tion See E. Silberschlag: *Saul Tschernichowsky* (London, 1968).

84. See Shimoni: *Idylls, op. cit.*, p. 11.

martyrdom: 'That is the trouble, that an ancient people, afflicted and great, looks askance, delighted with its children, who are sick of the shame, the shame of exile.'[85] Exile is not merely a burden, it is a positive disgrace.

Like Lamdan's *ḥaluẓim*, and in accordance with actual practice, Shimoni's characters express the sublimity of their lives in dance. The dance is the climax of the idyll *In the Hadera Forest*, and even the terminology of its description is similar to Lamdan's: 'so light were their feet'. Like Shlonsky, he finds that he cannot adjust himself easily to city life, though he does not hate it as does that poet. He admits to the metropolis: 'You have become very dear to me, though the open spaces are seven times dearer.'[86] The countryside is what really draws him: 'What have I to do here, and whom have I in the murmuring cement city? Has not my heart been drawn even since distant childhood, to forests and fields with [their] tremendous, mysterious power.'[87] Not only is this mood appropriate to the poet's pioneering theme, but it is also in the pastoral traditions set by Y. L. Gordon in his poem 'David and Barzilai',[88] with its theme of the corruption of big-city life.

We see from these idylls that Shimoni is, on the whole, at ease in Zion. What a contrast Lamdan presents in our poem. Even the joy here is hysterical. He is homesick, and therefore, maladjusted. He still remembers his father's house with affection, for it represents warmth and security, however soundly his faith in its attendant values was shaken: 'And as for me, what is to become of me? In my blood do distant winter nights still howl, and the complaining, psalmic melody of my father murmurs in it; the sinking of Sabbath rest brings tears to my eyes, and coals of destruction glimmer in them.'[89] Here, he nostalgically recalls his past by the use of religious images which are no longer relevant for him in the present. The religious background is associated with the exile to which he

85. *Ibid.*, p. 59.

86. *Ibid.*, p. 33.

87. *Ibid.*, p. 27.

88. This poem is discussed in the chapter, 'Four Biblical Poems'. first section.

89. *Masada*, p. 53.

belongs no more, but for which he sometimes yearns. His father's voice is the voice of security, and when finally determination to withstand all seeps through at Trumpeldor's cry of *la menazeah*, he at first compares the cry to his father's comforting voice at prayer: '*La menazeah* ... how sweet is the voice, and how comforting. Thus did father sing Psalm tunes on Sabbath mornings, and I listened with frustrated longing.'[90] Since *La menazeah* is a psalmic heading, the voice reminds him of the singing of psalms at home. It is only on second thoughts that the poet realises that this is not the old, traditional voice, like his father's, but a new, rebellious cry: 'No! Thus did they sing there when the rebellion was raised, and when flags were unfurled ... thus sang I too when I ascended to the wall.'[91] The contrast here is between the old and the new; he is learning to acclimatise himself by renouncing his nostalgia for the past, and looking with confidence to the future.

Lamdan felt ill at ease with the landscape and climate of Palestine. For sensitive people, the process of major adjustments, such as to a new country, is complex and difficult. The environment sinks deep into the poet's soul, and he becomes intensely attached to it; the writer has a particular need for deep roots, and for familiarity. It may be that the strangeness of of a new country paralysed Bialik's muse after he left Russia for Palestine in 1922: he wrote almost no poetry from that date until his death twelve years later. Palestine was so very different from Russia. Also, Hebrew writers dreamed of Palestine from afar, and naturally, the reality was very different from the dream. As we see from his first poem, 'To the Bird',[92] Bialik dreamed of a land 'where Spring reigns eternal'.[93] Even though his enthusiasm must afterwards have been modified with the onset of maturity, the actuality of the country certainly shocked him. And in spite of the fact that Lamdan emigrated as a young man, he too found it difficult to adapt himself. He speaks despairingly of the shagginess of the landscape: 'As an

90. *Masada*, p. 74.

91. *Ibid.*

92. Bialik: *Poems* (Dvir, Tel-Aviv, 1944, p. 1).

93. *Ibid.*

unwanted object does the empty cup of my youth roll at my feet. I have faithfully poured all its wine on the rocks of Masada.'[94] The startling intensity of the sun strikes him, the sun that will tolerate no secret: 'Nothing is shut up in it, nothing is hidden from the light of the sun.'[95] This sun is still strange to him,[96] and the weather constantly takes him by surprise, even the cold: 'And I said that there was no Autumn in Masada, that the sun is constantly warm'.[97] Lamdan's unease in new surroundings can be compared to Shlonsky's. Shlonsky also looks back nostalgically to the past. This, in transit, on a train: 'I heard the tune . . . [when] did I hear it in trembling? Perhaps in my youth as the coffin [ark] proceeded, so black, in which they took my grandfather somewhere far away, like [to] a blind horizon.'[98] The expression 'as the coffin proceeded' can mean also 'as the ark travelled', and it is taken from the Pentateuch (Numbers 11:35), where the ark of the Covenant leads the children of Israel into battle. Here, the poet adapts the phrase, to use it as a play on words with 'coffin'; the God of Israel is dead. Shlonsky too associates the past with tradition. But for him, it really is dead, for he says of it explicitly that it is 'like an inscription on the dead in a black frame'.[99] Lamdan too tries to make a definite break with the past, i.e. with all pre-Masada history. As he says at the end of the poem: 'As from now, a new book of Genesis is opened on the wall.'[100] Masada opens a new chapter.

The Title

One of the most significant things about the poem is its title. *Masada* is not an image taken from the history of modern Palestine, where that mountain had not played an outstanding role; nor is it one taken from Biblical history. The fortress of

94. *Masada*, p. 58.

95. *Ibid.*, p. 33.

96. *Ibid.*, p. 34.

97 *Ibid.*, p. 58.

98. See A. Shlonsky: *Collected Poems* Vol. 2, the poem 'Mahalakah shlishit'—'Krakiel', p. 14.

99. *Ibid.*, p. 22.

100. *Masada*, p. 82.

Masada had overwhelming significance at only one period of Jewish history, and that was in the war against Rome. The Jews, of course, were then defeated, and Masada, the last fortress held, fell. Masada served as the focal point for the most determined and unremitting of rebels, it was 'a hotbed of insurgents'.[101] The fortress was under extreme Zealot leadership, and the fighters committed suicide rather than fall into Roman hands; the leader was the Ben Yair[102] mentioned in the poem (p. 44). Lamdan's choice of Masada as the central symbol is of special significance, because it is, of necessity, a symbol of defeat. The poet would not have been hard pressed to find another and more successful point of Jewish history on which to hinge the poem; he could have chosen a title from the halcyon days of independence in Biblical times, or from the period of the second commonwealth, after the successful Maccabean revolt. It seems that a point of history marked by failure was chosen deliberately. The Masada struggle of history has two outstanding characteristics, (a) the determination to fight to the end, and (b) eventual defeat, and suicide. The picture we receive from the Masada struggle is of a people throwing its entire energy and resources into the battle, but which it is fated to lose. And this is the unspoken implication of the choice of title. The people must fight, and fight to the last. But they will not win out in the end.

The poem is governed by these two moods, that can be crudely designated optimism and pessimism. We swing from the burning faith of the dancing pioneers who assure us that 'never again shall Masada fall'.[103] to the constant thought of suicide, the suicide that is considered in the recognition of defeat, that marked the original Masada fighters: 'Ah, who knows if all of us here, one by one, will not slip away to the abyss'.[104] Enthusiasm alternates with despair, and is born of hatred: 'On my image have the sharp nails of disbelief engraved convulsion and a tattoo of enmity, towards everyone,

101. See Graetz: *op. cit.*, Vol. 2, p. 293.

102. *Ibid.*, p. 316.

103. *Masada*, p. 44.

104. *Ibid.*, p. 73.

everyone, everyone . . .'.[105] Disillusion with the other solutions brought the poet to Masada, a belief that 'the graces of the world have disappeared'.[106] The old country, symbol of the old solutions and failures, must be left, although it is all too easy to remain in 'this terrible refuge', 'drawn to the cold, consuming flame' of 'this chaos'.[107] The fighters go to Masada, but their battle is regarded with indifference by those down below: 'There is no one to substitute for the weary and stumbling amongst us; when one falls, there is no one to take his place.'[108] And even of those who are in Masada, 'many slip away into hidden places in the darkness, and secretly descend from the wall'.[109] Inexorable Fate seems once more to be getting its grip on the people as it has always done before. But then an appeal is made for supernatural intervention, in 'The Prayer', and 'the heart is lightened'.[110] The assurance is made that 'there is a great, merciful Father. He has not called us to chaos from the depths—Masada will not fail.'[111]

The conclusion of this poem does not sustain this note of optimism. But determination is asserted: 'Let us smite foreheads on rock, smiting until blood squirt out.'[112] It is true that 'the hand of Fate, happy to embarrass, crouches constantly behind us',[113] but at the moment, it does, at least, remain in the background. The Masada solution is asserted to the extent of the admission that no other path is viable. There is no way back: 'This is the frontier; from here onwards, there are no more frontiers, and behind—to no single exit do all paths lead'.[114] At the beginning of the poem, we heard that 'a final banner of rebellion' had been unfurled, and now, at the end, the sense of revolution is pressed: 'As from now, a new book of Genesis is opened on the wall.'[115] Something entirely new is afoot, so new departures can be expected. But the people must

105. *Ibid.*, p. 22.
106. *Ibid.*
107. *Ibid.*
108. *Ibid.*, p. 63.
109. *Ibid.*
110. *Ibid.*, p. 71.

111. *Ibid.*
112. *Ibid.*, p. 79.
113. *Ibid.*
114. *Ibid.*, p. 82.
115. *Ibid.*

shoulder their own responsibility. Traditionally, God has been the decisive factor in Jewish history, now the people themselves must substitute for Him. God is ousted from His position as arbiter of the Fate: 'Praise is not due from us to God, creator of the world.'[116] It is the people whom the poet addresses, when he concludes: 'Be strong, be strong, and we shall be strengthened.'[117]

The two factors of the poem's title and the assertive conclusion seem to be at odds. The title seems to be a deliberately ambiguous symbol pointing to eventual defeat, and the conclusion of the poem leaves room for hope. Perhaps, the poet like the Masada fighters, will not admit defeat even as he is going down; or perhaps, the poet chooses the symbol to contradict its implications, to assert the mutability of Fate, and the power that man can command against the forces of Determinism.

Form of the Poem

From the point of view of form and content, Lamdan has been characterised an expressionist poet,[118] and it is only on the basis of this poem that the definition can stand. 'The expressionist style is explosive and erratic' not descriptive; it emphasises the dynamic and ecstatic'.[119] *Masada* is the only work of Lamdan's that at all suits this definition, that is 'erratic' and sometimes reaches points of ecstasy. Expressionist literature refused formal laws, taking over, amongst other things from the Symbolist movement, free, i.e. metreless verse,[120] for it was felt that the means of expression were lagging behind the thing to be expressed, and that metre itself was not an essential

116. *Ibid.*
117. *Ibid.*
118. Ben Or: *op. cit.*, Vol. 1, p. 291.
119. See Cassell's *Encyclopaedia of Literature* (London, 1953), Vol. 1, p. 214.

120. For origins of free verse amongst the French symbolists, see E. Dujardin: *Mallarmé* (Paris, 1936), essay: 'Les premiers poètes du vers libre'.

component of poetry.[121] Traditional forms were felt to be exhausted—'the skeleton of the arts had so long been buried under a mush of traditional and effete forms that only some violent effort such as we have lately seen could disengage it'.[122] Dramatically, August Strindberg, regarded as a forerunner of Expressionism,[123] began to deploy types rather than individual characters. The leading characteristic of Expressionism is its reaction to Impressionism; unsatisfied with recording the world as it was, the artist strove to shape it.[124] The movement attained its momentum in the early part of the twentieth century, mainly as a reaction to the cataclysmic events of the First World War.[125]

Masada is a product of the violence of the war, of the riots, of the revolution and of the emigration. To describe such an epoch-making adventure, Lamdan had to burst the bonds of traditional verse. The whole is transmitted with great intensity; emotions, whichever way they tend, are always extreme. We hear the constant apocalyptic use of the words 'final' and 'end'. Slaughter introduces the poem, and death follows constantly. There is a consciousness throughout of a new and final act in human history. Also, the poem has the expressionist liking for abstractions, and for ideas played out in dialogue, as in the ideological clash at the opening of the poem, where the ideologists present their cases. Despite all the voices in the

121. For the essential nature of poetry in the Symbolist view, see *ibid.*, p. 115: 'Le vers devait toujours être un jaillisement, le jaillisement étant le propre de la pensée poétique', and p. 116: 'l'instauration du vers libre a correspondu à retour à la pensée poétique pure dans le vers'.

122. J. Rodker: *The Future of Futurism* (London, 1926), p. 92.

123. H. F. Garten: *Modern German Drama* (London, 1959), pp. 102, 103.

124. *Ibid.* 'Man was no longer a product of his environment, driven by forces beyond his control, but he was himself the driving agent, capable of transforming the world according to his vision.' See also chapter, 'The New Hebrew Literature', first section.

125. *Ibid.*, pp. 105–7. Expressionist drama also foreshadowed the war, as it witnessed the alarming growth of 'the ugly aspects of modern civilisation'.

poem, there are no people; there are only protagonists. The characters have no names, and nothing bears its own title. Communism is not called Communism, Zionism is not called Zionism, and Palestine is not called Palestine. They all have symbolic names; Gordon, Brenner and Trumpeldor are all introduced by pseudonyms. The nearest approach to an everyday event is the invasion of the shores by the 'pedlars' (page 64), and even this sounds flat in the context of the poem. A high level of emotional intensity is sustained, and it is a tribute to the poet's powers that he never becomes inarticulate or banal. The language matches the sentiment. The poem is ambitious, and it achieves its ambition.

Although it seems that the poem is a prolonged shriek, it is not a monotonous one. As the mood changes, and as the protagonists speak by turn, so does the structure of the poetry vary. Lamdan uses short, fast-moving phrases when the description warrants, as in 'The Chain of Dances' (page 39), which has a rhythm similar to that of Longfellow's 'Hiawatha'. But when the overbearing, dull reality is seen, the lines lengthen as if the heat slows down the pace of the poem: 'There are nights in Masada, heavy nights of evil portent. Like black, heavy-winged birds, they descend on to the wall.'[126] He sometimes adopts a rhythm with a pace midway between fast and slow. In the passage following 'The Prayer', there is some relief: 'The crags of rock absorb the last tears. The supplicator raises his head; and it is as if the nightly heavens are not as black as before the prayer.'[127] Though the poem has no metre, it is full of rhythm.

Masada is the only poem of Lamdan's written in this vein. His later poetry is quieter, less apocalyptic, and very often in metre. Although the overall tone of the later poetry is often gloomier than *Masada*, there is not the polarisation of violent extremes of emotion found here. It is more reflective, and less ideologically orientated; it is also more personal and lyrical. But *Masada* is a fine product of a literary movement that was comparatively short-lived, and expressed a certain very significant mood in world literature.

126. *Masada*, p. 57.   127. *Ibid.*, p. 71.

Chapter 4

'IN THE THREEFOLD HARNESS'

Introduction

'IN THE THREEFOLD HARNESS'[1] is the overall title of three series of poems that Lamdan wrote soon after he had finished *Masada*, but did not publish until 1930.[2] Thematically, Lamdan limits himself to the framework of *Masada*, though he develops certain moods, and omits others. As Ben Or says: '[the series] sounds like additions to the poem *Masada*, but broadened and deepened'.[3] The poems were written after Lamdan had been in Palestine for several years,[4] and had experienced the new life in its darker aspects. Here we find that the elements of 'enthusiasm' and 'dance'[5] have been left out; only the gloom looms large. The theme that is later to dominate *Bema'aleh 'aqrabbim* is already central here; viz. the peculiar and special destiny of the Jewish people, the *yi'ud*. The *yi'ud* places special demands on the poet, and one of these demands is that he should devote himself completely to the new country. *Masada* was the literary record of the spiritual struggle towards this decision, and the conclusion there was: 'Here is the border. Further on, there are no more borders, and further back—all paths lead to no exit.'[6] Lamdan reiterates the hold that the new country has over him in 'In the Threefold Harness', e.g. 'Blot out, O winds, my footprints up to this point. Close after me, O world, every gate and entrance. I make a circle round me

1. Written between the years 1924 and 1928, with the exception of three poems.

2. Lamdan: *Ba-ritmah ha-meshuleshet* (Berlin, Tel-Aviv, 1930).

3. A. Ben-Or: *op. cit.*, Vol. 1, p. 286.

4. He immigrated in 1920. See above, Chapter 2.

5. See above, Chapter 2, and below, Chapter 7.

6. See *Masada*, p. 82.

like Honi[7] the Circle maker, and close it with the explicit word—"here".[8] To this extent, in spite of all his qualifications and reservations, Lamdan here, as in *Masada*, takes a patriotic stand, although it is a stand based on the negative nature of the Jewish destiny. Lamdan is doubtful whether the Jew can avoid his tragic fate even in Masada, but it is in Masada that he is determined to stay.

Lamdan himself defines for us explicitly what he means by 'the threefold harness'. These are the three functions imposed upon him, as is a harness upon an animal, not to let him escape. The first function is 'to carry the heavy chain of Abraham, Isaac and Jacob, with the whole body, tensing every vein',[9] i.e. to be the traditional Jew, bearing his traditional destiny. The second function is 'to roll a bared heart over the gravel and twisted paths here as an ungirdered wheel',[10] i.e. to expose what he sees, to be the poet of his generation. And his third function is 'to bear under an agonised armpit—as one carries a lamb with no pasture or flock—the Hebrew scroll.'[11] Ben-Or writes of this scroll that in it 'a major place was appointed for pioneering, whose green dreams and agonised struggles, the poet saw through his flesh and soul together',[12] i.e. the 'Hebrew scroll' that Lamdan would bear is the contemporary drama, of which 'pioneering' was a major component. The three tasks that Lamdan wants to fulfil in this collection of poems are then: to be faithful to his inheritance, to give written expression to the events and mood of his era, and to unfold the Zionist drama in which he so fervently acted. These three functions have been allotted him by Fate,[13] and he cannot escape them, the harness 'is stuck to my body, like the armour to a tortoise'.[14] But the 'harness' is negative, because 'it has rusted my blood with the

7. Figure of Rabbinic times, who drew a circle round himself in a time of drought, and refused to move till rain fell—Ta'anit 23a. See below, Chapter 6, Section 'The Pioneer'.

8. *Ba-ritmah ha-meshuleshet*, p. 169.

9. Introductory poem to *Ba-ritmah ha-meshuleshet*, p. 3.

10. *Ibid.*

11. *Ibid.*

12. Ben-Or: *op. cit.*, p. 287.

13. *Ba-ritmah*, p. 3.

14. *Ibid.*

love of suffering'.[15] There is no hope of mercy either, all the 'bars of mercy's gates' are rusted, and only the 'enclosure of wounds' is opened out to the plagued.[16]

The only thing to do is to lick the wounds, since they cannot be cured by any other means. The last line of this prologue is: 'Oh, lick. Day and night lick.' Lamdan in *Masada* also speaks of wound-licking as a cure, when he invokes Brenner: 'You who taught us to lick our wounds in order to cure them, and mercilessly exposed our great deprivation and failure.'[17] Here also, exposure and licking are spoken of together, and Lamdan praises Brenner for his practice of bringing out into the light all the weaknesses of which he spoke, and wallowing in them in order to effect a cure. Lamdan wants to do the same thing, for there is no other 'gate of mercy'. But he can entrench himself in his situation. His poetry, in this instance then, is the public licking of his wounds. Poetry, for him, has a therapeutic effect as it does in the poem 'Lyric',[18] where poetry is seen as a last resort when all other potentialities of human expression have been exhausted,[19] and the only possible comfort to man in time of his extreme distress.[20] The paradox of curing by pain is finely expressed in that poem: 'Oh, you poetry of the deep, heard by man in every era, you hurt and comfort, reveal and hide. You are Noah's dove, which bore the gospel of comfort in his wing, but a bitter olive leaf in his mouth.'[21] Lamdan also bears a bitter leaf in his mouth, which is the lash of his poetry. But through this might come relief.

'With Wrapped Face'

The first series of the three series of poems is entitled 'With Wrapped Face', an image also used in the poem 'The Covenant between the Pieces',[22] to express horror at the revealed truth. The first section of the series is addressed to his father, and in

15. *Ibid.*
16. *Ibid.*
17. See *Masada*, p. 66.
18. See *Bema'aleh 'aqrabbim*, p. 135.

19. *Ibid.*
20. *Ibid.*, p. 136.
21. *Ibid.*
22. See *Bema'aleh 'aqrabbim*, p. 15.

the first poem he speaks of a shipwreck. The shipwreck is a
metaphor for his situation, in which he has lost his tradition
'(I have forgotten the travellers' prayer which you taught
me)',[23] and his own substitutes and improvisations have proved
of no avail—'my sails, spread out to the four heavenly winds,
have been torn'.[24] But now, not only can he not move, because
he has no vessel, but he has nowhere to move to. Only nothingness lies ahead: 'To the broken arm of the mast, stretched out to
nothingness, is my despairing eye attached.'[25] The shipwreck
expresses Lamdan's feeling of aimlessness at this point. We often
find in his poetry that the poet has lost the faith of his father
without finding a suitable substitute. In the poem 'A Lost
Diamond', the poet laments the fact that not only is he himself incapable of receiving his father's inheritance, but that
there seems to be no one else capable either: 'Where will your
diamond come or arrive, Father? Who will draw it from the
depths of the sea? There are no fishermen any more on the
beach. The storm has chased them away.'[26] The storm that has
chased the fishermen from the beach is presumably the contemporary turmoil that has turned people away from tradition.

Bialik too notes a similar situation, and uses similar terminology to describe it. In his poem 'Alone' he says that he
has been left by himself with his Tradition, and that as for the
others, 'The wind has borne them all away, the light has swept
them away,'[27] the light being that of modern Enlightenment.
Lamdan's tradition has been disturbed not so much by the
Enlightenment, as by the cataclysmic events of his life. So it is
not 'light' with him that swept people away that they cannot
reach for tradition, but storm. In the poem 'Without the
Sabbath', he still hears the traditional sounds, but they are the
sounds of the past: 'In ruined temples, an invisible loving hand
played on the buried harps of the past, and sounds stole through
to my ears.'[28] But the Sabbath, here a symbol of the Tradition,

23. *Ba-ritmah*, p. 7.
24. *Ibid.*
25. *Ibid.*
26. *Ibid.*, p. 8.

27. H. N. Bialik: *Poems* (Tel-Aviv, 1944), p. 147.

28. *Ba-ritmah*, p. 9.

is unable to get through to the poet, because 'secular nails have torn from my windows the eyeballs of holiness: the Sabbath candles'.[29] The Sabbath is indeed sought still, 'In its paths, [i.e. of the world], camps of strangers wander, seeking the Sabbath.'[30] It is sought because it is a protection: 'When is the royal robe of its [the Sabbath's] kingdom to cover with its trains our nakedness, trembling with cold?'[31] Without the tradition, the poet feels naked, he has found no substitute, and wants to return to the Tradition. But he cannot, because that world is dead: 'There is no answer for the nocturnal wanderers, and there is no camp follower. But I follow at their feet, on my neck—the arms of a kneeling world, with its "Kaddish"[32] on my lips—for the departed Sabbath.'[33] The Sabbath, the old world of faith, is dead. Everyone mourns and is sorry, but no one can resurrect it.

In 'God Hides Himself', Lamdan describes the collapse of traditional Judaism in very similar terms to Bialik in his 'Before the Bookcase'.[34] The type of imagery they use is similar to evoke a similar mood; sometimes they even use identical images. Lamdan witnesses the death of his tradition, and the last breath of life is described as 'only one string trembling in grief'.[35] Bialik images the same phenomenon in the words 'a last ember hissed on the stove'.[36] Lamdan talks of his father's books: 'And if the letters flew from the parchments of your books when the Cossacks laid bonfires with them—they have flown forever.'[37] Bialik also addresses his books: 'Or are you rotten, ever dead, with no remnant left in the land of the living.'[38] Lamdan speaks of the smashing of the synagogue windows: 'smashed were the panes and windows of the house

29. *Ibid.*

30. *Ibid.*

31. *Ibid.*, p. 10.

32. 'Kaddish' a traditional Jewish prayer recited by the relatives of a dear departed, on every day for a year following the death.

33. *Ba-ritmah*, p. 10.

34. See Bialik: *op. cit.*, p. 211—'Lifne aron ha-sefarim'.

35. *Ba-ritmah*, p. 11.

36. Bialik: *op. cit.*, p. 213.

37. *Ba-ritmah*, p. 11.

38. Bialik: *op. cit.*, p. 213.

of prayer',[39] and Bialik also in a synagogue writes 'the shutters were broken and, with their iron bars, all the devils of the pit cracked the walls'.[40] Lamdan has 'and the everlasting lamp[41] went out above the pillar',[42] and Bialik makes this light the central symbol of the dying Tradition. He writes: 'Only the flame of my lamp was still dying, wandering and meandering, and jumping the jump of its death. Suddenly the window burst open, and everything went out.'[43] Lamdan notes the departure of the Holy Spirit (*Shekhinah*) from the place: 'And the *Shekhinah* gathered up its protective wings,'[44] and Bialik earlier in his poem had spoken of the departure of the *Shekhinah*: 'And I saw the *Shekhinah* of God leaving its place, sneaking out under the altar cover.'[45]

In both Lamdan's and Bialik's poems, the poet has attempted to image the world of a dying tradition. They are both witnesses to the death of God. But both mourn the situation. Bialik addresses the 'Stars of God' at the end of his poem, and asks them why they are silent. He feels the need for communication for after the death of his tradition, he feels lost. He has been thrown into the night: 'And I am a young chick cast from its nest into the night and its darkness.'[46] The darkness is a symbol for Bialik of bewilderment, as light is of enlightenment. Bialik wants to strive for the light, but he cannot communicate. He says to the stars: 'Has your golden eyelid nothing, not the slightest hint to give me and my heart? Perhaps it has—and I have forgotten your language.'[47] Perhaps Bialik has so changed that he no longer receives the message of the Tradition. Lamdan, in this poem, also feels the break with Tradition, and wants to fight his way back: 'Where has the God of generations hidden, Father? Twilight is descended, call the hiding God.'[48]

Lamdan's only link with the past is his father, to whom he

39. *Ba-ritmah*, p. 11.
40. Bialik: *op. cit.*, p. 212.
41. A lamp kept burning constantly above the holy ark in the synagogue.
42. *Ba-ritmah*, p. 12.
43. Bialik: *op. cit.*, p. 212.
44. *Ba-ritmah*, p. 12.
45. Bialik: *op. cit.*, p. 212.
46. *Ibid.*
47. *Ibid.*, p. 214.
48. *Ba-ritmah*, p. 12.

pleads here. And in the following poem 'From the Banks of the West' he continues his plea, still in the same world as Bialik. He tells his father: 'Alone do you shelter me with your broken wings over the embers of a burnt nest and on a lone coal, still whispering in the ash of ruins.'[49] The images express almost complete impotence. The wings, symbol of protection, cannot protect properly, because they are broken. Bialik uses the identical image in his poem 'Alone': 'I was left entirely alone, and the *Shekhinah* held its broken right wing tremblingly over my head.'[50] In Bialik's poem, it is the Divine Presence whose protective capacity is defective, and in Lamdan's it is his father: But both images point to the same problem, the problem of faith that can no longer be upheld, because the object of faith is no longer invulnerable. Bialik's break is with the tradition in which he was reared, which he does not identify with any particular person. But Lamdan addresses his father, and it is his father who is symbolic of the tradition from which he is now separated.

We saw in Bialik's 'Before the Bookcase' how Bialik identified Tradition with Light, i.e. security; that when cut off from it, he was left in the darkness. Lamdan identifies Tradition with tranquillity, as he says that in being separated from it, he will know tranquillity no more: 'On the banks of the West, the wanderers of an age bring tranquillity to burial, and I am one of the mourners',[51] and later, 'tranquillity is dead for us, and its soporific lullaby is forgotten.'[52] It has been decreed that he rest no more: 'The decree of wandering and meandering has been engraved on my flesh, at every shadow, roof, and tent, that they gather me not in.'[53] He asks his parent why he still troubles: 'Why, Father, do you still keep a lone, whispering coal that will be warm for the pigeon [i.e. the poet] when he comes back, and visits its fire?'[54] Lamdan now realises that he will never be able to know comfort again; his Destiny has marked him out for suffering. There is still a dying ember of

49. *Ibid.*, p. 13.
50. Bialik: *op. cit.*, p. 147.
51. *Ba-ritmah*, p. 13.

52. *Ibid.*
53. *Ibid.*
54. *Ibid.*, p. 14.

the Tradition left, but it is not for the poet. He will not be able to enjoy its warmth.

In the poem 'My Days and Nights', his father asks him of his life in Palestine: 'How do you pass days and nights, my son?'[55] Then the poet tells his father: 'My days and nights are wounds in the body of my plagued generation, that open their mouths, spitting blood with a roar for the non-existent cure.'[56] Here he tells the truth of the pain and the hopelessness he has felt at times. Here all apparent medicines are illusory. The ideologies of the moment are not permanent cures, although they are intended as such: 'the magicians of the age hiss over their pain, and drip over them [the wounds] the balm of the future—but they cannot heal them.'[57] The magicians of the age are the propagandists who justify present suffering with promises of future bliss. Although, the propagandist here spoken of is not Communist, the Communist propagandist in *Masada* used a similar argument: 'The free horsemen of the morrow will send the daggers of its lightning into the dragon of yesterday, shaking the earth with final, thunderous roars.'[58] But any Utopia is false: 'I close them [the wounds] up with temporary tow',[59] but 'their roar will cease for a moment and after that with a spit will the bundles [of tow] be ejected, and with contempt for their despicable cure'.[60] This bitter confrontation with the truth and the communication of it to his parent may be contrasted with a later poem of Lamdan's where the same situation exists. In 'With Laughing Countenance', the poet's father asks his son to tell him of his life in Palestine: 'Tell me of your life there in the land of Israel. Is it really good for you, and are you content?'[61] In that poem Lamdan's answer is: 'It is good for me there, Father. Good, so good.'[62] For he says: 'Could I relate otherwise to a father laden with grief who expects relief and comfort from his son?'[63] He lies out of consideration for his

55. *Ibid.*, p. 15.
56. *Ibid.*
57. *Ibid.*
58. *Masada*, p. 15.
59. *Ba-ritmah*, pp. 15–16.

60. *Ibid.*
61. See *Bema'aleh 'aqrabbim*, p. 49.
62. *Ibid.*
63. *Ibid.*

father's feelings, a consideration he seems to have learnt with the years, for he shows none of this delicacy in the earlier poems.

In 'Onto the Yoke of Night', the poet asks what he can do now that God no longer exists for him: 'Father, what can the son do without sinning now that God is not in His heaven to be loved, feared, and prayed to? How can I not fall for every temporary flickering fire when all the lights of my generation have failed?'[64] Direction has been lost: 'the hand on the rudder has become weak'. The poet contradicts Isaiah's message, for he says: 'this generation of children will not draw its joy from the wells of salvation—the wells have dried up' . . .[65] If there are true lights, then he must take the false, 'how could a moth not long for the protruding flames, when the sun has left it on the yoke of the night?'[66]

The poem 'In the Corners of the Fields' expresses Lamdan's pioneering and Zionistic purpose, and here he speaks for his generation explicitly. His generation is wandering, always seeking answers, and always disappointed: 'Oh, these worms who work in every nest of man, and succeed in the work of none of them.'[67] His people have been so eager to grasp, but they can never get a grip. The same sentiment is expressed in *Masada* where he characterises his people's activity: 'they are the hands of Israel, which grasp everything, and from which everything falls' . . . 'Ah, these hands, the first to raise the flags of every gospel, and the last—its solaces.'[68] And here, we arrive at Lamdan's view of Jewish history: 'a generation of children was scattered, and wherever it moved, the planet of Israel was on its head—the star of wandering . . . and I with the few remnants emigrated to the ancient homeland, to rebel against this mocking star, and smite it in the sun'.[69]

Lamdan's *aliya* was a determined attempt to escape the plaguing destiny that he had always suffered. The Jews had been constantly wandering, but if they had a home to go to,

64. *Ba-ritmah*, p. 17.
65. *Ibid.*, pp. 17, 18.
66. *Ibid.*, p. 18.
67. *Ibid.*, p. 19.
68. *Masada*, p. 30.
69. *Ba-ritmah*, p. 18.

then surely the wandering would cease. He had to make the home a fit place to live in though, and he stresses that he concentrated on building life, not on living off the dead: 'I did not hurry to the wailing wall when I came here and bury my head in the bosom of its stones. I did not stretch myself out on the graves of the Ancients or on ruined relics to listen to the echo humming like a dove.'[70] This ancient God, the past, is in misery, and the poet wants a new, fresh God: 'Father, I did not seek the tearful, pained God here: I went out to the field to greet the God of great comforts (My rebel comrades told me he was there)' . . . [71] This God is one worthy of the rebels' faith and trust: 'broad are His wings and secure, and He covers a group of roots that suck and bear this great source of rest'.[72]

The poet wanted to devote himself wholly to this God: 'At the feet of this God have I crouched, and become attached to the broad furrows of the field, to be, even I, one root amongst many and a grain amongst grains.'[73] But, even then, the poet was disappointed: 'he did not turn to my meal-offering', i.e. this God did not accept the poet's sacrifice, and did not favour him. The poet has no option but to blame himself for the failing: 'It must be that I am still too impure to enter his holy places.'[74] Lamdan asserts 'The mocking star up above is still not dimmed.'[75] i.e. the traditional Fate persists, even after such steps have been taken to avoid it. He had not yet become adapted to the new life of the fields; as he says: 'The God of the homeland walking around in the field has not yet absorbed me.'[76] The God 'walking around in the field' is another version of 'the voice of the Lord God walking in the garden'. (Gen. 3 :8.) He is the pioneering God to whom the poet with his comrades would devote his life. But he is unrewarded and remains a 'rejected stalk in the corners of the fields',[77] still unfulfilled.

70. *Ibid.*
71. *Ibid.*, p. 20.
72. *Ibid.*
73. *Ibid.*

74. *Ibid.*, p. 21.
75. *Ibid.*
76. *Ibid.*
77. *Ibid.*

In the series of poems 'On one of my Nights',[78] the poet attempts to justify his pessimism, for his colleagues rebuke him, and think his poetry out of place: 'For whom and for what does this heavy stench press so heavily on the light of this our sun, here in the homeland?'[79] They think pessimism misplaced in the new country. The poet's answer is: 'O reproachful liars, He who changes the times [i.e. God] did not bless me as He did you with the corn of pleasure and with the falling quails of joy. From the cup of perplexed times did I drink whilst still a boy.'[80] Lamdan tells us that it is not so much a personal matter as a common trait of those whose fate is as his: 'I am not alone —a sad, aching poet is every lad here, every Israelite.'[81] Then he describes the characteristics of these enquiring people, and asks: 'whose head would not be struck dizzy at the mockeries of the enquiry, and who would not enwrap the face at the terror of the solution?'[82] But the special virtue of this small group of people, the Israelites in Palestine, is that they are the active and creative representatives of the whole Jewish race, and this is the function of the poet—'we are a congregation of poets. There is living and alert in us what is dead and gone in the people.'[83] The Jews as a whole have tried to forsake their destiny, but 'what it [the people] has divested, we have assumed, and with few people, we shoulder and carry everything—a homeland, love, God, man'.[84] These four words are the words around which major ideals centre, and they are the concern only of 'the congregation of poets'.

This idea of an elect amongst the people is also present in *Masada*. There, the haluẓic A. D. Gordon in the person of Abtalion, comes to the poet—with his advice. The poet had been regretting the whole Zionist project, because there seemed to be no support from the ranks of the people. But Gordon there says: 'Neither ask nor enquire, my son, you redeem your own soul, and tell your friends that each man

78. *Ba-ritmah*, p. 28.
79. *Ibid.*
80. *Ibid.*
81. *Ibid.*
82. *Ibid.*, p. 29.
83. *Ibid.*
84. *Ibid.*

should redeem his own soul in the battle. For you are the *Shekhinah* of the people, and your head is its head.'[85] The sense of the word *Shekhinah* here is clearly élite. Gordon advises the pioneers to persist in their task, regardless of anyone else. Since they are the élite of the people, higher standards are expected of them. But the poet finds himself wavering in his task, for his common, worldly needs are too powerful for him: 'A home-land, love, God, man, but meanwhile the body is hungry for bread, cries out for a little rest.'[86] It is all very well to bear such exalted purposes, but the pioneers, like everyone else, have more basic appetites, such as for food and for rest. This thought makes the poet uneasy, and he needs wine to blot it out: 'Come up, wine, in honour of the guest who has come to me for a night, who goes after me like a shadow, allowing no rest.'[87] This guest is his 'mood' (the title of the poem), which he hopes is temporary. He is sure that he will overcome it, that he will not always place such a high value on these basic, material things, but, for the moment, it must be borne.

Lamdan did not admire abstract ideologies, and did not unreservedly embrace any. In the poem 'With the cries of the people',[88] he tells us why: 'For the cries sound to me like a sterile tree that will never know the feel or weight of fruit, but light-textured, moves with every wind.'[89] The ideologists make a lot of noise, and move easily and quietly whenever the wind changes, but they produce no fruit. The poet is also swayed by the change of wind, but not so much; he is like the stock of the tree, not the top: 'And I like a stock with no top in the packed forest, move with every wind, move with all of them so, but make no noise.'[90] In the last stanza, he answers the same question thus: 'I have been stripped of all the swathings of flags, and coloured prayer shawls.'[91] The flags and shawls are of ideologies; images used extensively in Lamdan's work. Though the poet has often been moved by various ideologies,

85. *Masada*, p. 65.
86. *Ba-ritmah*, p. 29.
87. *Ibid.*
88. *Ibid.*, p. 39.

89. *Ibid.*
90. *Ibid.*
91. *Ibid.*, p. 40.

he has never been completely swayed by them. So he ran naked to Palestine: 'In the hands of the lover of a generation, I left my last coat, and fled here naked, to sew a belt for my nakedness from the green Spring leaves.'[92] His demands are very modest. He has cast off all the gaudy shawls, the ideologies that catch everyone else's fancy, in search of simple green leaves, a partial ideology, just to cover his nakedness. But even in this the poet is disappointed, because 'behold the stock even here turns yellow, and there is no green leaf for the belt'.[93]

But in the second part of this same poem, Lamdan seems to be persuaded of the justice of these cries. If you cry loud enough, you will hear no dissenting voice: 'even the heavens will submit to the wondrous cry, and drop down medicine in spite of themselves'.[94] They are right to cry out in joy: 'for what is the good of the whole world and the fullness thereof compared with this great, terrible good that is seen in your restraint at the bad?'[95] At this point, Lamdan gives complete affirmation to the Zionist ideal, an ideal which was unique in its time, and unrepeatable: 'No child will know, no grandchild understand how great was the vision in a visionless generation, and how much poetry flowered in our roaring nakedness, in the stock.'[96] All this crying and shouting might be quite sterile, but what matter? Enough is in the experience of the wonder: 'What is a blossom to me, what is fruit, when I have the skies of the day thick with wonders, and when the heavens of the riddle of the people with all their glorious clouds are spread over me?'[97]

In a group of poems, 'When a Man Prays', the poet tries to achieve contact with God, and to be at peace with Him. In a short poem 'Only the Few'[98] he starts to climb 'the ladder set in the ground' that reaches up to God, but the climb is very difficult: 'how numerous are the rungs in the ladder of your world, O God, and if only I could set my foot properly on one

92. *Ibid.*
93. *Ibid.*
94. *Ibid.*, p. 41.
95. *Ibid.*

96. *Ibid.*, p. 42.
97. *Ibid.*
98. *Ibid.*, p. 49.

of them'.[99] Here, the poet accentuates one difference that he has with his people; he wants urgently to be at peace with God, which is the good. 'To be at peace with you and with life'.[100] No one else seems to share this desire: 'My people—has already, has already forgotten this, and my generation—does not want to know. And though I am a loyal child of both—I am still distressed, distressed to breathlessness at the forgetfulness and unwillingness of both.'[101]

In the last series of poems in this first section 'Of Days Abroad', the poet's constant theme is the unease which he feels away from Palestine, and the desire to arrive back home. He says: 'I have been here like a sheep that has wandered from its flock, pasturing somewhere in a dangerous, desolate landscape.'[102] He longs for his own landscape, even though it may be desolate still: 'Carry me, make me tranquil, until I return and go out in the track of the rising flock in the desolation of the homeland.'[103] He wants to suffer in his own country, since that is the demand made of him there: 'I will return soon, O my country, to enter the yoke of your suffering.'[104]

'In the Shadow of the Thorn Bush'

On the first poem of this second series of poems 'Scales', the poet balances the positive sides of the pioneering personality against the negative: 'Our extended arms are the balances of a scale suspended on our plagued and wearied body. One rises, rises—with all our merit in it. But the other descends, and is decisive.'[105] But even if the positive side of the personality were to be effective: 'Where would the miserable balance of our credit rise to, when the heavens are so distant, and we have no heavens?'[106] Even if the pioneer could reach up, and had the capacity to fulfil his aspirations, there is nowhere within reach. But if there is nothing to aspire to, or rise to, there is also

99. *Ibid.*
100. *Ibid.*
101. *Ibid.*
102. *Ibid.*, p. 52.

103. *Ibid.*
104. *Ibid.*, p. 60.
105. *Ibid.*, p. 67.
106. *Ibid.*

nothing further that they can sink to: 'But where would the balance of our debit descend to, still sink, when below there is no earth, and we have no basis or foundation?'.[107] There is no earthly security, and no heavenly hope. The pioneers have fallen between the two stools of the holy and the profane, and they must suffer: 'The immoral and evil-intentioned dread sorceress stalks amongst us, laughing at the naked terror, and dries the last crust in our basket with the breath of her mouth. Woe, that this dry crust is constant food for us.'[108] The crust is a symbol of hard living, and that it is dried reduces it to almost below subsistence level. The poet is neither in heaven nor properly on earth.

Lamdan was often occupied by the problem of the pioneer who does not reap the fruits of his labour—the sower who does not reap. In the poem 'The Cry of Grandfather', he addresses another poet who wrote of the same problem, though with respect to a different theme, Y. L. Gordon (1830–92). Gordon, writing some forty years before Lamdan, was worried about the disuse to which Hebrew was falling. In a poem entitled 'For Whom do I toil?',[109] Gordon asks himself why he works so hard to write in a dying language, and wonders if he is not the last poet to write in Hebrew, and if his readers are not the last readers: 'Oh, who can tell the future, who can inform me that I am not the last of Zion's poets, and that you too are not the last readers?'[110] Lamdan adopts Gordon's slogan 'for whom do I toil?' for his own purposes, because the Palestinian pioneer was also unsure if his successors would appreciate his efforts, or indeed if there would be successors at all.

But at first, Lamdan employs the slogan to contradict it, for he says: 'Ah, late Grandfather [i.e. Y. L. Gordon], your off-spring knows for what and for whom he is toiling and sickening',[111] and he goes on to say that he knows why, though he was not a born Palestinian, he decided to devote himself to the

107. *Ibid.*
108. *Ibid.*
109. Y. L. Gordon: *Writings* (Tel-Aviv, 1953), p. 37.
110. *Ibid.*
111. *Ba-ritmah*, p. 71.

country and to the Hebrew language: 'I know why I stopped my ears from hearing the sound of my blood and its roar, and went at the sound of a single lilt, the lilt of the renewal of our beginning.'[112] He asserts this with confidence, and yet still feels uneasy, and he still hears the persistent question: 'I knew, and I still know—but exhausted, I bury my head in the scroll and listen to the roar that smites me with trembling For whom do I Toil. This roar is not yours alone, Grandfather, it is not only your voice that walks dreadly with it.'[113] The question is echoed everywhere. But the Hebrew poet should not feel himself different from anyone else: 'O scroll of afflictions of the solitary Hebrew poet, gather up your curtains as a bereaved bird gathers up her wings in mourning, and accept with love your sentence that our late grandfather knew! For why should your lot be better than the lot of anyone else living and aching here?'[114]

In the poem, 'The Organ of Perplexity', Lamdan asserts the unique importance of the Hebrew poet. He gives expression to an experience that no other poet can know: 'Players of the world and fiddlers of the nations, you do not know what is that melody of perplexity, so terrible in sound "At our place!" Only the solitary Hebrew knows it, of his soul and flesh he knows it.'[115] The Hebrew is a poet by the nature of his experience, which is so deeply felt: 'his body is the organ, his wounds—the notes, and his nails play. So is the terrible tune "at our place" played.'[116] This perplexity is not a desideratum: it is not something that the poet has imposed on his work to give it its peculiar character. On the contrary the poet has done everything possible to normalise his poetry. He has travelled and written in all parts of the world to allow foreign spirits to penetrate his work, without success. And now he has come to Palestine: 'What more can I do to the organ [i.e. my poetry] that I have not yet done to rid it of its perplexity? I have hung it on the willows of all the ways, and abandoned

112. *Ibid.*
113. *Ibid.*, p. 72.
114. *Ibid.*

115. *Ibid.*, p. 73.
116. *Ibid.*

its chords to all the playing winds, and I have allowed foreign hands too to direct its sounds until I brought it here to hang it on the neck of the final sun with a plea.'[117] Again, we have here the familiar, apocalyptic use of the word 'final'. This sun, i.e. this hope, is the last. As he says in *Masada*, 'here is the border, further on there are no more borders'.[118] It may be that this 'border' will be insufficient, or that this 'sun' will fail, but there is no other on which any hope may be pinned. The poet finds that all his exercises are of no avail in changing the nature of the Hebrew muse: 'Great is the perplexity still in the organ and terrible is its tune.'[119] He has now given up hope of normality and relaxation: 'Shake, shake my couch, thin stubborn, Hebrew hand, for there is no rest for the agony, there is no forgetting or tranquillity, and there is no sleep for the body that was organ for the tune "At our Place".'[120]

He repeats his comrades' complaint at his incessant moaning in the poem 'With the First Steps'. He too would like to be happy, but he is too much aware of impending doom: 'I thirsted like them, but what can I do now that the crouching knife of fear is stuck into my flesh?'[121] His fault is that he sees too clearly. He sees harshly, but he sees true. My comrades and compatriots hate me because I see hard things, but O, my brothers, this I did not want. But what can I do if our invisible Leader forgot to blind my eyes as I go, and walk, open-eyed, falling and then going on.'[122] It is much worse for the poet, because though he is just like anyone else in that he falls, he suffers more because he sees the fall coming, and the actual fall itself. If he could blind himself to it, it would not be so bad, but: 'Woe to the visionaries that fall whose vision is not closed to them whilst they fall.'[123] But even as he is falling he sees prospects of hope. 'What do you see, O falling visionary? I see wells of comfort, and their waters of salvation, drawn up in broken jugs.'[124] A broken jug can hold no water, so his thirst

117. *Ibid.*
118. *Masada*, p. 82.
119. *Ba-ritmah*, p. 73.
120. *Ibid.*, p. 74.
121. *Ibid.*, p. 75.
122. *Ibid.*
123. *Ibid.*
124. *Ibid.*

will not be slaked. The vision is seen, comfort is in the distance; but fulfilment is never to be had. Though the experience is hard, life is still possible: 'Surely I do see the great wonder and look upon it. We, the clowns of the world, who can jump over chasms . . . will learn to walk.'[125] We have already heard the Jews spoken of as clowns in *Masada* in the speech of the resigned nihilist protagonist. 'What would this mad dictator [i.e. the world] do without a clown, beggar in his temples to dance and sing before it?'[126] The Jew must act like a clown to keep alive. The poet believes that it is the only way for him to succeed, although it is desperately hard at first. As he puts it: 'the first steps are also the rhythm of the old wedding march— "at our place" '.[127]

The trouble is that Lamdan has lost his faith, otherwise he would do what Honi did: 'If I only knew that we still had God in our distant Heavens, like Honi the circle-maker would I make a circle round me, and not move from it, and not stop kneeling till He hear my prayer.'[128] Then the poet would pray for salvation and help. But this is a theoretical proposition, because the poet is not Honi, and is not sure that God is in His heavens. Nevertheless, he does include the text of the prayer which he would like to make and he says: 'Teach us to walk, with the whole sole of our feet to walk on the earth without smiting its restful grass with baldness.'[129] In the poem *Masada*, he includes a similar prayer, a prayer for help and mercy in unbearable circumstances: 'As for those who have dropped from foreign gallows, and ascended the wall [i.e. of Masada], steady their step, O God, that they stumble not, nor fall, for they are still stumbling and falling.'[130] Both prayers are written in a like spirit, and in similar circumstances. But both prayers are made theoretically. In our poem here, he appends the condition that he be sure of God's existence, which he is not. And in *Masada* the prayer is made by one of the other pioneers. It seems that the poet is still not completely

125. *Ibid.*, p. 76.
126. See *Masada*, p. 17.
127. *Ba-ritmah*, p. 76.

128. *Ibid.* See also above, p. 52.
129. *Ibid.*, p. 77.
130. *Masada*, p. 69.

ready to pray himself, for prayer requires faith in its own efficacy.

Since the present is so harsh, the poet looks for his hope to the future in the poem 'Those who go toward the morrow'. And so, to find out if his hopes are liable to be justified, he asks those who might know what the future will be like, those who bear the future within them. He asks a child: 'Tell me what you have to tell me, little one. Perhaps it will hush my tearful speech.'[131] He then goes to a baby in its cradle, to a young plant, even to a madman in the market place (who is perhaps a prophet and a fortune teller), to ask of the future, and his question is: 'Is this the sun that is being born? And if it is born will it rise without the stain of generations—at our place?'[132]

This 'at our place' is the chorus of this group of poems, the haunting refrain that dominates every hope and expectation. For 'at our place' is the weight of History, the Fate that has accompanied the Jews at all times. The poet is deeply aware that if his people are to break the spell, it will require a tremendous impetus, because of all the force of the past. And as often as not, he views the attempt with scepticism. But his mood constantly changes within a fixed spiral, and in the poem 'On the altar', he attempts to justify the Jewish experience. He says: 'We must not close our eyes at the sight of the terrible writings engraved on our wall', and 'come, let us not be deterred from this dreadful inscription "at our place".'[133] Everything he is prepared to sacrifice: 'There is still one whole tooth—let it be inserted into its clods and—broken in justifying the judgement.'[134] The poet thinks that his sacrifice of himself will justify the Jewish Fate. But too many questions should not be asked, not even whether the sacrifice is a worthwhile one, 'Here are we all bound, and with our own hands we have brought the wood here. Not to ask or enquire if the offering will be favourably accepted.'[135]

The questions need not be asked, because the poet has faith

131. *Ba-ritmah*, p. 78.
132. *Ibid.*, p. 79.
133. *Ibid.*, p. 80.

134. *Ibid.*

135. *Ibid.*

that 'there certainly is a father who wants it, [i.e. the sacrifice] there is certainly a mother who will not forget us. Let us roll our necks then, on to the altar in silence.'[136] Thus we have seen a progression in faith on the part of the poet from 'With the first steps' when he doubted the existence of God in the heavens, and when he would have prayed like Honi, to the present poem where his faith in a good Providence seems to be complete. He is also unreservedly prepared to suffer. And in the last poem of this group: 'The morrow of agony', he reiterates this. For he says that Providence has two sides. The same Being that comforts also makes demands: 'The hand that here binds the wounds of generations and carries the seed of comfort to souls, also reveals and unrolls stones from the closed wells of our agonies.'[137] Realising this, the poet requests more pain as if he might get pleasure from that in itself: 'There is of the pleasantness of the sting of alcohol for a heart completely despaired, in you, O marrow of agonies.'[138] Just as alcohol gives pleasure though it burns, so does the agony of the poet. He thinks of it as only one side of the coin, while the other comforts and eases.

In the person of 'Who knows not to ask', the traditional fourth son of the Passover reading, the poet presents another aspect of his faith. The poet differs from his comrades in respect of his faith, though he accepts their brotherhood because of the bond of common experience. 'As if I were one of them do they call me "our Brother". But I am not of them because I wanted their way, but because their tragedy is the tragedy of my life.'[139] Or as he puts it in the next verse: 'I am one of them because one Destiny has called us.'[140] The difference between the poet and his comrades is seen in the next line, where he says that they reject the Destiny. But this difference is comparatively unimportant beside what they have in common: that they have both been elected by the same Destiny, and they both feel by it: 'And even if they stone it [the Destiny—*yi'ud*]

136. *Ibid.*
137. *Ibid.*, p. 81.
138. *Ibid.*

139. *Ibid.*, p. 89.
140. *Ibid.*

with the stones of their unbelief, I, like them, have too been orphaned.'[141]

Here, the poet has reverted to his theme of the death of God, which is the special Destiny (yi'ud) Both the poet and his companions are conscious of Its death, but the poet's suffering is greater!—'my pain is two-fold: I have been orphaned in their bereavement, but my mourning is not theirs'.[142] His fellows too have lost their God, but they do not mourn Him. His mourning is peculiarly characteristic of the poet, for, as he said earlier in the poem, they try to deny their God of old, and cast stones at Him. Lamdan differs, not by denying this God's death, but my mourning rather than despising Him: 'I am a resident in their community where my God was burned. Both His ashes and the place where they were seated are sacred to me.'[143] Perhaps this stanza can be seen as central in Lamdan's poetic thought, and the mood that characterises his verse most deeply. Because here he asserts loyalty to a dead God. It seems to be more than nostalgia too that binds the poet to his past, for it will let him move in no direction. He receives neither the joy of belief, nor the freedom of unbelief. He is like the man who remains faithful to the memory of a wife he never enjoyed. And this loyalty has become a trust: 'Therefore, I cannot go, to break the covenant of the orphan, to unload the sin of brothers and seek foreign Gods.'[144] He will ever be loyal to a God in whom he has no faith.

'From our Deep Distress'

In this third series of poems, the theme that we are already familiar with recurs. The special nature of Jewish destiny, and its ambiguous implications; the Zionist solution and its dubious validity. The poet swings from the positive to the negative pole and back again and often writes at determinate points in between. In the first poem of the series 'A Hebrew Tramp', the poet echoes the philosophy of the Biblical Koheleth (1:9):

141. *Ibid.* 143. *Ibid.*
142. *Ibid.* 144. *Ibid.*

'What was will be, and what has been done will be done. For there is nothing new under the sun.' The poet sees these words of Koheleth as true, for 'the stalks of solution, I see have already turned yellow, and have still not yet raised a blossom of fruit.'[145] The pioneering movement, the stalks, have already become old and will soon die and they have still had no positive effect. Soon they will die without having achieved anything. Life is a long round of suffering and every proposed cure is illusory: 'With a strip of gospel flag does man bind his wound, already the thousandth dressing and it still hurts.'[146] People incline to forget Koheleth's truth, but it is always whispering in the background: 'Street lamps are taken as funeral torches, and the grass of forgetfulness covers the grass of vision. Quiet is the hand of Koheleth, but someone [says] with a sob—"What has been done will be done".'[147] But the poet is stubborn in the face of the rational truth. An obscure urge drives him on to defy the words of the preacher: 'The eye of understanding is perplexed when it peeps into my depths. Logic bows its head when about to block my way.'[148] The poet is not like any other man; 'in my human book there is a special chapter . . . written not by experience but by Fate, which engraved it with its nails from A to Z.'[149] If he were to have learned from experience, he would have long since forsaken his struggle, for experience teaches the lesson of Koheleth.

But experience is not the only teacher. Far more important for Lamdan are the forces of Fate (*goral*) and Destiny (*yi'ud*). These have no explanation and the poet never even attempts a rationale of them, but they are the dominating factors in his life and poetry. Here again we see that Lamdan is driven on by Fate in the teeth of reason, to find solutions. Such is the nature of his heritage: 'the knapsack of our inheritance has stuck to my back, and the harness of a new Destiny has clung to my flesh'.[150] He cannot escape the weight of his Past which he carries with him into the present and in addition he has to

145. *Ibid.*, p. 103.
146. *Ibid.*
147. *Ibid.*
148. *Ibid.*, p. 104.
149. *Ibid.*
150. *Ibid.* p. 105.

fulfil the new Destiny, which is to build up the land of Palestine. There are two factors in Lamdan's sense of duty—devotion both to the old and to the new. The old factor is Jewish destiny and the new factor is Zionism. These are the first and third points of the harness which he must bear.[151] So the poet asserts his determination to fight to the end: 'I am again for the way, though the hand of Koheleth is now writing on the ways of the world the last word.'[152]

In the poem 'Poverty', the poet speaks of his people's lost faith, but this time his theme is how they have lost in stature because of this. A great and glorious God has been lost, and none has taken His place: 'We are impoverished, we have lost our Father that is in Heaven, and without His spirit do we walk around on earth. Prayer has been forgotten by mouth and heart, the synagogue paths are laid waste and when an Israelite feels distressed he turns to nothingness—the glory has gone from Israel.'[153] We saw in an earlier poem, 'He who knows not to ask',[154] that the poet feels himself amongst the pioneers in that he alone mourns rather than curses the dead God. In this poem, we learn what the poet feels that he is missing: 'Our golden spirit that we bore through the dangerous forest of generations and on paths littered with troops from nation to nation and from one state to another—has disintegrated.'[155] The people have lost their self-respect, and in spite of their great and hallowed tradition borrow from infant nations: 'Ah, how is our great head bent now—just like the orb of the sun straying and wandering, rising and sinking and rising above the products of the earth—to take instruction from the stammering mouth of infant nations.'[156]

Lamdan's national pride is repelled by this phenomenon. A great nation has been stripped of its culture which was based on a tradition of Faith, and wanders round the world, looking for more suitable vestments amongst much younger and more

151. See Introduction to this chapter.
152. *Ba-ritmah*, p. 105.
153. *Ibid.*, p. 196.
154. *Ibid.*, p. 89.
155. *Ibid.*, p. 104.
156. *Ibid.*, p. 106.

inexperienced nations. There was once some splendour in the wanderings of the Jew, who took his spiritual treasures with him, and always left his mark on the world. But the modern Jew takes nothing with him, gives nothing to the other nations and is totally insignificant: 'There is no more splendour in these wanderings, since there is no spiritual gold in our knapsack: "No aspirations press, so our feet are light and their steps have no echo and every passing wind covers the footprints of the poor man on the paths".'[157] However unfortunate the Jew has been in the past he has never previously been spiritually impoverished. But the modern Jew is not only physically unfortunate, he also has none of the spiritual strength of his ancestors. He is an empty vessel, a truly deprived person.

Although Lamdan has often told us of the oppressive nature of Jewish Fate and of its inevitability, he has never before expressed with such clarity the dual feeling of attraction and repulsion with respect to it that he expresses in the poem 'The Mastery of Our Fate'. The question that Lamdan puts to Fate is: why does he, the poet, not only not reject the terrible Fate whose nature he recognises, but actually feel attracted to it, as though it were altogether different? He knows and fears his Fate, but loves it too at the same time. He cannot escape, but at least he should resent his captivity. However, he does not: 'From our deep distress, I call to you, our only Fate, as the one sun in the sky: You are like a spider weaving the involved net of our ways, and we, like trapped flies, flutter in it—answer me! Answer me, what is this longing that burns and yearns for you, O destroyer?'[158] The poet turns to Fate on two fronts, one positively, as to the 'only sun in the sky', as light, and one negatively, as a destroyer. For Fate apparently serves both functions, as the only possible guiding light for the poet, and as the Adversary who deprives him of all pleasure and hope.

The poet asks: 'Why do I rejoice at your sorrowful way, and seek your torturing closeness? Reveal to me the secret of your great mastery, that rules over all my worlds, though I have not

157. *Ibid.*, p. 107.   158. *Ibid.*, p. 110.

anointed it!'[159] This same Fate oppresses the poet even far
away from Palestine, on foreign soil: 'The breast of a foreign
country still suckles my soul in private. The tattoo of my
ancient race has been rubbed from my countenance . . . what
then is this heavy stone that is stuck to my soul, and draws me
to our dark depths of distress?'[160] But in spite of this, the poet
is not freed: 'Why do I bury my head deep into your thorny
bosom, as into the soft pillows of a cradle that had been laid
out for the baby?'[161] Because the bosom is not really a bosom:
it shows no tenderness or mercy: 'I know well that you do not
know mercy.' There is no answer, and the poet does nothing
more than to state the paradox.

In the poem 'Invitation', the poet invites all the 'thinkers of
the world' to consider the Jewish problem as one of the great
problems of the world and one that defies understanding. It is
also a problem to which Lamdan claims to be especially sensitive. His table in Palestine is 'like a central radio station for
the reception of every shake and tremor of the scattered pieces
of our existence on all the ways of world.'[162] The vision of the
wisest man does not comprehend the special situation of the
Jews, who have the problems of men in duplicate. The poet
tells the philosophers: 'You consider only one chasm: the soul
of man that is deeper than the deep. But you do not know that
there are two chasms, and we, we are the second—a chasm
placed within a chasm.'[163] The Jew shares the problems of other
men, but has additional ones peculiar to himself.

The philosophers are concerned with the great questions of
life and death, and love, but the question of Lamdan's people
demands special attention and does not receive it. Only the
poet himself is disturbed by it: 'You [i.e. philosophers] sink
into the mystery of three riddles—death, life and love are the
three. But the fourth—us—you do not know, its riddle does
not govern your sleep. You do not knock your thinking head
at its locked gate like I do. Its burden I bear alone.'[164] This

159. *Ibid.*, p. 111.   162. *Ibid.*, p. 113.
160. *Ibid.*   163. *Ibid.*
161. *Ibid.*, p. 112.   164. *Ibid.*

burden that the poet thought that he was bearing alone in its several aspects is the theme of Lamdan's poetry. For the poet does not treat these other great 'riddles', of life, death and love. His concern is with the fourth riddle, the one neglected by others. And although he does not draw conclusions or arrive at solutions, he devoted his literary life to knocking his head against 'the locked gate of the riddle', to afford it the treatment neglected by other philosophers and poets.

In this same poem, the poet goes on to characterise his nation, and he observes that it is possessed of a unique sensitivity, that tracks pain unfelt by other people: 'The solitary Hebrew has a sixth sense, with which no man apart from him has been cursed. With which he breathes in the painful abstract and at whose touch even a dumb object would be scorched.'[165] Because of this unique gift, or, as Lamdan has it, curse, the 'solitary Hebrew' can feel pain of which other people are totally unaware. The mystery is why this Jew has this particular attribute and this is the mystery that Lamdan would solve. He had been alone in his self-imposed task, but he would like help. So he extends this 'invitation' to the philosophers: 'Come, philosophers of the world, deep thinkers amongst the nations. Bow your philosophic heads to the riddle, as my body bows its back, to bear this additional weight that is borne by no man but me.'[166] Perhaps their greater intellect and penetration will help to throw light on this problem to which the poet is so devoted, but which he has never succeeded in illuminating.

In another group of poems in this third section of the book, 'Of the Poems of One of those who Walk Here',[167] the poet's problem is that of his pioneering immigration to Palestine and the mysterious forces that caused him to take this step. His motives are obscure and he does not know whether he has been deluded (perhaps deluded himself), or whether he is walking in the right direction, for he sees a sign: 'everyone who goes here [goes] as if with closed eyes.'[168] Perhaps he too

165. *Ibid.*, p. 114. 167. *Ibid.*, p. 117.
166. *Ibid.* 168. *Ibid.*, p. 119.

is walking 'with closed eyes'. In the poem 'In the Halter', in consideration of the question why he came, he asserts: 'I did not hear the word of God out of the tempest.'[169] The tempest is the furious onset of the modern world which 'extinguished' the traditional. It is this tempest which symbolises Lamdan's twentieth century in the poem already discussed, 'The Hiding God'.[170] And in this poem Lamdan makes an anti-prophetic statement that he did not hear the voice of God out of the turmoil. In the Bible such cataclysmic events induced prophetic inspiration as in Job (38:1, 40:6), where God makes his great speech from the storm. The poet received no supernatural guidance in taking the quasi-religious step of immigration to the holy land.

But if he did not hear the voice of God in the tempest, he did hear the cry of man: 'In the thundering, and in all the metamorphoses of their sound, I only heard the wailing of man ever bereaved of comfort.'[171] And then the poet heard a message, the gospel of Masada. But this gospel which preached future redemption turned out to be false: 'I also went according to the voice of the gospel, but the song of redemption immediately died on my lips.'[172] His hope died for what he beheld was the same dismal spectacle as he had known all his life: 'On the chopping block of eternity, the Fate of the people bound.'[173] This poem reaches the lowest point of the scale accessible to Lamdan. There is simply no way out: 'Then I knew that all tears flow to a sealed bottle, and all our palms are stretched out to nothingness.'[174] The poet can find no answer to the question of what impulse brought him to Palestine, except that it was 'a secret hand'. It is that 'secret hand' that the poet implores to keep a tight hold on him, for it is only this hand that keeps him in check. He might otherwise be reduced to anarchy: 'Lead me here, secret hand, lead me, grip the halter of my life. Do not leave go for a moment, and

169. *Ibid.*, p. 11. Reference to Job
    38:1 and 40:6, where God speaks
    to Job out of the tempest.

170. *Ibid.*, p. 11.

171. *Ibid.*, p. 120.

172. *Ibid.*

173. *Ibid.*

174. *Ibid.*

believe no more in its self-discipline. For who can know the nature of a harnessed life, which, without halter or guide, has once imbibed chaos with wild roars?'[175] The poet has no faith in his own judgement. He believes in nothing, so he must be unquestioningly subservient to an omnipotent leader. Otherwise, he is liable to collapse into hopelessness and nihilism.

The poem 'Our Sun' again treats the special problem of the Jews, and is related to the Zionist 'solution' which is no solution. He has heard two things: that the sun is setting in the West, i.e. in Europe, and is rising in the East, i.e. in Palestine. But this belief that Zionism would eradicate the traditional Jewish Fate is rejected by the poet. He believes neither in the setting of the old sun, nor in the rising of the new: 'I did not mourn there [i.e. in Europe] with the mourners of the setting. I will not shout here [i.e. in Palestine] with those who applaud the rising.'[176] For the poet, this is to miss the point, because it is a judgement based on normal standards. But normal standards cannot be applied to the Jews: 'I know, we have another sun, a different one. Why should we raise our eyes to seek it amongst the four winds, when it is not there? We have a fifth wind out of the range of the other four. To this, to the fifth, raise your straying hands, and our other, out different one, raise only from this one.'[177]

Though Lamdan has concentrated mainly on the negative side of the Destiny in this book of poems, the poet, as in *Masada*, concludes with an expression of determination to fight. In the poem 'Homeland' he says that he will never leave the new country, and he calls on the natural elements to support him in his determination: 'Blot out, O winds, my footprints up to here. Close after me, O world, every gate and entrance.'[178] Again, Lamdan takes the image of Honi the Circle-maker as a point of comparison to himself, this time positively, to express determination to remain where he is: 'I will draw a circle round me like Honi the Circle-maker, and close it with the explicit

175. *Ibid.*, p. 132.
176. *Ibid.*, p. 149.
177. *Ibid.*
178. *Ibid.*, p. 169.

word—"here".'[179] When he mentioned the person of Honi
before, it was in connection with his prayer: 'I shall not move
out of it [i.e. the circle] and I will not rise from kneeling until
He hear my prayer.'[180] Here, there is no mention of prayers,
and no contact with any superhuman element. But the poet has
decided to remain where he is.

But an even more completely positive aspect of the Palestinian experience is the revival of the Hebrew language. The
poet addresses it: 'every idiom of yours is a diamond, it has all
the colours of the rainbow . . . to what should I compare you?
To a deep well, into which when one looks one becomes
dizzy?'[181] There is a poem in 'Bema-'aleh aqrabbim' too, where
Lamdan addresses the Hebrew language in similarly ecstatic
terminology: 'As a flock of spring swallows are you to me, O
Hebrew words, that are blown from the mouths of small
Israelite children in forsaken townships.'[182] And in another
poem in that volume, the poet regrets every word spoken by a
Jew that is not Hebrew: 'I am distressed about every diamond
of speech that is not fitted into the twenty-two letters.'[183]
(There are twenty-two letters in the Hebrew alphabet.)
Lamdan here exults over the decisive part which the
Hebrew language has played in Jewish history, when 'you
comforted even when you were forgotten and foreign'.[184] But
even more important than the part played by the Hebrew
language in the past is the function that it can fulfil in the
future. For it can ever be a glory: 'Be raised, peak of splendour,
the glory of every generation. May your landscape still be
broad over the proud stock.'[185] In the poem 'As a flock of
spring swallows', Lamdan is optimistic about the future of the
Hebrew language, and as he hears children speak it, he considers its unimaginable potential. He tells the 'Hebrew words'—
'In your chirping, there is the first echo of the voices of the
morrow that we do not yet know. And in your chatter, there

179. *Ibid.*
180. *Ibid.*, see poem *Im ha-tse'adim
     ha-rishonim.*
181. *Ibid.*, p. 170.

182. *Bema'aleh 'aqrabbim.*
183. *Ibid.*, p. 111.
184. *Ba-ritmah*, p. 171.
185. *Ibid.*, p. 172.

is of the babbling of the stream that comes out of the great deep.'[186] The store of the Hebrew language is enormous, and will again be used to express the unique Hebrew message which is traditionally, in the prophetic writings, known as vision, and is now called by Lamdan 'Destiny': 'In the eyes of the whole world, for nation and man, visionaries will still deliver their vision and word of Destiny through you.'[187] (i.e. Hebrew.)

186. *Bema'aleh 'aqrabbim* 3.   187. *Ba-ritmah*, p. 172.

Chapter 5

FOUR BIBLICAL POEMS

For a translation of the text of the four Biblical poems discussed here, see pp. 235 ff. below.

The Use of Biblical Motifs in Literature

IT HAS BEEN very common for writers to use classical themes in their work, either adapting the myth to a modern context, or treating the theme directly in its own setting. We will deal only with those who use Biblical motifs in their own setting, i.e. those who apparently enter into the Biblical world. This does not mean to imply, however, that the writer on a Biblical theme identifies himself completely with the world of the Bible. On the contrary, he may well be more concerned with his own contemporary situation. But at the same time, the Biblical motif is seen to offer useful illumination of that situation. The illumination may be illusory. The writer may misunderstand the original, or he may place upon the original text a revolutionary and surprising interpretation. Since Biblical narrative style is so concise, a great deal of room is left for imaginative treatment. It is because of this that we learn more of the writers who adapt the theme than of the theme they attempt to adapt.

Sometimes, a Biblical protagonist is used as an undisguised ideological tool, and sometimes genuine psychological depths are revealed that may be common both to the Biblical figure and the poet. But it is always the poet's world that we view. The Biblical base certainly has a use, but it is that of a catalyst that can touch off poetic inspiration. From the reader's point of view, the traditional motif is useful because it is well known. Personal poetry can use the heroic persona as a disguise; the poet can apparently identify himself with one aspect of the figure's personality, and develop it to the exclusion of others. In Balladic poetry the Biblical figures may offer a congenial parallel with the poet's contemporaries, but in all cases it is interesting to observe the manner of the author's treatment of his story. If he departs from the story, it is certain to be significant and those aspects stressed are naturally those that primarily interest the poet.

It was because the Biblical framework suited Dryden's satirical purpose so admirably that the poet adapted it for his poem 'Absalom and Ahitophel'.[1] He feels no great affinity with his characters, but treats them with classical detachment as equal counters for those whom he wants to satirise. Each figure in the poem has his precise counterpart in real life. The poem was written in 1681–82, twenty years after the Restoration, and the story of Absalom afforded Dryden a marvellous parallel with the contemporary political situation. Dryden, who wants to defend Charles II's honour, is, in the poem, on the side of King David. As before the Restoration, civil war reigned in Palestine after the death of King Saul. The plot, by the Earl of Monmouth, son of Charles by Lucy Walters, is paralleled by the plot of Absalom, son of a minor wife of David-Maacah. The Ahitophel of the poem is a portrait of Anthony Ashley Cooper, i.e. the Earl of Shaftesbury, who was alleged to be implicated in the plot, and who was at that moment in the Tower on a charge of high treason. Another parallel is afforded by the fact that as David reigned in Hebron before he was elected King over all the tribes, so Charles II was crowned in Scotland, ten years before he was crowned in England.

But in Dryden's poem, Ahitophel is portrayed as the instigator of the plot, prepared to use Absolom as a tool:

> 'But, for he knew, his title not allowed,
> Would keep him still depending on the crowd.'

Of this the Bible gives no hint, as indeed Ahitophel's motivation appears obscure altogether. Here we see how a poet by departing from his text places his own interpretation on events.

1. See John Dryden: *Selected Poems* (London, 1926), p. 94.

Dryden despises the treacherous popular movement whose 'general cry' is 'religion, commonwealth, and liberty.'[2] Behind all this cant, Dryden descries only naked ambition, and Absalom has no will to resist Ahitophel's rationalisation:

> 'If you, as champion of the public good,
> Add to their arms a chief of royal blood,
> What may not Israel hope and what applause
> Might such a general gain by such a cause.'

The failure of the plot is a clear lesson to revolutionary upstarts.

Milton's treatment of his protagonist in 'Samson Agonistes' clearly displays the identification of the poet with the hero. Milton has much in common with Samson; they were both blind (at this stage of Samson's career), they had both been unhappily married, and they were both, in Milton's view, lonely champions of morality. This last quality of Samson's is an invention of Milton's own; the Biblical figure is not conspicuous for nobility of purpose or profound religiosity. Milton transmutes Samson from a tribal leader into a religious leader, who is jealous for the true God. Even after his terrible punishment, Samson asserts: 'My trust is in the living God.'[3] Milton sought a protagonist worthy of a sacred play,[4] and he created Samson for the part.

In Hebrew literature, Biblical motifs are employed frequently. Characterisation of a figure in a particular manner is often used for ideological ends. Ahad Ha'am's Moses[5] fits in very well with this twentieth-century rationalist's pattern of thought. Moses's magical act of lifting his hands to enable the children of Israel to win the war against Amalek[6] is interpreted

2. *Ibid.*, p. 95.

3. Milton: *Poetical Works* (London, 1874), Vol. 2, p. 134.

4. Milton was at pains in his preface to the Poem to defend the morality of playwriting. As a Puritan, he had some sympathy with those who would ban the theatre. He wanted 'to vindicate Tragedy from the small esteem, or rather infamy, which in the account of many, it undergoes to this day.' Preface to *Samson*.

5. See *Writings* (Tel-Aviv, 1947), p. 342, essay 'Moses'.

6. Exodus 17:9–12.

by Ahad Ha'am as the encouragement of a leader to his soldiers.[7] This also suits Ahad Ha'am's view of the spiritual nature of Moses, who was not a man of war.[8] Moses was a prophet, and to be a prophet means not to be in transcendental communication with God,[9] but to be a seeker of 'absolute justice'. The prophet pursues truth and justice without compromise.[10] In his description of the incident of the burning bush, Ahad Ha'am says that Moses 'hears the voice of God within him'.[11] This is more than an adaptation of the Biblical passage. It is a rereading of the verse 'And the Lord saw that he [Moses] turned to see, and God called to him from the bush.'[12] The voice of God has become the voice within, the voice of conscience acceptable to the rationalist thinker. Ahad Ha'am was a theorist of Zionism, and he made the supreme virtue of Moses his aroused national consciousness. He had not been fulfilled because he was living amongst strangers, but now he could go to his own people.[13] The timing of Moses's death is also rationalised. As a prophet, he would not be the right person 'to carry out the ideal in deed. The prophet cannot stand at the head of the people, but must make way for another. Because from that moment a new epoch begins, an epoch of rejection of prophecy, of renunciations and compromises.'[14] Ahad Ha'am has here created a Moses in his own image.

It is precisely the physical element of Moses rejected by Ahad Ha'am that appeals to Bialik in an early portrait of him.[15] Moses here also displays justice and modesty, but it is stressed more that he displays these qualities from on high.[16] His

---

7. See Ahad Ha'am, *op. cit.*, p. 343.

8. *Ibid.*

9. Ahad Ha'am does not say this. But in his characterisation of prophecy, he makes no mention of any supernatural functions.

10. Ahad Ha'am, *op. cit.*, p. 343. See also characterisation of the prophet as contrasted with the priest in his essay *Kohen ve-navi*, p. 91.

11. *Ibid.*, p. 344, *op. cit.*

12. Ahad Ha'am, *op. cit.* (Ex. 3:4).

13. *Ibid.*, p. 344.

14. *Ibid.*, p. 346.

15. See the poem, *'Al Rosh Harel*, p. 27; Bialik: *Poems* (Dvir, 1944).

16. *Ibid.*

exaltation is awe-inspiring, and it seems to be this that made him the greatest of the prophets.[17]

In a later poem, *Metei midbar ha-aharonim*, Bialik again makes Moses the focus of attention. Bialik imposes his Zionist ideology on the story. But here, Moses is a symbol of the past, giving them a fixation, because he asserts his authority even as a dead man. The children of Israel have been wandering in the wilderness for forty years, and they have become captivated by their past: 'They seek the Moses, the dead Moses'[18] says the poet after he finds that he is unable to rouse them. He tells them: 'Rise, wanderers in the wilderness, go out of the wasteland.'[19] The past is dead, and the dead must be forgotten— 'let not the corpses of the enfeebled hinder us, those who died in their slavery—let us hop over the carcasses.'[20] They are going into a new land, where a new life awaits them, and Joshua (the Biblical Herzl) is prepared, 'full of strength and power', to lead them. But the people now seek their old leader, Moses, 'their loyal, exalted shepherd'.

Bialik repudiates the complacent longing of the people for the comfort of Egypt, the dream of 'much onions, garlic, many great pots of meat'. This is Israel's complaint in the wilderness, that they had left so much good behind. But this longing is the longing of slavery, and the goods longed for are phantom. These things are to Bialik 'the corn of heaven' (*degan shamayim*), i.e. insubstantial spirituality, which may be contrasted with the solid food that is worked for: 'Eat the bread of pain, the fruit of the work of hands.' Passing to a 'new land' is a symbol of the new outlook. But who tells the people to go? 'Each man in his own heart hears the voice of God speak: go.' The voice of God speaking in the heart is an Ahad Ha'amic adaptation of the objective speech of God to be found in the Bible. Biblical

17. *Ibid.* This is an adaptation of the belief enshrined in the *Yigdal* hymn based on *Maimonides* 'Thirteen Principles of Faith', Singer's *Prayer Book* (London, 1954), p. 3.

18. *Ibid.* Poem *Metei midbar ha-aharonim*, p. 59.

19. *ibid*, p. 51.

20. *Ibid.*

revelation has been reduced to the modern voice of conscience. Bialik here, in an early poem, rationalises the Biblical command, after his mentor's fashion.

In a still later poem, *Hozeh, lekh berah* ('Seer, go flee'), Bialik identifies himself with Amos in his quiet prophecy of doom. Amos (7:18) asserts that 'Israel will surely be exiled from its land', and the poet tells the people that 'tomorrow the tempest will carry you all away'. They have no resilience, they are 'rotten wood'. All that the poet wants now is to return quietly whence he came—'I shall return to my habitation and its depths, and cut a covenant with the sycamores of the forest.'[21]

Saul Tschernichowsky, who so admired physical strength, often used the figure of King Saul in his poetry. His first Saul poem, 'At Ein Dor' (1893), is concerned with the encounter between Saul and the witch before the king is defeated on Mount Gilboa. The poem follows the Biblical account faithfully, except when Saul reflects on his situation, and reviews his past idyllically—'And the king remembered hills and his youth, the Spring of his world before his sky darkened . . . a broad meadow appeared, pasturing cows . . . there the young shepherd rested at ease.'[22] This naïve contrast between the delightful unambitious pastoral life and the cares of power is also pointed by Yehuda Leib Gordon in similar terms.[23] The poem follows the Biblical story from there and closes with Samuel's angry prophecy to Saul that he, the king, would join him the following day. In Saul's eyes glitters 'terrible despair'.

The same poet composed a much more powerful poem that is based on the battle of Gilboa, when Saul dies. It consists of a dialogue between Saul and his weapon-bearer. Saul hears of the constant decline of his fortunes, but refuses to lose heart. In spite of the fact that 'the uncircumcised are more numerous than us now,'[24] the chorus in every verse, to the end, he

21. *Ibid.*, p. 216.
22. S. Tschernichowsky: *Poems* (Tel-Aviv, Dvir, 1968), p. 7. *Be'ein Dor.*
23. See Y. L. Gordon, Writings,

David u'varzilai (Dvir, 1953), p. 95. Barzilai's lot is seen as idyllic.
24. Tschernichowsky: *op. cit.*, p. 159—'Al harei gilboa.*

commands his men to continue the fight, and 'take the place of those who fall and stumble'.[25] In this poem, Tschernichowsky is much less bound by the Biblical framework than in the 'Ein Dor' poem, and his greater control is reflected by the lack of sentimentality. The situation gathers momentum through the recounting of events, the rhythm, the choruses and the repetitions of words.[26]

In 'Visions of a false prophet',[27] Tschernichowsky identifies himself with the false prophets, because he thinks that the (true) prophets have a debilitating effect on the people—'the seed that you have sown will become a worm, and will consume my people till they disappear.'[28] In contrast to the prophets of the Lord, he is the 'philosopher of Life'; he preaches the physical life as against the over-spirituality of the prophets.[29] 'If you should ask me about my God'—'Where is He that we may serve Him in joy'—'He is also here on earth . . . His image is also in a pretty tree or furrow.'[30] The poet voices his vitalistic philosophy through the so-called 'false prophets', and those Biblical figures that he regards more favourably as being against the mainstream of traditional spirituality.

'The Covenant between the Pieces'

Lamdan uses Biblical motifs in a group of four poems to present his view of the Jewish Fate and the nature of Jewish history. The three figures treated—Abram (Abraham), Jacob (in two poems), and Jonah—face the same problem, the imposition of an unsought destiny. In these figures, Lamdan portrays the elected Jew, elected presumably for a prophetic purpose, since the prophet Jonah is one of the men involved, but

25. *Ibid.*, last line.
26. E.g. the word *tak'a*, which occurs many times in four of the six verses. Where the word is not employed in the two middle verses, the spirit of the verses is more subdued.
27. Tschernichowsky: *op. cit.*, p.

177, *Ḥezyonot 'akum*, first part *Me-ḥezyonot nevi ha-sheker*.
28. *Ibid.*
29. *Ibid.*, p. 227. Compare the poem 'I believe' in which he says that 'the life of the spirit is not enough for it [the people]
30. Tschernichowsky, *ibid.*

unwilling to bear the yoke of election, who wants, like Jacob (in *Vayikaz Ya'akov*), a simple, normal life—'a song for the heart, a sight for the eye, stones of rest, a crust in hunger, and in thirst—a jug of water.'[31] Jonah does not want to bear the prophecy to Nineveh, and so becomes an object of hatred—'I no more want to be an undesirable object on your earth.'[32] There is a rejection of the special destiny of the Jewish people, which is similar to the unwilling prophecy we find in the Bible,[33] the twofold functioning on heaven and earth,[34] in favour of normalcy. The normality to which the poet aspires is a very common aspiration reflected in modern Hebrew literature, and in the Zionist movement.

'The Covenant between the Pieces' well expresses this feeling. It achieves its effect by its polarity; the expectant Abram of the first stanza is counterpointed by the distraught figure in the last The setting is taken from the Genesis story of the covenant (Gen. 15), but the covenant is given a significance that is not found in the original. After the first awe of God's appearance (verse 12) 'a great awe fell on him', the tone of the Biblical passage is optimistic, when Abram receives news of his inheritance, he merely asks confirmation 'How shall I know that I will inherit it [the land]?'. They make the covenant, then God tells him that his descendants will suffer first in a foreign land for four hundred years, but will then 'go out with much property'. As for Abram, he will die at a good old age. Thus the upshot of the covenant both on a national and on a personal level seems happy and positive. Abram receives news that he will live a long time, and more importantly, that his children will enjoy a great land—'On that day, the Lord cut a covenant with Abram saying "I have given this land to your seed, from the river of Egypt to the great river, the river Euphrates".'[35] Not only is there no reaction recorded on Abram's part but the terms of the agreement seem eminently

31. *Bema'aleh 'aqrabbim* (Tel-Aviv, 1944), p. 21.

32 *Ibid.*, p. 24.

33. Jeremiah is another unwilling

prophet, see Jer. 1:6, and so is Moses, see Ex. 9:11.

34. *Bema'aleh 'aqrabbim*, p. 21.

35. Ex. 13:18.

satisfactory, and after the initial four hundred years' discomfort, no negative elements are mentioned.

But in Lamdan's version of the covenant, Abram is distraught by the end. In contrast to his initial optimism there is 'Fateful expectation'.[36] Like a large lone torch raised in a magic hand, Abram kneels on the hearth of vision, and covers his face'.[37] Lamdan uses similar terminology for both instances to point the contrast between the two moods. It was during this fateful interval that Abram made the covenant with God. This event Lamdan invests with a terror absent from the Biblical text. No words are spoken initially. Abram is left to regard the scene in silence. He sees 'vista upon vista drawn' to his eye 'as to a magnet', 'Scene upon scene sink into its pupil'.[38] The vastness of the vision, coupled with the awefulness and splendour of the setting—the first lines of the poem are: 'bathed in the purple sunset, sparked by the light of the future, Abram stands against the horizon—fire kisses fire'[39] seem too much for Abram, and he cries out: 'Not all at once, O my God. The sign is too strong, too heavy.'[40] The only hint of Abram's reaction here in the Biblical text is the original 'great awe falling on him'. In Lamdan's poem, Abram has not as yet heard anything of the covenant, and it is only implied that he does hear. For all the additional material that Lamdan incorporates in the story, he leaves out what is most vital in the original, and that is, the actual substance of the treaty. The nature of the covenant is presumably implied. But, more important than the covenant to Lamdan were the circumstances that accompanied it, and the crux of the poem comes at the beginning of the third stanza. Abram has, after noting the awe of the scene, just asserted 'Between my pieces, I am alone.'[41] God, at this moment

36. *Bema'aleh 'aqrabbim*, p. 14.
37. *Ibid.*, p. 15.
38. *Ibid.*, p. 14.
39. P. 14.
40. *Ibid.*
41. The pieces of animals that Abram divided as a symbol of the covenant with God (Ex. 15:10). It was customary in Abram's time to make contracts by dividing up animals each into two parts, and arranging them in two lines, through which the partners of the contract would walk.

answers him—'You are not alone, Abram! Look, three of us wander there within the cloud; I, you and this—see how it encircles and examines.'[42] It is this third figure, that Abram recognises, that dominates the scene—'The vulture ['ayit], Great God, why is this again between us?'[43] The vulture here has a powerful symbolic function,[44] and attracts Abram's attention to the exclusion of everything else. God tells Abram that the vulture 'is a witness, an eternal witness to the covenant between the pieces'.[45] The details of the covenant are subordinate in importance to the terrible omnipresence of the vulture, which is the negative element of the special relationship between the Jews and God. The chosenness of the Jewish people in Lamdan's eyes carries curse more than blessing, and in this poem, the 'ayit bears all the symbolic weight of Lamdan's view of the negative side of Jewish destiny. There may be a somewhat dubious positive element present too, but it is always accompanied by the certain negative element. Abram asks in dismay—'And so always unceasingly are the covenant and God to be together?'[46] And God's answer is 'This is the covenant, Abram.' The positive, God, can only come to Abram, with the negative, 'ayit. And the covenant must be accepted. In addition to the polarity of optimism and pessimism that we have in the poem, we also have the polarity expressed here. God and 'ayit go together, but the 'ayit dominates; the trembling expectation of the first stanza becomes the dismay of the last. Abram will not enjoy a carefree life.

The 'ayit has its source in the Biblical text, where we read that after the pieces had been laid out—'the vulture ['ayit] descended on the corpses, and Abram drove [lit. blew] them away' (Gen. 15:11). Lamdan takes this unobtrusive sentence as the pivot of his poem. The important thing to the poet apparently is not the promise enshrined in the Biblical text;

42. *Be ma'aleh 'aqrabbim*, p. 14.

43. *Ibid.*

44. See note on *'ayit* in chapter on imagery, Chapter 7.

45. *Bema'aleh 'aqrabbim*, p. 14.

46. *Ibid.*, p. 15.

that Israel would eventually leave Egypt and inherit a great land. The important thing is the burden and suffering that come with responsibility, the Fate of the Jewish people which is not even implied in the Bible. Neither has this concept support in other Biblical passages, where happiness and prosperity is made dependent on observance of God's commands.[47] Lamdan mentions no prescriptions that can be applied to avoid this terrible Fate, and he does not mention any demands other than those that are the cause of the suffering. God can only come to Abram in suffering. He says 'I shall always be revealed to you at night and in thick darkness'.[48] The Bible tells us that the revelation came at night (Gen. 15:12). Lamdan takes the night, plausibly, as another negative symbol. God can now only be seen at night. Blackness is another attribute of the 'ayit, who is the 'black of wing'. The 'ayit will always be present in the covenant—'Wherever the blood of the pieces is spilled, there will it return and again descend.'[49] Abram laments his loneliness as pitted against the two great powers, God and 'ayit: 'The two of you constantly on one side and I [on the other] alone.'[50] God makes no pretence that the covenant is an easy one for Abram, and He does not attempt to justify it. He knows it is a 'yoke', but His command is that Abram bear it: 'This is the covenant, Abram! Rise, go out and bear its yoke.'[51]

Now, Lamdan for the first time hints at the terms of the covenant, when Abram comes to inquire about the country. The text of Genesis is exclusively nationalistic; no religious duties are imposed, and no promises are made other than the nationalistic one that the land will be given to Abram's descendants.[52] This trust was of course of particular interest to Lamdan as a latter-day settler in the promised land. He makes Abram here ask God whether the same Fate that must befall the Jews will also befall the land. Or will the people suffer as much in the land as they do outside?—'And this land that You have given me for myself and my seed, is it also for You and the

47. E.g., Deut. 47:26.
48. *Bema'aleh 'aqrabbim*, p. 15.
49. *Ibid.*, p. 14.
50. *Ibid.*, p. 15.
51. *Ibid.*
52. See above and Note 41.

vulture, pieces for the both of you?'[53] To this, God does not even answer, and there is no need of an answer, as the 'ayit immediately manifests itself: 'Only the flapping wing scratches, threateningly in the silence, and there is a shadow on the pieces.'[54] The presence of the 'ayit is already well understood by Abram, although no interpretation has been offered. The 'ayit is the terrible Fate, and he can bear to regard it no more— 'Enough. Close the window of scenes. Show me nothing else. O my God. I do not want to see.'[55] He knows his Fate well by now. The 'sign' that was rising in the first stanza, becomes the 'sign of Fate' (goral) in the last. And 'Fate' in Lamdan's poetry is negative. 'The sign of Fate is cut round about,'[56] he writes. Through everything Fate could be seen, clear, unexposed. Abram, who has entreated to be shown no more, that he should not see, can only cover his face.

'For the Sun had Set'

The poem 'The Covenant between the Pieces' ended with Abram dismayed by the prospects held out for his people in the future. But though Abram 'kneels and covers his face', he offers no protest. The protest, only implied in the previous poem, is made explicit by the protagonist of this poem, Jacob. Jacob too is faced with the predicament of special election by God, but he differs from Abram in offering articulate dissent.

The poem takes its setting from the Biblical story of Jacob's dream in Gen. 28:11-19. There, Jacob receives the revelation equivalent to that made to Abram, which was the setting of 'The Covenant between the Pieces'. Once more, the Biblical story is quite neutral, and the purport of the revelation is again the promise of the land. The promise is ebulliently optimistic: 'The land on which you lie will I give to you and your seed. And your seed shall be as the dust of the earth, and you shall burst out Westward, Eastward, Northward and Southward, and

53. *Bema'aleh 'aqrabbim*, p. 15.   55. *Ibid.*
54. *Ibid.*   56. *Ibid.*

all the families of the earth shall be blessed in you and in your
seed.'[57] No negative element is introduced, and no conditions
are made. There is no mention even of an equivalent of the
'dark terror' in the revelation to Abram. In spite of this, Lamdan so far departs from the spirit of the Biblical original as to
make the encounter exclusively negative. As in the previous
poem, no covenantal terms are specified, and there is a complete concentration on the atmosphere of the revelation. The
dominant image is the night, and the special character that
this possesses. The 'ayit of the previous poem was 'black-
winged'; the night, blackness and the thick darkness have
the same function here. God only communicates with Jacob
in the dark, and the communication is always of terrible
import.

In the poem, we read in the first line—'Where am I? Terrible
is my lover, he has fenced me round with darkness.'[58] The
darkness here is clearly not the natural darkness of night, for
Jacob feels its dread significance. The darkness has been made
especially for him, so that the message can be communicated—
'This must mean that you have another loving message for
me.'[59] The idea that God created the darkness especially for
Jacob, Lamdan bases on a Midrash[60] that he quotes at the head
of his poem.[61] The Midrash deals with the verse (Gen. 28:11):
'And he happened at a place, and lodged there for the sun had
set', speaking of Jacob on the eve of the night of revelation.
The Hebrew for 'for the sun had set' consists of three words

57. Gen. 98:13, 14.

58. *Bema'aleh 'aqrabbim*, p. 16.

59. *Ibid.*

60. I.e., allegorical interpretation of
a Biblical passage. The literary
device of Midrash comprises a
formidable amount of Rabbinic
literature, the Hebrew literature
of the post-classical period, from
circa first century C.E. onwards.

It is a Jewish Commentary on
Scripture which seeks to bring
out a deeper meaning than lies on
the surface of the text. The two
types of the Midrash are the
Halakhah interpreting legal
points and the *Aggadah*, em-
phasising folklore, lessons, par-
ables, anecdotes, and the like.

61. Taken from *Bereshit Rabba* 68:10
2.

ki va hashemesh.[62] The Midrash reads the first two words *ki va* as one word *kibah*.[63] and changes the spelling, to give an allegorical meaning. The meaning of *kibah* is 'he extinguished', and the sentence thus translated—'he extinguished the sun'. The Midrash learns from this that God made the sun set early so that he could speak to Jacob in private.[64] This is Lamdan's basis for presupposing a special act on God's part for Jacob's benefit. The Midrash also gives the reason for this act of God. It is because God so particularly loves Jacob, and can be compared to a King who requests that the lights be extinguished because he wants to speak to a special friend. This 'love' is understood ironically by Lamdan, when Jacob calls God his 'terrible lover'. God's love seems to be an entirely negative quality and is accompanied by terror. The lover, i.e. God, is also a seducer, he loves against the will of the person loved. Jacob does not want God's advances; this love is a scaffold: 'I want to be dragged no further against my will to the scaffold of your love, O my lover and seducer.'[65] This sort of love is unsought; Jacob would reject it—'None of your love, and none of its torments.'[66] 'If this is love—then hate me, friend of my soul,'[67] he pleads. In this poem, God seems to take on the function of rapist, all-powerful, but feared, and unwanted.

Jacob recognises his peculiar situation, that his people has been chosen by God. But he is afraid that this closeness of God involves rejection by man; the two seem inseparable one from the other. When called by God, he answers—'No, I do not want to come to hear, and to be, once more, despised by man though loved by God.'[68] The uniqueness of the experience does not make it any more pleasurable—'As one unique, appointed person am I called to you, and whilst I come—I have no countenance and no sound spot. I am like the worm of the earth.'[69] Ahad Ha'am too recognised the twofold implication

62. *Bema'aleh 'aqrabbim*, p. 16.
63. *Ibid.*
64. See heading of poem in translation.
65. *Bema'aleh 'aqrabbim*, p. 16.
66. *Ibid.*, p. 17.
67. *Ibid.*
68. *Ibid.*
69. *Ibid.*

of selection, though with him it is a peculiarly prophetic interpretation of Jewish existence—'They [the true prophets] saw in it [i.e. the people of Israel] the chosen people.' The function of the chosen people, in this view, was to pursue 'absolute justice', and to be a paragon for the rest of the world. This positive function that Ahad Ha'am ascribed to Jewish existence is not implicit in Lamdan's work. Election for its own sake would make no sense to Ahad Ha'am, who thought that the prophets were prepared to suffer indignity and hurt for the sake of a greater ideal, that of justice—'And this task, great and exalted, though neither pleasant nor honourable, the prophets saw (as they always saw their innermost desire as already in existence in the visible world) as on the shoulders of their small nation . . . that the whole people should be a basic force, a force for justice in the compound harmony of human life in general.'[70] Ahad Ha'am in his appreciation of the negative side of election, says prosaically here what Lamdan has been saying in verse. But whereas, to Ahad Ha'am, the negative element is subsidiary, to Lamdan it is all-important. Lamdan nowhere even mentions a positive element that could justify election. The Jew is chosen; he knows not why, but must unwillingly submit to a greater will.

A closer approach to Lamdan's view of Jewish election is made by the German dramatist Richard Beer-Hoffmann in a play *Jacob's Dream*,[71] which he wrote between 1909 and 1915, many years before Lamdan wrote 'When the sun set'.[72] The affinity is so great between the two works that there are even verbal parallels. Beer-Hoffmann uses the same Biblical setting (also Gen. 28), and chooses as his theme the doubtful character of Jewish election, as in Lamdan's poem, an allegorical reading of the Biblical text. Jacob says in the play 'I would bear it [Judaism] as a crown, not as a yoke',[73] and more protestingly, 'Why did He choose us without asking us if we want to be

70. See Ahad Ha'am's essay *Kohen ve-navi*: *op. cit.*, p. 92.

71. See translation into Hebrew by Joseph Lichtenbaum in the volume of plays *Yisrael ve-yi'udo* (Tel-Aviv, 1954).

72. Written in 1942.

73. See *Ḥalom Ya'akov*, p. 239.

chosen?'[74] In the play, Jacob hears a dispute between Samael and the angels. The angels tell him that, if he accepts election, he will be eternal.[75] But Samael argues that what appears to be a blessing will turn out to be a curse. The angels say that he will be 'a light to the nations'. Samael argues that this will involve suffering, and invite hatred, although it might be God's wish—'You will be, though beloved of God, hated by the whole world.'[76] The wording here is almost identical with Lamdan's plaint in the poem—'[I don't want] to be once more despised by man, though loved by God'. But even Beer-Hoffmann views the function of Jewish existence in a positive light. Jacob will be a scapegoat,[77] a sacrifice.[78] He will serve the function of purgation for the rest of mankind, and be a Jesus figure. Beer-Hoffmann's Jacob accepts the covenant willingly in the end—'Let God heap upon me what he will . . . like a wreath will I wear it [his imposition], not a yoke.'[79] Beer-Hoffmann sees a positive function in the existence of the Chosen Race where Lamdan does not.

Jacob would be pleased to listen to God's word in Lamdan's poem, were God prepared to speak to him openly, in the light of day. But he chooses darkness, and it is the darkness that is symbolic of terror. So Jacob pleads: 'If there is anything that you want with me, a precious and great loving matter, spread it out at my feet like a grassy, spring carpet.'[80] Let everyone hear of it—'With all the sounds of the Universe [let it play] in all men's ears.'[81] But in reality, God's love is not like this, and is not so communicated,' if in all the fullness [of its] stores, there is no crumb of kindness or any glimmer of light . . . its touch is the sting of a nettle, strangulation its embrace,'[82] then Jacob will have none of it, and he begs to be hated, not loved.

74. *Ibid.*, p. 240. The same idea is repeated in Jacob's answer to Adnibaal, his servant, who tells him that God has chosen Israel, p. 254.

75. *Ibid.*, p. 296.

76. *Ibid.*, p. 298.

77. *Ibid.*

78. *Ibid.*, p. 299.

79. *Ibid.*

80. *Bema'aleh 'aqrabbim*, p. 17.

81. *Ibid.*

82. *Ibid.*

Jacob here goes on to say what it is that he would like—
'Leave me to join the community of the small', he requests,
'I would cross the paths of life unheeding like them all . . . be
one strand amongst many.'[83] What Jacob is expressing here is
a rejection of his special nature, i.e. the special nature of the
Jewish people. And we can read here the yearning for normality that characterises so much Hebrew literature of the period.
To be 'one strand amongst many' and to have no unique
relationship with God is the desire of many writers of the time
and is one of the aims, often unexpressed, of the Zionist
movement. Bialik, for example, regretted the fact that he
never enjoyed the normal pleasures of youth, or love. 'What
is love?' and 'where is my youth?'[84] he asks. Brenner's hero
asserts that he cannot love, because he does not believe in it.[85]
Tschernichowsky complains of the strangulation of the human
spirit by unworldliness,[86] and this leads him to the exaggerated
worship of strength, already noticed.[87] Berdichevsky, a
contemporary of Ahad Ha'am, voiced a similar feeling in
prose, in his attack on Ahad Ha'am's concept of a national
morality—'In my view, Ahad Ha'am wanted to lean on the
past. The people of Israel are too spiritual.'[88] Haim Hazaz[89]
asserted through his mouthpiece in the story 'The Sermon'
(Haderashah) that Jewish history since the Bible is unworthy of
being called a history, because it had always been created by

83. *Ibid.*

84. See H. N. Bialik: *Poems* (Dvir, 1944), p. 41. *Hakhnisini taḥat Knaphekh.*

85. J. H. Brenner: *Selected Works* (Tel-Aviv, 1953), Vol. 1, p. 187, *Mikan umikan.*

86. Tschernichowsky, *op. cit.*, p. 227: his poem *Ani maamin.* Spiritual life is insufficient with reference to the Jewish people. See also his poem, *Lenokhaḥ pesel Apollo*, with reference to the

spirit of the people. 'And they bound him with the phylactery strap.'

87. See above, first section of this essay, on this series of poems.

88. See M. J. Berdichevsky, *Collected Essays* (Am oved, 1952), *Me-ḥezyonot 'akum*, Section *Maḥashavot* the essay on Ahad Ha'am's *At the Crossroads* ('Al parashat derakhim).

89. A contemporary novelist. See Chapter 2.

others. The people had been too weak and passive to form its own.[90] This dual accusation of passivity and over-spirituality is the principal motif of ideologically orientated Hebrew literature of the period; and the Zionist belief is that this un-natural situation prevailed because of the unnatural conditions in which the Jewish people had been living. If they had their own homeland, not only would they be able to create their own history, they could also live normal lives without having any special pressure placed on them. In Beer-Hoffmann's *Jacob's Dream*, Jacob's only request of the angels is that they let him sleep restfully once more.[91] He wants no dreams, no impositions, no covenants, and no special relationship with God. Brenner's aspiration for his people is unspectacular in the same way, even anti-spectacular. He wants a renaissance, but not a renaissance in the exalted, Italian sense—only a renaissance to normality, 'life on the earth'.[92] And so Lamdan has Jacob make a similarly simple request—'Let bread with salt taste pleasant, O God, let the waters of the earth from earthen-ware jugs be sweet to me.'[93] He would rather taste simple food, i.e. enjoy an unspectacular life, than be made giddy 'by the strong and bitter wine of God'. Like Beer-Hoffmann's Jacob, Lamdan's Jacob wants no dreams—'mocking dreams', as he called them. For these dreams are about the 'untilled corn of heaven'.[94]

This same expression 'corn of heaven' is used scornfully by Bialik in his Zionistic poem *Metei midbar ha-aḥaronim*, men-tioned above, to describe the insubstantial spirituality that the people have been feeding on too long—'No, not insubstantial bread, quails and corn of heaven—the bread of hardship you shall eat, the fruit of manual labour.' Bialik is tempting them out of the wilderness, the diaspora, where they have fed on spiritual food, to their own land where they would eat the fruit of real work. Both Bialik, and Brenner in a more sober

90. See *Sippurim nivḥarim* (Dvir, 1952), p. 184.
91. Beer-Hoffmann, *op. cit.*, p. 292, 2.
92. See Brenner: *Selected Works* (ed. Poznanski), Vol. I, p. 170.
93. *Bemaʿaleh ʿaqrabbim*, p. 18.
94. *Ibid.*

mood, seek the rejection of this spirituality for another end, a nationalistic one, where normality or glory, depending on the shade of the writer, will be restored.

Lamdan also seeks to reject over-spirituality, but for the unambitious purpose of living a normal life. There is here no implication of nationalism. He would reject the covenant, because it is illusory, it is 'black soil' with the black of hopelessness. In the following verse enclosed in brackets to indicate that it is a side issue, Jacob tells us of the effects of drinking 'this unearthly wine', of fulfilling the covenant, for till now he has drunk of this wine. He has been thrown into sewers, made 'a target for stones of hatred', and has been then cast out 'empty-handed' to beg at 'foreign gates'. The parentheses that Lamdan puts round this verse indicate his total concern with the present situation, for it is completely inappropriate to the story of Jacob. The poet here casts down the barrier he himself has erected by deploying a Biblical figure. Described here, of course, is the modern Jew who, totally occupied with God, has been trampled on by men. The 'foreign gates' are all the countries of the dispersion to which the Jew has to seek right of entry, 'to stretch out the hand'. He has been dreaming of the 'corn of heaven', and has starved on earth. For the first time also, Lamdan openly calls the covenant a lie—'a seductive, lying vision'.[95] God has become not only a seducer, but a liar as well. The poet's disillusion is complete.

The last stanza reverts to the situation of the first. Again, there is darkness, and Jacob infers from it that God would speak with him again. We saw in the poem 'The Covenant between the Pieces' how Lamdan makes the final stanza echo the first to sharpen the change of mood, as the pulse of the protagonist is slowed down. Here too, the final stanza echoes the first, and here too the mood has changed in the interim, for though Jacob has pleaded for normality for 'bread with salt', he has received no hint that he will ever enjoy a normal life. And now that God's presence is manifesting itself again, he probably

95. *Ibid.*

begins to realise that his protests are in vain. But protest he does until the end—'Leave me', he cries. He wants to disperse the darkness that has again fallen everywhere: 'Let there be light. Raise up your sun, O God.'[96] Light is hope, the antithesis of darkness. Jacob uses the words from Genesis in the creation story, when God said 'Let there be light, and there was light.'[97] Light was the first thing that God created in the world. Everything had been 'waste and void', chaos. Light dispelled the chaos. As 'light' is a positive symbol in Genesis, so it is generally in literature a positive symbol. Light and its instruments, sun and day, are what Jacob craves, and it is his grievance against God that he is denied them. The simple man enjoys light, and Jacob wants to be such a simple man, and have nothing of any special relationship that precludes normal, justified pleasure. He holds out, and his last cry to God, also the last line in the poem, is: 'I want to come no more, I do not want to hear.'

'And Jacob Awoke'

This second Jacob poem, though written considerably earlier than the one just described, follows it in historical sequence from the Biblical point of view, and also presents an emotional development. 'When the sun set', gave us, albeit allusively, the revelation of God to Jacob. This poem describes Jacob's mood after the revelation when he awoke. In 'When the sun set', we leave a rebellious Jacob, asserting weakly—'I want to come no more; I do not want to hear.' Here, no question of defiance arises. Jacob makes his protest in much the same terms once more, but is resigned to his fate, and is prepared to fulfil the obligations placed upon him by God. But in spite of the deeper pessimism that colours this poem, in which no protest could possibly be effective, the mood is not so oppressive. The lines are shorter, and the rhythm is lighter. There is not the same emotionally charged symbolism that characterised the previous poem, where night, darkness and

96. *Ibid.*   97. Gen. 1:3.

horror were so conspicuous. The emotional pressure is much lower here.

Once more, the Biblical base gives Lamdan no support for his conception of the character of Jacob and the nature of his experience. The Bible does indeed record that Jacob was much impressed by his dream and revelation. But since, as we have seen, the revelation was a positive one, there was no cause for him to be distraught. He did say 'How terrible is this place',[98] but the reaction was that of a man who had been vouchsafed the special attention of the Almighty. Indeed, we see from Jacob's reaction to the dream on the following morning that he now felt a special affinity with God—'And Jacob vowed a vow saying: If God will be with me and guard me on the way that I go and give me bread to eat and clothes to wear, then shall I return in peace to my father's house, and Jehova will be God for me.'[99] In the Bible, Jacob is so impressed by Jehova that he would adopt Him as a God. After all, He did promise him the land.

In this second poem of Lamdan's, once more we find no mention of this entirely positive element, but we do find the introduction of the negative element characteristic of all Lamdan's poetry, that is totally without scriptural foundation. The poet, in fact, entirely reverses the scriptural account of Jacob's fortunes. Lamdan has Jacob say at the beginning of the poem: 'Joyful and light of step did I leave the house of my father', whereas the Bible tells us that he fled from the wrath of Esau on Rebecca his mother's advice: 'And now, my son, listen to my voice. Rise, flee to Laban, my brother, to Haran . . . until the wrath of your brother turns from you . . .'[100] Lamdan contradicts the scriptural account and makes Jacob's early state happy for his own doctrinal purposes, because he wants to assert that Jacob afterwards felt burdened by God's revelation of election, and yearned for his carefree youth. The revelation is indeed crucial in Jacob's life, but the Bible does not slant it in Lamdan's way. The first four and a half verses of

98. Gen. 28:17.   100. Gen. 27:43, 45.
99. Gen. 28:20, 21.

'And Jacob awoke' are occupied by an idyllic appraisal of the joys of his unburdened existence the simple pastoral life. This idealisation of the pastoral life we have already noted in two other poets in their treatment of Biblical themes, Y. L. Gordon and Saul Tschernichowsky.[101] This too is foreign to the spirit of the Bible. But for Lamdan the Bible provides only the barest narrative skeleton here.

That Lamdan places Jacob's carefree existence in his youth, although it was only very recently that he had been burdened with the *yi'ud*, the special task, can be seen when he has Jacob say—'My youth cheered my path from pace to pace.'[102] Song, brightness, and light are symbols of joyousness. He had been exposed to the open air—'wreathed round above my head was the distant firmament in bright purple'.[103] Nature was friendly—'As the lambs of my father in the plain of Beersheba and its meadows, did the clouds, bright with faith accompany me from a broad height.'[104] Nature is here made sympathetic to the poet's mood as it had been on the awesome occasion of God's revelation to Abram.[105] Everything conspired to make his environment 'a homeland of happiness'. His headstone was soft for him as sheep's wool before shearing.[106] This 'headstone' later became a source of foreboding, because it was on a headstone that he lay when he dreamed his dream.[107] He had lain down on his headstone in the quiet security that his peace would continue—'the good of the morrow is still plentiful'.[108] But this was the night of the dream, so his hopes were rudely disappointed: 'I fell asleep until the dream, and after it, God was standing over me, so

101. See above, 'The use of Biblical motifs in literature', and Note 23.

102. *Bema'aleh 'aqrabbim*, p. 19.

103. *Ibid.*

104. *Ibid.*

105. E.g. the first stanza of the poem 'The covenant between the pieces'.

106. *Bema'aleh 'aqrabbim*, p. 19.

107. See Gen. 27:11. 'And he took of the stones of the place, and placed them at his head.' This is the linguistic basis for the unusual expression *Even meraashot*, meaning 'headstone'.

108. *Bema'aleh 'aqrabbim*, p. 20.

exalted and terrifying.'[109] The sleep was the sleep of peace, and he had been able to enjoy it up till the moment of revelation. For then, God appeared to him, and God was not only great, but terrifying as well. His negative side was recognised immediately. Jacob had been happy, carefree, before he knew God, but never again would be know that same peace of mind. It seems from this poem that knowledge of God is negative, that happiness can only be had in ignorance of Him. God demands and imposes; He does not bestow. The revelations of both Abram and Jacob are for them the moment of crisis. Life is not to be enjoyed; there is a duty to be carried out. But this duty is not the normal religious duty that carries with it reward. It is not the Biblical duty that makes laws for the purpose of God's gratification and man's benefit. It is the modern duty, the duty to No-God, duty becoming Duty, self-justifying and still all-demanding. This Duty Lamdan views as a peculiar Jewish curse, by which Jewish existence is justified, negatively and tragically. The Jew is bound to the yoke of a graceless, irrational Power.

Jacob realises this when he awakens: 'Now that I am awake, I know. I was not here alone with the joy of the sight of my eyes, with my expectation of the future. The large demanding eye of God has set its ambush for me here.'[110] Here again the dual character of God is noted, His size and His awkwardness. His eye is both great and demanding. His demands will allow Jacob no more rest. The Jew will no longer be free to satisfy his own desires, he will be an instrument of God's. He will not be able to escape, because he will be cut off by ambush. The eye of God will see him wherever he is—'It (I do not know why) watches my step.'[111]

The nature of the landscape too has changed—'And this landscape that yesterday fondled me with its kind ways is, alas, no more a nest of happiness for man.'[112] All had been brightness, light and trust, and is now changed, has become 'a gate

109. *Ibid.*
110. *Ibid.*
111. *Ibid.*
112. *Ibid.*

to heaven, a ladder to its terrifying angels'. The nest of happiness has become the ladder of Jacob's dream, the nest being a symbol of security, and the ladder of its opposite, as it was a ladder that set up the connection between heaven and earth, between God and man, and it is this that Jacob so fears. The ladder of the Biblical verse[113] has been interpreted symbolically, and has become the instrument of revelation. The nature of the revelation is deplored, it is 'a trap set by God for me, and a far-ranging ambush'.[114] Jacob now hints at the substance of the revelation, the land that had been promised to him—'And this land is given to me'. But he will never enjoy the land 'because when I clutch the bosom of my earth—I am reminded with trembling: it is a gate of heaven, a ladder to the unseen'.[115] The unseen is the Duty that has been forced on him. Jacob complains that he will never be able to till the soil like an ordinary worker, because immediately the Terrible One would descend on him with the command 'Cease to grovel in the earth! Rise, ascend to the stars'.[116] Every time he tries to occupy himself with worldly tasks, heavenly duties will be imposed on him. He contrasts his present situation with his previous innocent state—'The stars! Last night, everything in me was quiet and slept as they twinkled to me so quiet and good, And I said, these distant things demand nothing.'[117] It is God's insistent demands with which Jacob cannot cope.

But just as Jacob cannot be wholly devoted to earthly activities, so he does not belong entirely to Heaven. He is like the angels of his dream on the ladder, both in ascent and descent. He is neither entirely Heaven's nor Earth's, but uneasily belongs to both, and is accepted by neither—'always unceasingly, in this great hollow of a sling between Heaven and Earth, to be slung from here to there, to be rejected by both, and to bear the

113. Gen. 27:12. 'And he dreamed and there was a ladder fixed in the earth whose top reached to the heaven, with angels of God ascending and descending it.'

114. *Bema'aleh 'aqrabbim*, p. 20.

115. *Ibid.*

116. *Ibid.*

117. *Ibid.*

yoke of both.'[118] Jacob the Jew has become the uneasy middle-man. We saw in 'When the Sun Set' that he did not want 'to be despised by man, though loved by God'.[119] Here it seems he is not even loved by God. There is no mention of 'love' in this poem, though in both 'When the Sun Set' and 'The Covenant between the Pieces', God's love for his chosen one is men-tioned, even if the love manifests itself in a peculiar way. Jacob regrets now that he came: 'Is it for this that I went out? . . . You promised me great things and they are very frightening, and your generosity casts terror into me.'[120] As in the previous poem, Jacob now articulates his simple desires: 'I sought a human inheritance: a song for the heart, a sight for the eye, stones of rest, a crust in hunger, and in thirst a jug of water.' Here again is expressed the now familiar longing for normality and the wording is almost identical with that in 'When the Sun Set', already examined: 'Let me enjoy bread with salt, O God. Let the waters of the earth be sweet to me from earthen-ware jugs.'[121] It was a simple life that Jacob wanted, and love—'I left my father's tents in the south to seek love'[122]—but he has found neither: 'But now the heavens have grown heavy, of a sudden, over my head. The earth scorches my feet . . .'[123] He can no longer even walk in peace—'every path and track in it bites the heel like a serpent.'[124] His past is dead, and so for him are its pleasures—'no more will rocky couches be tender to my back.'[125] He is full of foreboding for the future, and knows that it holds nothing of delight for him—'The way does not cause its countenance to shine upon me.'[126] He can do nothing about his Fate, however, for he is prisoner—'prisoner of subjugating Destiny, and bound by the word of God'.[127] His spirit is subject to another will. He can no longer even protest, and has become resigned to his lot.

118. *Ibid.*, p. 21.
119. *Ibid.*, p. 17.
120. *Ibid.*, p. 21.
121. *Ibid.*, p. 18.
122. *Ibid.*, p. 21.

123. *Ibid.*
124. *Ibid.*, p. 22.
125. *Ibid.*
126. *Ibid.*
127. *Ibid.*

'Jonah Flees from his God'

In mood, this poem about the prophet Jonah, is closest to the second Jacob poem: 'And Jacob Awoke'. The awe of revelation is not manifest as in the Abram poem, and no hysterical protest is offered as in the first Jacob poem. As in the second Jacob poem, the mood is quiet and a further development is noted in in the state of the protagonist's depression. He does not cry out in furious protest as in 'When the Sun Set'—'I want to come no more, I do not want to hear', because he knows that such protest is ineffectual. And he is not content with being 'bound by the word of God', because such a state is intolerable. His desire is to exercise the only freedom that is left to a man in his position, the freedom to die—'Let waves finish me in their anger, let the great deep swallow me.'[128] This death is preferable to his present status as 'servant of God and His truth, bound to the train of His splendour, who is dragged in the dust of the earth'.[129] The language here presents an even more disenchanted picture than the 'tied to dominant Duty, and bound by the word of God' of the poem 'And Jacob Awoke'. The picture is one of complete degradation. The prophet, fulfilling the word of God, is seen as contemptible, dragged through the dust. For the first time in this series of poems, the Biblical text is in accordance with the mood here. After his prophecy has failed, because the people of Nineveh have repented, Jonah feels betrayed. He acted as an instrument, eventually fulfilling God's wish against his own will, and even then is let down. He is made to look a fool. As Lamdan expresses it (if he is speaking of the same or a similar incident, though in the Biblical source it occurs later), 'They say Vision has been closed off from Jonah.'[130] The Bible presents Jonah as such a disappointed man that he requests to die: 'Now, O Lord, take my life from me for it is better that I die than that I should live.'[131]

Lamdan has Biblical support throughout for the mood of his poem, and for the first time works within the Biblical

128. *Ibid.*, p. 26.
129. *Ibid.*

130. *Ibid.*, p. 24.
131. Jonah 4:3.

framework. From the point of accuracy, his subject is a far more plausible one than his other two as an instrument for his particular view of Jewish existence. We might not see, from the Biblical text alone, that Abram and Jacob were any more than tribal leaders and folk figures, and they may give no hint of religious, missionary or moral zeal. The prophets, on the other hand, were the representatives of the Lord on earth to Israel. They received direct communications from God,[132] and they transmitted this communication to the people. This fits in with Lamdan's view of the Jew as the link between heaven and earth. Also in support of Lamdan's outlook is the involuntary nature of prophecy. Rarely does the prophet choose to prophesy. He merely cannot avoid it, it is inevitable. As Amos says, 'If a lion roars, who will not fear; if the Lord God speaks [i.e. so commands], who will not prophesy?'[133] Jonah too did not choose to carry out God's command. In fact, he displayed greater unwillingness than any other prophet, for as soon as God spoke to him, he fled—'Then Jonah rose to flee to Tarshish from before the Lord.'[134] But his flight was useless because God caught him—'And there was a great storm at sea.'[135] There is no escape from God. Thus, there are four reasons why Jonah was a suitable protagonist. Firstly, because Jonah was a prophet and it is the function of a prophet to act as a link between man and God. Secondly, that Jonah was unwilling to prophesy, and displayed this unwillingness to a greater degree than any other prophet, in fleeing. Thirdly, that Jonah was eventually caught, and discovered that one cannot flee from God, and fourthly, that Jonah, even after fulfilling the word of God, was betrayed, in his view, and made to appear foolish before men, despised and rejected. These four characteristics, in Lamdan's poetry, mark off the chosen Jew, and constitute the theme of his work in general, and of this group of poems in particular. In Jonah, Lamdan found the ideal protagonist, the archetypal Jew.

Lamdan presents Jonah as addressing us at the position he

132. E.g. with Jonah, see Jonah 1:1.   134. Jonah 1:3.
133. Amos 3:8.   135. Jonah 1:4.

arrived at in the Biblical book, Jonah 1:3, i.e. at the time of his attempted escape. But the wish to die of Chapter 4 is advanced to this stage of his career. A storm has come. He reflects on the recent events. He had tried to escape, but 'can a man flee his shadow, or can a tree tell its roots: "Let go of me, my dark children that I, the stock, may wander far off".'[136] He had wanted to sleep unconcerned in 'the recesses of the boat'.[137] The The 'recesses of the boat' here are what the 'nest of happiness' was in 'And Jacob Awoke', a symbol of security and protection from the necessity to fulfil his Duty. The boat, he says later in this poem, tried to offer a refuge (*miklat*), but this attempt was doomed to failure, because he was not supposed to enjoy refuge.[138] Jonah's complaint is identical with that of Jacob—he no longer wants 'to be a mediator between God and man, between Heaven and Earth, and a constant target for the arrows of both together'.[139] This in concert with the next phrase—'I no longer want to be constantly slung between the two of them as in a sling,'[140] shares a great deal with the stanza expressing this feeling in the previous poem—'unceasingly to be slung in this great sling between heaven and earth, between here and there, to be rejected by both, and to bear the yoke of both.'[141]

Both figures are uneasy of their status. As intermediaries, they do not know where they belong, but they feel uncomfortable in both places, that is both in their relationship with God, and in their relationship with other men. They are hated by both, and get no benefits from either. Jonah complains, 'I receive neither the corn of the land nor the choice fruits of heaven'.[142] Jonah admits the possibility that God might love him. But he asks 'If I am very dear to you, why do You not let me go free, O my God, without Your yoke that bends my life and draws it with its weight to the terrifying depths?'[143]

136. *Bema'aleh 'aqrabbim*, p. 23.
137. *Ibid.*
138. *Ibid.*
139. *Ibid.*, p. 24.
140. *Ibid.*

141. See previous section *Bema'aleh 'aqrabbim*, p. 21.

142. *Bema'aleh 'aqrabbim*, p. 24.

143. *Ibid.*

He wants to be simple, 'a person with no yoke, with no double world or life',[144] a man who owes no particular debt to anyone and can live normally. He is 'fed up with being a vain mark, an ineffective stumbling block . . .'[145] He is not even effective in his unwanted task, because God reverses his decisions. But the prophet seems to have fewer rights than a murderer, because there is nowhere that he can escape—'Is there nowhere amongst the crannies of Your world a retreat and a refuge for me as well, as there are cities of refuge for every murderer?'[146] It seems that there is not. Jonah requests to die.

This poem is the most rhetorical of the group of four poems, and the most rambling. Unlike the others, too, it is written in free verse, and in this instance the technique does not achieve the economy of expression that characterises his more formal work. But the motifs of the poem are familiar, and the greater affinity between Lamdan's Jonah and the Biblical figure makes the use of a Biblical motif more pointed. Here Lamdan's work seems to become both an interpretation of the text of the Bible, and a uniquely personal expression of the archetypal contemporary Jew.

144. *Ibid.*, p. 23.
145. *Ibid.*, p. 25.
146. *Ibid.* In Deut. 35:11–13, cities of refuge are appointed for those who murder accidentally, that no blood-avenger should be able to touch them as long as they remain there.

Chapter 6

OTHER THEMES IN LAMDAN'S
LYRIC POETRY

Two Faces of the Poet

SO FAR in our consideration of Lamdan we have been presented with what seems to be a monolithic obsession in his poetry; the problem of the Jewish Fate. At times, it has seemed to the poet that there is a possibility of escape from it, that *Masada* could wave 'a final banner or rebellion',[1] and at others, that the Jew must remain 'prisoner of subjugating task, and bound by the word of God'.[2] But whether viewed with hope or despair, there has been one central concern: the existence of the Jewish nation in the face of an unspecified Destiny (*yi'ud*) and a tragic Fate (*goral*). This concern might be called political, since it centres on a national and historical pivot conceived in terms of world forces. We have as yet seen little of the poet's concern with the personal, with those aspects of consciousness specific to the individual. The poet conceived it as his function to record the strange phenomenon of Jewish national existence, with particular reference to its condition in his own lifetime and to the revolutionary revival in Palestine.[3]

But the poet did not arrive at this decision without conflict. There were forces drawing the poet in another direction, away from the discussion of political issues and 'solutions', towards the world of the private imagination, where these issues are irrelevant. The poet's conflict is recorded in the second series of poems in the volume *Bema'aleh 'aqrabbim*, entitled 'In twofold

1. See *Masada*, p. 11.

2. See *Bema'aleh 'aqrabbim*, p. 22.

3. See chapter on 'In the Threefold Harness', discussion of the poetic frontispiece.

image' (*Be'khephel demut*). The 'twofold image' is the two sides of the poet's countenance, the one intricated with the turbulent events of his day, and the other associated with 'the landscape of childhood', possibly his true self, the heart,[4] that has since been estranged from his other self. Nowhere else in his poetry does the poet afford such a clear picture of his ambivalence. No solution is proposed, no synthesis is reached; both aspects of the countenance cannot be shown at the same time. We have seen that the poet elected for what we conveniently call 'the political', but he still yearns for 'the personal'. He fights off his deepest desires in order to fulfil an obligation.[5] He takes an option which leaves him incomplete personally, and yet he feels that the alternative may not be chosen. In this series of poems, we are faced with the naked and irremediable tragedy of the situation.

The two poles of attraction assume in these poems different names, according as to how their various aspects present themselves. In the first of the series of poems, 'Ballad of my other self' (*Baladah 'al ha'ani halaz*), he aspires from 'the revealed' to 'the hidden'. The life to which he is now accustomed is commonplace, and he is constantly aspiring to the other: 'In every sealed-up, revealed thing, he tears a lattice to the hidden.'[6] The mood of dissatisfaction is set immediately, in the first lines of the poem, for, as for this other ego: 'His spirit is a wheel of changes on the axle of disquiet.'[7] The characteristic of a wheel on an axle is that it may easily be turned in either direction. The poet, though moving firmly in one direction, as we have seen from his other work, is now tempted by other vistas. These vistas are appealingly uncharted, and the poet 'would sail to the unseen from the shore of solutions'.[8] Earlier, the poet had wanted to dance the dance of solutions,[9] in that case, the Zionist solution. The Zionist solution was a political and social answer to the problem posed by the Jewish Fate. And this is precisely the world which the poet now wants to escape;

4. *Bema'aleh 'aqrabbim*, p. 40.

5. *Ibid.*, p. 35.

6. *Ibid.*, p. 33.

7. *Ibid.*

8. *Ibid.*

9. See *Masada*, p. 38.

the world of 'solutions' is the world of politics. In that it is a 'shore', it represents the known to the poet. But he now aspires to the unknown.

Changing the image, the poet goes on to say: 'An exit to another entrance he seeks at every entrance; a vision of dread is the appearance of every yoke to him.'[10] We see now that the poet would avoid the 'yoke' as well as 'solutions'. The 'yoke' is what Jacob complained of in the previous series of poems, when longing for normality. He said that he had to bear the yoke both of Heaven and of Earth.[11] In the following poem, Jonah desires to be simply 'a person with no yoke, with no double world or life'.[12] The yoke is not a thing borne by every man, but only by the elect, who, with Lamdan, are the symbol of the Jew in modern times. To shuffle off the yoke is to escape the Fate, and these two series of poems aspire to just that. Jacob and Jonah wanted the simple life, simply to be left alone. Here the poet wants more, especially as a poet, for 'the unseen' is also 'the wondrous parable': 'Of all the dialects of man and his words on earth, he chooses the wondrous parable.'[13] The 'wondrous parable' is the literary instrument whereby the writer arrives at 'the unseen'. The poet tells of the time when he was devoted to it, when he was young: 'When I was young, my love was given to it alone. To somewhere mysterious and to nameless legend did it steer my yearnings on a far constant voyage.'[14]

We do not know much about this 'somewhere', since it is 'mysterious', but its vital property is that it is 'a place where the heart forgets burden, duty, and statute'.[15] This is a negative characteristic, but it is the negative sought by Jacob and Jonah: relief from this special burden that is anyway not laden on the rest of mankind. And it had the quality of cheering the general aspect of things: 'It revealed to me the rainbow of pacification in every cloud of sorrow. I loved it. It once was me.'[16] The

10. *Bema'aleh 'aqrabbim*, p. 33.
11. *Ibid.*, p. 21.
12. *Ibid.*, p. 23.
13. *Ibid.*, p. 33.

14. *Ibid.*
15. *Ibid.*
16. *Ibid.*

child could find comfort in things that are no longer available to the adult. Speaking of this other self, the *alter ego*, he says: 'I sent it from me, and brought my life into the yoke of a generation that walks contrariwise with nation and God.'[17] Again the yoke, now, we hear, deliberately imposed by the poet on his own neck, not, as with Jacob and Jonah, imposed from outside on an unwilling bearer. The poet has deliberately committed himself to the people and to the land, to pioneering Palestine: 'And I entered a covenant with a land poisoned with Fate, hard of spirit and aspect.'[18]

But now the poet is faced once more with the clash, for the other aspect or 'image' returns to lure him: 'Now it sneaks in day by day, knocks on my door, whilst I shrivel up silently and do not call "Come in".'[19] The poet is unwilling to admit the image, for 'it is too late . ... the miracle will not occur again'.[20] He has been spoilt; he is no longer capable of pure delight and love as he was as a child: 'How can I raise my face to it, when I have killed my love, have throttled its echo in me?'[21] The poet is now too deeply entrenched in the world around him. Since he has known delights of the other 'image', he can understand its temptations, but the other cannot understand him, the lyrical infinite cannot understand the involved political: 'It will not understand me, its eyes are only to the vista, and it neither sees nor knows what is near at hand.'[22] One wandering in 'the landscape of childhood' would not notice the political concerns of the poet; he would be otherwise occupied in grander speculation. Whereas the poet can comprehend the other view, the other could not stoop to him: 'It would not know that there is a sorrow too heavy to take to wing, and a yoke beside which every ranging freedom is small.'[23] The poet not only dons the yoke willingly. He does it in the face of this enormous lure that the 'unseen' presents to him. But the constant knocking is an image of lurking

17. *Ibid.*
18. *Ibid.*
19. *Ibid.*
20. *Ibid.*
21. *Ibid.*
22. *Ibid.*
23. *Ibid.*

temptation that the poet recognises, though he heeds it not: 'I, as if unhearing, do not call "Come in". I am as if unseeing, and my heart, ah, is not with me.'[24] The poet can only ignore the temptation by a conscious effort of will that distorts his faculties.

In the next poem, 'The Poet', Lamdan deploys a different main image to illustrate this same theme of the division in the poet's soul. The image is of a poet sitting in an enclosed room (where later a single window is opened), whilst round about is open space, the vistas where children play. The poem opens and closes with the children playing outside: 'Outside did children play, gay with sun and wind. And they flew coloured paper snakes up high.'[25] The children have limitless space and unbounded ambition with which they can aspire to the heights, and make their creations, the paper snakes, soar into the sky. The contrast is presented with the poet's room, where 'the walls are deafened, the view of the windows blinded'.[26] But then the poet has a chance to see out, for 'in the thick silence, a single window is opened'.[27] The opening of the window here is the equivalent image to the knocking on the door in the previous poem. For these two occurrences represent the sudden awareness in the poet of the 'unseen' of his childhood world, on which he had turned his back. In the previous poem, the poet did not open the door, i.e. return to the 'landscape of childhood'. And in this poem, he does not go out to join the children. But he is presented with the problem: 'He looked through it [the window], and saw a terrifying, unknowable vista stretching out round about, and in it like a question mark was the world cast bound and twisted as in a convulsion.'[28]

And then the poet is tempted; he would recapture the past: 'And into the air he stretched out his hand as one thinking to gather in from the vistas, and to bring back everything that he had sent away from himself until that day, and to call out: "It

24. *Ibid.*, p. 35.
25. *Ibid.*, p. 36.
26. *Ibid.*

27. *Ibid.*
28. *Ibid.*

is not my fault. I did not send it away!" '[29] The poet does not understand his new mood, and is uncertain how to react: 'He did not know whether to cry, rejoice, roar, or keep quiet in the stillness till his breathing stopped.'[30] So he does nothing: 'Into the depths of himself without echo he sinks, and is submerged like a heavy stone.'[31] He says of himself: 'He knew only one thing more; that he would not know himself.'[32] The poet here, faced with the sudden challenge of the 'unseen', is completely divided. In this poem, he seems to be less sure of the issues than in the previous. There, he was clear as to the choice before him, and opted for the 'yoke'. Here, it appears otherwise, and he chooses nothing, saying that he does not know himself. He concludes as he begins, with the image of the children playing outside. The poet is becoming more alienated from his origins.

In the next poem, 'The Missing One', the central image is that of a mirror which is broken for reflecting a self that belongs to the poet no more. He has sacrificed all to his political life, to the 'God of trial': 'This was when he had poured a last libation of the heart to the God of trial that would know no satisfaction. And when thirsting at eventide, he saw that he had not left for himself a single drop.'[33] He complains to this God: 'You have emptied out everything, that I am now as a stranger in my own eyes.'[34] It is too late to return to himself, so he breaks the mirror.' This action symbolises the complete break with himself; it really is a different person inhabiting his body now: 'From then on, it seems that, like all his contemporaries, he threshes about in the swirl of the times with no one noticing his absence, and unaware that this is not he but someone else.'[35] The only link between what he has become and his original self is the patch on the wall, which is the mark left by the mirror now broken: 'And in his house, when he sees that the space for the mirror is white—the bare patch on the wall—then he knows that this single, dumb

29. *Ibid.*, p. 37.

30. *Ibid.*

31. *Ibid.*

32. *Ibid.*

33. *Ibid.*, p. 38.

34. *Ibid.*

35. *Ibid.*

brightness commemorates the missing one.'[36] But he otherwise
has no clue as to his own identity, does not know who he is.
When they ask him, his answer is: 'How could I know when I
have not seen myself for so long?'[37]

In 'The Missing One', the poet has made no attempt to re-
discover his identity and return to it, although he is aware of
the situation. But in the following poem, 'On the Threshold',
he does make the effort, although it is much more difficult to
go back than it was to leave: 'Seventy-seven ways he fled from
himself, but, with the passing of the days, he returned by only
one way. In fleeing, his feet were so light, distances behind him
they pushed. But on his return, they have become heavy and
wind slowly.'[38] And he is uncertain whether such a return be
possible: 'To knock on his door, or not? Will it be opened?
And if it is opened, will they tell me to get out, or ask me to
come in?'[39] His courage flees him; he cannot get beyond the
threshold. He remains in a constant state of indecision: 'So sank
he on the threshold of himself, knelt on the sill of his heart.
Thus waited, waited shamefully, and dared not enter.'[40] He is
now afraid that he has stayed away too long, and that any
return would be an unsuccessful one. Would he be the same
after the period of absence: 'What shall I tell myself when I
come back? That the broad places led me astray? And if the
heart should be estranged from me after my tarrying, and in
the face of the one who returns too late it should close its
doors?'[41] So the poet does nothing, and remains painfully
where he is. Here, we notice another change of mood in the
poet, since he is now apparently eager to recover his old self
and no longer speaks of the sacrifices that he feels bound to
make. Apparently, he would now return, if he could.

In the following poem, 'Ballad of an anonymous stumbler',
the poet localises more closely this other self that he has been
seeking; it is the self from the 'landscape of childhood'. Here
he characterises this landscape a little: 'It is the landscape in

36. *Ibid.*, p. 39.　　　　39. *Ibid.*
37. *Ibid.*　　　　　　　40. *Ibid.*
38. *Ibid.*, p. 40.　　　　41. *Ibid.*, p. 40.

which the picking of the borders of the firmament caresses the clods in the field of man. And on the ears of days lit with expectation lean wondrous nights which tell their secret.'[42] In the choice and synthesis of these images, Lamdan captures at once the sense of longing, ambition and comfort that this 'landscape' induced. The 'firmament' is the feeling of unbounded capacity that the child possesses, and the caress comforts in the 'fields' of man; not to the harsh noise of the city, but against a gentle, pastoral background. This is the self to which the poet tries to return. But 'alas, spoiled are the ways thither, and one can neither enter nor exit; the arrogance of man and the mockeries of peoples and tribes have overgrown every path that ascends to its goodness.'[43]

Now we know why the poet cannot return; the political life in which he has been involved has obscured that other life. He is too much involved in the social context to be able to isolate himself with unconcern. This landscape has been destroyed: 'Woe! In the tears of grief-stricken children is its destruction reflected.'[44] It is the landscape of childhood to which the poet would return, so if even children, who should be now where he was, are 'grief-stricken', what hope can there be for him? It seems that this past is not only dead for him personally, but for everyone in general: 'There is nothing to seek any more. The generation of the precious has been bereaved of everything precious.'[45] There is nothing more to hope for; the only thing that the 'anonymous stumbler' requests is: 'Let me be quiet, and silently mourn the death of a legend.'[46] Here is the conclusion of this series of poems. The poet recognises the division in his soul, and yearns for his past. But now he discovers that this idyllic past is dead. He at first would not acknowledge it, fearing it. He then ignored it. He then began to doubt his own identity, and after attempting to return to it in 'On the threshold', he recognised the impossibility of such a thing. The past is dead, so he mourns.

42. *Ibid.*, p. 42.
43. *Ibid.*
44. *Ibid.*, p. 43.
45. *Ibid.*
46. *Ibid.*, p. 44.

The Function of Poetry, and its Limitations

Associated with the alter ego to which the poet aspires is the 'wondrous parable'.[47] We have already characterised it as the literary instrument through which the writer arrives at the 'unseen'.[48] In other words, it is poetry, the particular poetry that held the writer's love as a child, and that wafted him to 'a place where the heart forgets burden, duty and statute'. The image of the 'heart' is used later as well to represent the essence of the youthful author in the poem 'On the threshold', where the poet strives to go back: 'And if the heart should be estranged from me after tarrying . . .' And in the introductory poem to *Bema'aleh 'aqrabbim* as a whole, the heart is once more the spirit of poetry, or the poet himself: 'Only that which has utterance and image, which can be named with exactitude, does the Heart plant in Its world in the sight of all.'[49] Here we have Lamdan's view of the function and limitation of poetry. The poet can record the surface, that which can be named 'With exactitude', i.e. as it is,[50] without difficulty or ambiguity. This is the function of poetry, and its limitation is recorded in the next lines: 'But that which is buried in the soul, hidden in the depths—its existence may not be estimated, not brought up amongst what is,'[51]

Poetry is limited in that it cannot reach into the depths of the soul; it cannot probe the human personality. This it would aspire to do, and is obsessed by the attempt. As the poet continues: 'Although round it [what is buried in the soul] alone, like a moth round fire, does the Heart whirl dizzily until It expires.'[52] The tragic quality of poetry is that it aspires to do that

47. *Ibid.*, p. 33.
48. See above, previous section.
49. *Bema'aleh 'aqrabbim*, p. 5.
50. The Hebrew *kemo* usually means 'like', but see Ps. 73:15, where the verse reads: *Im amarti asapperah kemo, hineh dor banekhah bagadti*, being either a corruption of the text or where the word

kemo could mean 'as it is'., 'the whole thing'. This usage of the word was adopted by later writers. (See Eliezer ben Yehudah: *Thesaurus* (Jerusalem, Berlin), Vol. 5, p. 2418), and is Lamdan's usage here.
51. *Bema'aleh 'aqrabbim*, p. 5.
52. *Ibid.*

which cannot be done. The poet goes round and round his subject without ever approaching it; his object is within sight, but not within grasp. What can be executed by the poet is a function of secondary importance: 'Only its surfaces does the Heart plant in shade or in sunlight—in a lonely, silent corner, or in the turbulent public places.'[53] And even in this secondary function of recording the surface, the task is hugely complicated: 'And see, even they [i.e. the surfaces] have become entangled, have become a thick forest in which silence, storm and deep darkness reign by turn, in which the roots are invisibly tied up with its soil, and unearthly echoes stalk its secret places.'[54] Even what is apparently on the surface and seemingly simple becomes involved with what is below, and unattainable.[55]

So it transpires that the task of writing poetry is confronted with a twofold obstacle. Firstly, the thing that the Heart (poet) is really interested in is not capable of expression since it goes too deep beneath the surface. And secondly, even that which it expresses becomes inextricably involved with that which is not. Thus the possibilities of success are very limited. Bialik too mourned the fact that he did not manage to express all that he wanted to in his verse. In one of his poems, 'After my Death',[56] he imagines himself as having died, 'with the poetry of his life cut off in the middle. Alas! He had another song, but the song perished for ever, perished for ever!'[57] It never occurred to the poet that he would sing this song.[58] In spite of the articulateness of the poet and the will to communicate, the song still remained unsung: 'He [the poet] had a violin—a living, murmuring soul, and ever since the poet spoke to it, he told it all the secrets of his heart, and his hand moved all the chords. But one secret he concealed inside himself: round and round it did

53. *Ibid.*

54. *Ibid.*

55. For a discussion of the imagery, see chapter 'Lamdan's Imagery', first section.

56. See *Poems* (Tel-Aviv, 1944)— *Aḥarei moti*, p. 172.

57. *Ibid.*

58. The poet had thirty more years to live, as this poem was written in 1904.

his fingers tremble. One note remained silent, remained silent to this day.'[59] Bialik was sure that he would never produce this note nor this song though he was clearly obsessed with it, for 'round and round it did his fingers tremble'.

We have already seen that Lamdan similarly expresses the frustrated longing of the poet for the unutterable: 'Although round it alone, like a moth round fire, does the Heart whirl dizzily until it expires.' Both Lamdan and Bialik remain within orbit of this unattainable without approaching it. But with Lamdan, we are clear that the poet regarded poetry as incapable of expressing the Thing (see first lines of poem under discussion), whereas Bialik leaves us uncertain as to the obstacle before the fulfilment of his desire. We know that Bialik was much distressed by this failure,[60] but we do not know what brought it on. Rather than the incapacity of poetry itself, it seems to be an act of will on the poet's part deliberately to suppress knowledge of the thing round which he hovered. For he says 'but one secret he concealed inside him', implying a deliberate act of withholding. This note longed to be played: 'All its days did this note move, move silently, tremble silently for its song, its friend, its redeemer. It longed, thirsted, grieved, yearned, as the heart grieves for its due: and though it tarried, waited for it every day, and cried for it with a suppressed moan—yet it tarried and came not. It surely did not come.'[61] This unexpressed thing would have found redemption had it been expressed, but, for reasons unmentioned, this was not to be. Lamdan's view is that something, and that, the main part, is incapable of expression. The poet's situation is essentially tragic.

But leaving the problem of the incapacities of poetry, Lamdan, in the same poem, goes on to describe the poetry that can be expressed, and the materials of experience that he uses in his verse. We have here the essence of Lamdan's motivation in his writing; that is why the poem serves as a frontispiece to the

59. Bialik: *op. cit.*, p. 172.
60. The twofold mention of *ve-ẓar meod*, and in the last stanza,

'and very, very great is the pain'.
61. *Ibid.*

whole work. Here, he images his historic involvement with his people. The central image used here is 'a forest', which is the history that he records. The one who walks through the forest is the reader, and 'a leaf that rustles quietly at your feet off the stock',[62] is an individual poem. The reader is begged not to hurry on, for 'the soul of an obscure forest is rustling from its depths'.[63] The poem is not to be ignored because it proceeds from the depths; the branches stem from the roots. Although the poem may be superficial, it has its source in the great un-expressed. It is this forest, the poetry, which records the mark of history: 'The trembling of a nation and its God has rolled its echo here.'[64] Shattering events have taken place, and the forest bears their imprint: 'Here has the heavy stamping of Fates left its footprints.'[65] And it is not only material objects that have been damaged, but ideals and dreams, the hope of the human personality. Here are 'the trodden grass of dreams, broken-branched trees. Here were waved on high torches of vision as flags of rebellion'.[66]

Here, in the forest, in Lamdan's poetry, is human history and the ideals that have made it, but more particularly, the dis-appointment and despair in their collapse and defeat. And what is to be the human reaction to these turbulent events? A dichotomy is established in his soul: 'Here walked about a lost person, perplexed, driven mad by the times, his heart a haven of mercy in the shadow of a jealous God, his whisper—love and kindness, and his voice calling to battle.'[67] The person is well intentioned and kind, but his God is jealous, stern and makes rigorous demands. His whisper, which expresses what he would like, is gentle, but his loud voice answers to the demands of the times, and is harsh; so he calls to battle. Then the poet appears (who may be the 'person' of the previous stanza), and seems to live in time unbounded by contemporary history, in timelessness, in a dream: 'Sailing into itself, beyond border or time, here grieves the soul of man, and sings

62. *Bema'aleh 'aqrabbim*, p. 5. 65. *Ibid.*
63. *Ibid.* 66. *Ibid.*
64. *Ibid.*, p. 6. 67. *Ibid.*

unheard, fluttering in a web of will-not-be and was-not, swing-
ing up and down in hammocks of invention stringing pearls of
dew and tears on threads of dream.'[68] Here the poet seems to
fulfil the function of the child or the alter ego in the series,
'In the Twofold Image', for he is not troubled by the events of
his time, and not bounded by the concerns of the 'political'
man. On the contrary, he sails into himself, occupies himself
with his own personality, and lives in a period that never was
and will not be.

But although this is Lamdan's own picture of the poet, his
own verse, with some exceptions when he portrays the struggle,
would seem to belie this intention, because it is highly involved with contemporary events, and with the Jew in history.
The last stanza of this poem echoes Lamdan's effort more
faithfully. He tells the reader (the walker in the forest): 'If you
listen well—then you will know that the forest of man shoul-
dered stormy heavens here, and from the roots of its grass to
the tops of its branches, the tremor of a generation passed like
a mighty, wounding comb.'[69] Lamdan, in his work, seems to
be more the 'man' of the poem than the 'poet', though he
may aspire to be the latter. For his poetry bears the imprints
entirely of 'the tremor of a generation', and is not concerned
with the timeless. *Masada* records the actuality of the Zionist
experiment seen in historical perspective. 'The Threefold
Harness', as the title implies, and as the poetic frontispiece
states, attempts to draw from the poet's own viewpoint the
Jewish situation, including both its eternal (not timeless)
aspects, and its specifically contemporary character as it had
been affected by the struggle in Palestine. And 'On the Scorpions' Ascent' continues this line, dealing both with a definite
historical situation, as in the poems on the European catastrophe
(see section on 'The holocaust') on the visits to his homeland (see section 'Return home') and with the Jewish Fate,
which is also localised in history. The poet 'sailing into himself' is not Lamdan as we recognise him from his work. It may
be either the 'idea' of the 'poet' in the abstract, or what Lamdan

68. *Ibid.*   69. *Ibid.*, p. 7.

himself, would like to be. The conflict that raged within himself, as seen here in the discrepancy between the description of the 'poet' and the actuality of Lamdan as poet, has been discussed in the previous section.

There is one other place where Lamdan expresses his view of the function of poetry, and that is in the poem entitled 'Lyric' (*Bema'aleh 'aqrabbim*, pp. 135, 136). Here, the function of 'lyric', of personal poetry, is seen as comfort. In the moment of despair, Lyric may be successfully invoked: 'Where the head sinks, stuck between its rungs [of Lyric's ladder], lacking all, impotent, orphaned, in your teardrop is the world again reflected, shining with all the colours of the rainbow, for its comfort.'[70] Thus, when one has arrived at a situation 'where there is helplessness, and all sense has gone',[71] hope can be restored by Lyric. Its function is similar to that of the 'prayer' in *Masada*, where relief followed despair immediately after the prayer had been made.[72] Both Lyric and Prayer in these connections serve a therapeutic function. To Lyric the poet says: 'You hurt and appease'[73] The very act of hurting may bring consolation, as we saw in *Masada*, when Lamdan addressed the 'wallower', Brenner: 'You who taught us to lick our wounds in order to cure them.'[74] Brenner, as wallower, sank deep into the degradation that he portrayed. This, to Lamdan, had a health-giving effect. And thus with Lyric, which may speak harshly, and yet cure: 'Like Noah's dove are you, which bore the gospel of comfort on its wing and a bitter olive leaf in its mouth.'[75] Lamdan here, as often, makes great play with the ambiguity of a single image.

Lyric has another means of affording comfort and consolation; it can stand at a distance. Here, it is a peak. We have already seen in 'In twofold image' that the writer aspired to 'sail to the unseen from the shore of solutions'.[76] This 'unseen' is at once ambition and detachment. Here, Lyric is a 'peak' from

70. *Ibid.*, p. 135.
71. *Ibid.*
72. See *Masada*, p. 71.
73. *Bema'aleh 'aqrabbim*, p. 135.

74. *Masada*, p. 66.
75. *Bema'aleh 'aqrabbim*, p. 235.
76. *Ibid.*, p. 33.

which the desired can be seen: 'You are like a Mount Nebo to those who view from here onward, and bear in their soul what they have not here. From your peak they see what is yearned; from your peak they know that they will not get there.'[77] Mount Nebo is the point from which Moses surveyed the holy land, when he already knew that he would never reach it.[78] Similarly, Lyric affords a vantage point of the beautiful, though the spectator knows that he will never achieve it in actuality. Poetry provides a vision, an ideal, that, though never reached, may still comfort. It may be a refuge when all else has failed: 'When the knife of fear suddenly flashes in their eye, and the invisible pricks them with tremoring needles, with a confused stutter they then call by your name, and only your word stirs their tongue.'[79] When all other modes of speech have proved of no avail, poetry will prove strong and justify its existence, the same poetry previously mocked as 'an idle old woman'.[80] Lyric consists of the purest elements of language: 'Every holy expression, every simple primeval utterance that has been rejected from the inheritance of man's speech.'[81] Such words are not ordinarily uttered, and they have an extraordinary capacity. That Lamdan himself believed the assertion here may be seen from another poem of his when on a visit to his home country. There 'the pain is too great to bear'.[82] Then he says: 'Ah, good suffering father, I am like you (who make religious chants in time of suffering). From all the dread things of the world, the pitfalls of Fate and its fears I flee to poetry, and over chasms do I plait bridges of verse from the letters of the alphabet.'[83]

In our appreciation of the fact that the poetry of Lamdan is built on the rocks of contemporary reality, we must also take into account his own view of poetry as an escape. Lamdan's poetry is certainly not an escape in that it avoids unpleasant issues, or turns its back on ugly facts. But what Lamdan means

77. *Ibid.*, p. 135
78. See Deut. 34:1.
79. *Bema'aleh 'aqrabbim*, p. 136.
80. *Ibid.*

81. *Ibid.*
82. *Ibid.*, p. 53.
83. *Ibid.*

by an escape may be the very fact of the existence of poetry at all. Writing poetry is retirement to a peak, or, the licking of wounds in time of distress; it does not meet the causes of distress on their own terms, and fight them in their own language. It is not of immediate relevance to the situation, though the material for its composition may be drawn from it. But, by reflection on the situation, from above, or from the side, great comfort may be drawn. This is what Lamdan does when he 'flees to Poetry'.

The Pioneer

Central to Lamdan's poetic thought is the idea of the Palestinian pioneer (Heb. *ḥaluẓ*), who is the creative builder of Masada, and defender of the fortress. In the poem *Masada* we read that 'there are prophets wandering amongst the walls of Masada, prophesying redemption, and in the tents of the tabernacle, amongst the ramparts, levitical sects are singing *la-menazeah*, with tomorrow's echo answering, *amen, selah*. There young priests extend merciful arms.'[84] The 'prophets', 'levitical sects', and 'flowers of priesthood'[85] are the titles that Lamdan ecstatically ascribes to the Palestine worker, the pioneer. These are the people who bare the 'antagonistic breast', who dare to challenge seemingly inexorable Fate. These are the men who follow A. D. Gordon,[86] the 'seer of Masada', by redeeming their own soul, and constituting 'the vanguard of the people'.[87] The apparently pedestrian work of building the country from the soil upwards through individual labour and collective responsibility was exalted by Lamdan into a religious act. That is why the men of Masada bear titles taken from religious practice.

But it is the Fate of the religious ecstatic, the man inspired to a particular task, to suffer, as we have seen from Lamdan's

84. See *Masada*, p. 12.
85. For a discussion of the use of religious imagery, see chapter, 'His Imagery'.
86. See chapter on *Masada*, section on 'Gordon, Brenner and Trumpeldor'.
87. See *Masada*, p. 65.

poems with Biblical motifs. Such too is the Fate of the pioneer. We saw in *Masada* the extent to which the men of Masada were brought low. People, who often came to Masada only from the depths of despair,[88] were driven to suicide.[89] In the first poem of the series, 'For the Sun had Set'—in *Bema'aleh 'aqrabbim* called 'The Sower in the Darkness'[90]—just this theme is treated. The sower is the pioneer who works out of and in despair. He sees no fruit in his labour, and is unsure whether any is to be borne in the future. Here we have none of the exhilarating determination that fired the spirit in the poem *Masada*, only blind effort: 'Tired is his hand and aching, [but] it sows and sows as if caught by convulsions.'[91] Lamdan images the fight 'in spite of all' that the pioneers stage; but this poem is in a much lower key than the earlier *Masada*. The same Fate persists, and curses the land as well as the people. But love is also part of the Fate, and the pioneer cannot restrain his love, which is also an affliction, for the land: 'He [the sower] knows that God has forsaken this portion, and cursed it with rocks, drought, night [like the word 'darkness' of the title, a negative symbol] and hail. No one would dare to sow here who has not been inspired with the awe of Fate and love.'[92] Fate and love go together, and they constitute the background of the pioneering will.

The sower has made a great sacrifice, so great forces must be invoked to justify it: 'He knows that no one would approach, nor come to this blackness unless he had burned his peace, and until he had cast his hope[93] on perverse chance, and its derisive mysteries'.[94] It is in the realisation of his sacrifice that 'he sings his dismal song: "In spite of my hatred, in spite of night and God, on your clods, O portion, and on your cursed rocks, the seed of my love here falls".'[95] He loves in spite of everything, even in spite of God, who here plays the part of the devil. But

88. See *Masada*, ch. 2.

89. *Ibid.*, p. 73.

90. *Bema'aleh 'aqrabbim*, p. 11.

91. *Ibid.*

92. *Ibid.*

93. Heb. *Yehav* (translation based on usage in Ps. 55:23).

94. *Bema'aleh 'aqrabbim*, p. 11.

95. *Ibid.*, p. 12.

the major tragedy is that even were the sower to have success, he would not himself reap: 'Burrow, burrow in the darkness, sing and sow, O sower, and perhaps a stalk will yet shine golden here in the joyful morning light. Ah, even then your scythe will not sparkle here and ring—you shall not reap it [i.e. the stalk].'[96] But he continues to work until he drops: 'Whilst his hand raises its seed—he stumbles, totters and sinks, his head hitting a stone. On this barren patch, two fall as one: a palmful of tear and seed.'[97] The contrapunction of tears and seed is taken from the Biblical phrase 'they who sow in tears', but the tragic point is the non-fulfilment of the second part of the second part of the verse—'shall reap in joy'.[98] The Biblical hope is disappointed. The prisoner does indeed sow in tears, but fails to reap in joy.

The tragedy of the pioneer is carried one stage further in the poem 'Honi',[99] for here we are transported to a situation in which the pioneer can see the fruits of his labours several years after his death, and thus discovers that he, the sower, is forgotten. The fruit of his sacrifice is being enjoyed, but its source ignored. The motif of the poem is taken from the Talmudic legend of Honi the circle-maker,[100] who brought rain in a period of drought by describing a circle round himself, and saying that he would not move from it till God brought rain. Thus came rain. Another legend tells us that he came back seventy years after his death, and that the people, on seeing him, refused to believe that he was indeed Honi. He then sought to die. Even at the time of the miracle, he faced opposition, as we see from the fury of Simeon ben Shetach in the legend. So Lamdan takes Honi as a symbol of the rejected pioneer, this Honi who brought blessing to the land, and was yet unappreciated. In the poem previously discussed, the pioneer was prepared for sacrifice, but did not know of his eventual oblivion. Here, after the pioneering tradition was long

96. *Ibid.*
97. *Ibid.*
98. Ps. 136:4.
99. *Bema'aleh 'aqrabbim*, p. 27, 'Honi'.

100. See *Seder Moed* Mas. *Ta'anit*, *mishnah*, and *gemarah* 23A, 73. Also see above, p. 52.

established (the poem was written in 1937), even this was to be witnessed.

The poem is set at the time of Honi's return to life, when he found the world so changed. The poem opens: 'You are lost, Honi, and walk around as in a foreign country. Every brother's heart before you is as a closed door. You, who bore the whole burden of a generation, have become as a porter dismissed without wages.'[101] The pioneer has done so much, and has yet received so little; in the land that he has built, he feels ill at ease: 'It is not a foreign country here, Honi! This is the land to which you have been faithful as a dog to its masters. Now you sidle in it, take twisted paths like a thief wary of step, fearing to be seen or heard.'[102] He had not only been faithful to the land, he had also acted for the people: 'And these round about who turn their backs to you are not foreigners, Honi—they all are your brothers! Did not your prayer put bread in their basket? And was it not your circle that saved them in the drought?'[103] But after a man has given what he can, his existence is no longer meaningful or relevant. He is not needed, so he might as well not exist: 'Gather your things together, Honi. Go out and, seek nothing! After giving everything that you had, you exist no more, you are only an invention, crying with no one to hear on the rivers of the past.'[104] (This, in Hebrew, is a play on words.[105]) But reward is still to be had, not in personal gratification, but in the knowledge that the country has benefited, if ungratefully. Honi should welcome the blessing: 'Go out, declare your sorrow, Honi, far into the nothingness, and when you go out, bless this beloved and estranged landscape! And your love? Now namelessly, it pours down its brightness in every grinning and glimmering beam of a light with a teardrop.'[106] So the love given by Honi, the pioneer, has borne fruit, and he may have that degree of

101. *Bema'aleh 'aqrabbim*, p. 27.
102. *Ibid.*
103. *Ibid.*, p. 28.
104. *Ibid.*
105. Pun on the word which means 'already' (translated here as 'past) and is the name of the river on whose banks Ezekiel prophesied. See Ez. 1:1.
106. *Bema'aleh 'aqrabbim*, p. 29.

satisfaction. But there is nothing left for Honi personally, so the poem concludes, as does the Talmudic legend, with a request to die: 'Ends reunite: a circle. The gloom of supplication. Honi the circle-maker seeks grace to die.'[107]

Here is the central figure in the Lamdanian drama, the hero. The pioneer is the one who has the temerity to challenge the Fate that has dogged the heels of the Jewish people since its inception. His labour does indeed bear some fruit, but personally, he is doomed to suffer. He suffers throughout his lifetime, because he neither reaps reward nor sees any positive outcome; and he suffers in the context of history, for he is not to be appreciated after his death. He can draw no comfort from the thought of recognition to follow. As soon as his purpose is served, he becomes an archaism. His sole consolation is that other people benefit from his sacrifice, and he must welcome this, 'bless' the land that he so loved, and to which he had devoted his life. He should hold no personal resentment, because he has reward enough. He may now die, having fulfilled his function.

Return Home

A great deal of *Bema'aleh 'aqrabbim* is written in the context of 'exile'; that is, within the Jewish diaspora. Lamdan has already spent many years in pioneering Palestine, and he journeys home to the places that he knew in his childhood, to see how they fare. Two series of poems are occupied with meditation on the life that he sees in the old country, and with the contrast that this affords to the new, to Palestine. The first section, 'Holiday time' (*Bein zemanim*) is of his visit home, and the second, 'Amongst my people' (*Betoch 'ami*), is of his visit to areas of Jewish settlement in general.

This visit is, for Lamdan, more than a trip to a foreign country; it is a voyage into the past: 'Raise a grieved blessing, miserable homeland house. Open your door to me who am

107. *Ibid.*

visiting the remains of my past.'[108] Much has happened since Lamdan was there last. The year is 1931, twelve years since the poet left home. Lamdan remembers the ravages of the war and the riots,[109] and he now remarks: 'Repairs have not been made in you since those evil days. Bared is your destruction, without any hide or cover.'[110] But the poet remembers the good things of his home, its comforts, and he asks whether these are still to be found: 'Is your bosom still warm, does the shadow of your roof [lit. beam] still drop down tranquillity as in the days of youth?'[111] It seems not, for he says later: 'I saw the terminal saw[112] cutting and sawing a nest-destroyed, bare-topped tree right down, and as for what was still green and alive, still producing buds, that sucked its sap from other soil.'[113] And later, in conclusion: 'How poor, how miserable are your habitations, O Israel.'[114] This is intended to recall the Biblical verse: 'How goodly are thy tents, O Jacob, [and] thy habitations, O Israel,'[115] and point the ironic contrast. The habitations of Israel, far from being 'goodly', are in a sad state of desolation.

The great Hebrew novelist S. J. Agnon (1888–1970) made a similar revisitation of his homeland after being a long time in Palestine. He emigrated in 1909[116] and published his 'Guest for the Night' (Oreaḥ natah la lun) in 1938. This novel describes a visit the writer paid to his town of origin, called Shibush in the novel but based on Buczacz, his home town in Poland (once Galicia). This novel is based on an actual visit home made by Agnon in 1930. There the writer found a scene of desolation similar to that of Lamdan's poems, although Agnon is more concerned with religious disintegration: 'The great synagogue, which I thought in my youth to be the largest in the world,

108. *Ibid.*, p. 4.

109. See opening of *Masada*.

110. *Bema'aleh 'aqrabbim*, p. 47.

111. *Ibid.*

112. On page 47, he uses the parallel image of 'the saw of time'.

113. *Ibid.*, p. 70.

114. *Ibid.*, p. 71.

115. Nu. 24:5.

116. See A. Band: *Nostalgia and Nightmare*: A Study in the fiction of S. Y. Agnon (California, 1968).

seemed to be smaller in area and height . . .'[117] and more images of spiritual collapse: 'The form of the studyhouse [Heb. *bet hamidrash*] had been completely transformed. Cupboards that had been full of books had disappeared, and only about six or seven pages were left. And as for the heavy, long benches where the elders of the Law [Heb. *Torah*] used to sit—some were vacant, and some were occupied by those who could not find the place [i.e. in the prayer book].'[118] The synagogues have become smaller, places have fallen empty, books have disappeared, and the learned have been replaced by the boorish. This is the picture that Agnon paints of the Jewish religion as he found it on his journey back to his home country. But he also found general desolation: 'Everywhere you set eyes, there is either destruction or poverty.'[119] Jewish existence seems to be in an abject state altogether. The past is there, or at any rate bits of it are, but reconciliation to it is impossible. It has been said of Agnon's effort in this novel, that: 'The late return to the world of his ancestors did not succeed. What remains is bits of the past;'[120] bits of the past that are irrelevant to the present. Agnon soon left this world, as did Lamdan. Both have found it in a state of degradation and collapse.

Lamdan sees his father, who is naturally eager to hear from his son about his experiences in the new country: 'At last, it has fallen to my lot . . . twelve years or more . . . now tell me, my son . . . every little detail.'[121] The father asks for his son's view of Palestine, and the only answer he receives is: 'It is good, so good.'[122] This is clearly a lie, but the poet's excuse follows: 'Could I tell otherwise to a grief-laden father, expecting relief and comfort from his son? Should I tell of the crust of our lives that is very hard and bitter, not dipped in honey, and not spread there with butter?'[123] This is the unpleasant truth about

117. See S. J. Agnon: *Oreaḥ natah lalun* (Shocken, Tel-Aviv, Jerusalem, 1960), p. 10. Translated in English, *Guest for the Night*, by M. Louvish (Jerusalem, 1968).
118. *Ibid.*, p. 14.
119. *Ibid.*, p. 31.
120. See Baruch Kurzweil: *Massekhet ha-roman* (Tel-Aviv, 1953), p. 90.
121. *Bema'aleh 'aqrabbim*, p. 49.
122. *Ibid.*
123. *Ibid.*

the new country, which is no more kindly treated than the old. It too hovers on the brink of collapse: 'Shall I tell of the cart of Destiny, laden with the burden of generations, which winds heavily along the abyss? About the miserable motherland, without the mother's caressing kindness, that offers its children the breast of grief and loneliness?'[124] and in one of the most bitter moments of truth, the poet continues: 'Could I tell all, put on the veil of a smile, make the man, perplexed in the middle of his way, shout out the truth: "Oh, the burden that your son has laden on to his back is too great." I cannot bear it, Father, though I dare not unload it.'[125] So this is the real truth that Lamdan will not admit to his father in the dialogue between Palestine and the diaspora.

What an ironic contrast it presents to that other dialogue, this time led by the diaspora, with a representative of Palestine, 'the bird' that has flown from there. Bialik, when he wrote 'To the bird',[126] had, of course, never visited the country of his dreams. He was very young when he wrote it, and full of idealistic conviction of the perfection of the Holy Land. And it was written in 1891, long before the poet was to go there, and when he was only some eighteen years old. Nevertheless, the poem does represent a typical dream of the Jew in the diaspora. The youthful poet has formed an idyllic picture of the country, and he asks of the bird: 'Does the dew descend like pearls on Mount Hebron, does it descend and fall like tears? And how is the Jordan and its clear waters? And the mountains and the hills?'[127] Lamdan, speaking as a settler, has another view of the Palestinian landscape, and it is in damning contrast to Bialik's vision: 'For, like a stumbling deer was I entangled in the thicket of the landscape, whose heavens are brass, and whose earth is a hearth.'[128] This is an enlargement of what the poet meant in the previous line by 'miserable and very despairing love'.[129]

124. *Ibid.*, p. 50.

125. *Ibid.*, p. 51.

126. See Bialik: *Poems* (Dvir, 1944), p. 1—*El ha-zippor.*

127. *Ibid.*, p. 2.

128. *Bema'aleh 'aqrabbim*, p. 50.

129. *Ibid.*

The poet has an ambivalent attitude to the country; there exists both a positive and a negative pole. Abram's question regarding the covenant with God: 'And so always unceasingly are the vulture and God to be together?'[130] was answered in the affirmative. The Jew cannot carry out his special task without the negative implication of the vulture, and he cannot be in the promised land without suffering. We saw in *Masada* that the poet found difficulty in acclimatising himself to the new landscape and climate,[131] where the sun was strange to him,[132] and the 'rocks' (symbol of hostile landscape) were overpoweringly hard.[133] And it seems that here too, in these poems, the physical conditions are difficult: the earth is a hearth that can scorch the feet, and make life intolerable even on the most superficial, external plain. But retreat is still impossible, for the poet has become 'entangled' in this landscape. Although his 'love' may be miserable and despairing, it is still a love that commits him unswervingly.

So Lamdan returns to his home country as a committed Palestinian. The exile is a complete negative for the poet, who asks: 'Why should we always sow for hail and tempest?'[134] And we have this contrasted with the aspiration of *Masada* to revolutionise Jewish life. Lamdan speaks as one of those who left 'to seek the footsteps of the redeemer on drizzle-beaten ways, and to raise a new cheer in the twilight of times.'[135] The return home, for all its negative implications, is used by the poet to acclaim Masada once more as the challenge to History that he celebrated in his first poetic work: 'Blessed be this daring dream that dragged us with its storm from the fallen nests of generations, lacking hope and support, and commanded us: "Go out and seek the Change in spite of the primeval, mocking decree of Fate".'[136] The only positive result of the destruction is the dream that has emerged from it: 'And

130. *Ibid.*, p. 15.
131. See chapter on *Masada*, section 'Adaptation to the New Country'.
132. *Masada*, p. 34.
133. E.g. *Masada*, section 'The Prayer', p. 69.
134. *Bema'aleh 'aqrabbim*, p. 56.
135. *Ibid.*
136. *Ibid.*, p. 57.

as for you, ruin of a generation, what reason is there for your destruction if not the dream of your children that has adorned it with its shining?'[137] For no hope is left for the thing destroyed: 'I know that your destruction is a destruction without —hope.'[138]

The Holocaust

The holocaust that fell upon European Jewry during the Second World War was no surprise occurrence to Lamdan, the poet of the Jewish Fate; it fitted the pattern of Jewish existence in history as he saw it. The last series of poems in *Bema'aleh 'aqrabbim*, entitled 'From the book of days' (*Misepher hayamim*), contains poems written between the years 1938 and 1943, perhaps the high period of Jewish tragedy in the course of Lamdan's lifetime. For a poet such as Lamdan, inured to the idea of the 'vulture' dogging the footsteps of Jewish history, such a catastrophe could only deepen his confirmed sorrow rather than occasion shock. Nevertheless, as the full knowledge of the collapse dawns, the bonds of indignation begin to burst, and the poet's quiet lament is broken by the cry of 'hatred'.

The series opens with a hymn of praise to the future reader, who would not understand Lamdan's constant lament: 'Happy be the one who comes and understands not my murmur, which will be strange to him, unloved and unhated.'[139] The poet yearns for such a person to exist: 'Ah, you who are not as yet, an embryo of distance and legend: from the straits of the "now" do I send my blessing to you: Oh, that you understand not, oh, that you know not.'[140] It is possible that far in the future the tragedy will be unknown, for even in the present it is not fully appreciated. Mothers rear their children without knowing what is in store for them. This is indeed lucky: 'How good it is that the mother's hand is incapable of feeling the weight of every burden laden on her palm! If you [the mothers] knew the full weight of Fate in these sieves, then you would not

137. *Ibid.*
138. *Ibid.*

139. *Ibid.*, p. 191.
140. *Ibid.*

have sufficient strength to raise them and shake them, swaying shaking into the morrow.'[141] It is 'sieves' that they are shaking, because their children will fall through them into the 'jaws' of 'arrogancy' (Heb. *zadon*). But in spite of everything, the people are still optimistic, and trust in the arrival of the Messiah; they love hopefully: 'How many eyes failing with expectation and reddened by sleepless terrors are now fixed in the habitations of Israel between the cracks of slammed shutters and the lattices of bolted doors (as if a lock or bar could be trusted), and long for Tishbi [Elijah], the bringer of good things.'[142] But it seems that the Messiah has lost his way, and will not reach the Jews: 'It must be that the Tishbite has wandered into the streets of the gentiles, and that sharp-teethed dogs have surrounded him, and block his way.'[143] The Messiah does not come.

The second part of this series—'Tomorrow, Tomorrow' (*Maḥar, maḥar*) is written more in the awareness of what exactly was happening in Europe, for it took some time for the knowledge of it to seep through. In the poem 'Behold it is the Landscape as of Old',[144] the poet returns to his old theme of the persistent Fate; History repeating itself: it is the landscape as of old, and Fate is responsible: 'I see nothing more. The black assembly of Fate hides the light of day and the face of the sun from me.'[145] Now the poet can feel nothing but hatred, an emotion until now moderated by determination and fight: 'Ah, of all this abundance, only the red-flamed lily of poison is left for me: hatred, hatred, hatred.'[146] The next poem is a 'prayer for revenge', and this follows consistently on to the previous poem's appeal to the 'God of revenge': 'Enough, we are weary of suffering! Rise, go out to the campaign, stir, be raised. God of vengeance, appear.'[147] Here, in contrast to Bialik, Lamdan prays for revenge. For Bialik, in 1903, after the Kishinev pogroms against the Jews, wrote a poem entitled 'On the Slaughter' ('*Al hasheḥitah*), in which he said: 'And cursed be

141. *Ibid.*, p. 192.
142. *Ibid.*, p. 194.
143. *Ibid.*
144. *Ibid.*, p. 224.
145. *Ibid.*
146. *Ibid.*
147. *Ibid.* p. 225.

he who says: "Revenge!" Such a revenge, the revenge for the blood of a small child, Satan has not yet created—let the blood pierce the deep!'[148]

Bialik's reaction to the violence done to his people was to say that revenge is impossible, because ridiculously inadequate. Such revenge is inconceivable; the deed itself, the blood, must act, must 'pierce the deep'; no action of man will help. Lamdan quests revenge, though not in the form of death, which is too mild: 'Not death, O God! Would that in itself requite that which the weeping of a whole people does not contain?'[149] What he asks for his enemies is life, life in which they can suffer: 'Please give them life, God of revenge and retribution, in which may be multiplied seventy-seven times all that they have wrought against Israel.'[150] This leads to a declaration of pure love for his people, and a closing of 'the accounts of credit and debit': 'At a time like this, my people, I have nothing in my heart for you but love.'[151] In other circumstances, faults may have been considered as well as merits, but the present situation would not admit of it. Of all the turbulence, suffering and despair that the poet has recorded, this is the most intense. And it is here that the poet turns from bitterness against Fate to love for the victim.

148. Bialik: *Poems* (Dvir, 1944), p. 159.

149. *Bema'aleh 'aqrabbim*, p. 228.

150. *Ibid.*

151. *Ibid.*, p. 131.

Chapter 7

HIS IMAGERY

The Meaning, Function, and Significance of the 'Image'

THE WORD 'IMAGE' is derived from the Latin *imago*, meaning a representation or likeness. It can also mean 'pretence', i.e. something that is intended to resemble something else. The literary image, which is our present concern, has been defined as 'a picture made out of words'. But, not content with this general characterisation, the composer of this definition continues to qualify it by saying that the image, though apparently purely descriptive, 'conveys to our imagination something more than the accurate reflection of an external reality. Every poetic image, therefore, is to some extent metaphorical.'[1] This view is supported by a leading authority on the image, who insists on the metaphorical nature of imagery. Imagery is defined here as 'words or phrases denoting a sense-perceptible object, used to designate not that object, but some other object or thought belonging to a different order or category of being'.[2] When we speak of the image in this context, therefore, we shall intend not just any picture in words, but a picture that is necessarily metaphorical,[3] i.e. a word or phrase intended not in its strictly literal sense, but in a transferred sense from another order of being, that can nevertheless be used analogously to illuminate the subject under review. Thus it will be adequate

1. C. Day Lewis: *The Poetic Image* (Clark Lectures, 1946—London), p. 18.
2. S. J. Brown: *The World of Imagery* (London, 1927), p. 1.
3. The Oxford English Dictionary definition of 'metaphor' is—'the figure of speech in which a name or descriptive term is transferred to some object different from, but analogous to, that which it is properly applicable.'

if we think of 'image' as 'metaphor',[4] as is indeed the general practice.[5]

A distinction has been made between two types of metaphor, radical and poetic.[6] The radical metaphor is unconscious, and has passed into normal language to such a degree that its original meaning is no longer perceived or particularly remarked. When we speak of 'spirit', we no longer think of it as a metaphor drawn from wind,[7] if wind was, indeed, its sole meaning at one time. The new meaning has been absorbed into the body of the language. The poetic metaphor, on the other hand, is the conscious transference of meaning to produce a new effect. When Hamlet says 'we have shuffled off this mortal coil',[8] we may assume that until then, suicide or death had never been spoken of in these terms, but that through the use of this metaphor Shakespeare obtains particular effects. 'Shuffled off this mortal coil' is a poetic metaphor, taken deliberately from a different order of being.

The radical metaphor is not our concern, if indeed it can properly be called a metaphor at all.[9] The metaphor that has passed into common use can no longer serve its specific function for the poet; it can no longer arrest our attention, and make us think of the object in a new way. The purpose of the image is to illuminate by implied analogy. The poet applies to his primary theme language that is normally used in another context, but that here serves to cast light on the theme, and demonstrate its specific significance in the new context. In the example already cited, the metaphor of life as a coil gives us an

4. 'Metaphor' is from a Greek word (*metaphorein*), meaning literally 'to transfer from one place to another'.

5. This is amply evident from the invariable use of the words 'image' and 'imagery' by critics and writers. All authors cited here use them in this sense.

6. Max Muller: *Three lectures on the Science of Language* (London, 1891), Lect. 1.

7. See Murray's *New English Dictionary* (Oxford, 1883).

8. *Hamlet*, Act III, Scene 1, Line 67.

9. W. Bedell Stanford: *Greek Metaphor* (Blackwell, 1936), p. 83. Stanford holds that Muller's main error lay in treating words as fixed algebraic symbols.

awareness of Hamlet's desire for the release that is death. The image affords the poet a better means of apprehension than photographic description, although he apparently distracts his attention from the object of his immediate notice. He expresses the abstract more actually through the concrete—'the image is a drawing back from the actual (which is too big) the better to come to grips with it. So every successful image is the sign of a successful encounter with the real.'[10] The poet is not a camera; not only does he accentuate and omit, but he clarifies by association, and transmits private emotional significances. This he can do most efficiently by his use of the image.

Both classical and modern authorities are agreed on the great significance of metaphor in poetry. Aristotle went as far as to say that 'most important of all for poetic diction is a gift for metaphor. This alone cannot be acquired from others, and is a sign of natural genius.'[11] Here we see that Aristotle held the view that metaphor is what uniquely characterises an author, and that it is the single most important factor in his use of language. In his latest work, the image became Shakespeare's favourite mode of expression,[12] and with it, he built not only mood but also character.[13] Through a consistency of imagery, he also created a unity of atmosphere. He developed the use of imagery to an unprecedented extent by producing images that reverberate not only in themselves, but throughout each work.[14] But he was the only one of the Elizabethan dramatists

10. C. Day Lewis: *op. cit.*, p. 99.
11. Aristotle: *Poetics* (22, 1459a).
12. W. H. Clemen: *The Development of Shakespeare's Imagery* (London, 1951), p. 5.
13. This is argued by C. Spurgeon in *Shakespeare's Iterative Imagery* (Annual Shakespeare lecture of the British Academy, 1931), and *Shakespeare's Imagery and what it tells us* (Cambridge University Press, 1939), but is viewed with some scepticism by W. H. Clemen (see above), who thinks that images must be seen in the context of the play and the character portrayed, and should not be taken as representative of Shakespeare himself.
14. See C. Spurgeon above. She demonstrates, by counting and classifying the images, a central image in each play, which is

[continued opposite

to do this and to have a unifying, active image at the centre.[15] Images can be useful and illuminating on a lesser scale of consistency and inspiration.

It is virtually impossible to say why a successful image produces the effect that it does. It is because the image touches the unconscious that we cannot describe its operation effectively. Images are representatives of sensation, and on the relevance and completeness of the representation does their success depend, although communication is complicated by the fact that everyone receives different visual images.[16] The effect does not depend on the vividness of the image, but on its capacity for creating a psychological echo in the reader's mind. The image must reverberate to be effective. It has been said that the significance of particular images, or indeed of whole poems, that goes beyond any definite meaning conveyed, can be attributed to 'primordial images' or 'archetypes'.[17] This assumption is based on C. C. Jung's 'archetypal unconscious'. Jung posits the existence of 'psychic residua of numberless experiences of the same type'.[18] These experiences may have been undergone by the race to become determinants of individual experience, unconsciously absorbed. Whether this is so or not, we do know that the effect of some images goes far beyond the immediate text, and in the possibilities of association, we have a criterion for the image that is deeper than its immediate functions of precision and illumination. But it is a function that springs from the depths of the poet's personality, and of which he would probably be unaware. It is this criterion

constantly modified and expanded. E.g. in *Romeo and Juliet* the dominating image is light, and in *King Lear* the dominant image is that of the tortured body.

15. Spurgeon: *Shakespeare's Iterative Imagery*, p. 6. 'Only Shakespeare has a whole active picture in his mind that motivates images'; p.19.

16. I. A. Richards: *The Principles of Literary Criticism* (Kegan Paul, 1930), p. 114.

17. M. Bodkin: *Archetypal Patterns In Poetry* (Oxford University Press, 1935), p. 1.

18. C. G. Jung: *Contributions to Analytical Psychology* (Kegan Paul, 1928).

that distinguishes great from good poetry, and that is probably incapable of precise literary analysis.

'Imagism' in European and Hebrew Literature

In the early part of this century, it was felt that although the image was the vitalising principle of poetry, its life had been sapped, and that a reorientation was necessary. This feeling gave rise to the movement of 'Imagism', which placed the image right at the centre of the poetic production. But before we consider 'Imagism', it would be worth while to cast a brief glance at the fortunes of the image in the context of post-Shakespearean literature English. The eighteenth century, generally, considered the image subordinate: 'The Augustans were interested in ideas and in the versification of ideas: for them, the function of metaphor and simile was to illustrate ideas, not to create them.'[19] Dryden, who admired Shakespeare in other respects, considered his use of imagery excessive: "Tis not that I would explode the use of Metaphors from passion, for Longinus thinks 'em necessary to raise it; but to use 'em at every word, to say nothing without a Metaphor, a Simile, an Image, or description, is I doubt to smell a little too strongly of the Buskin.'[20] And Dr Johnson thought that 'the style of Shakespeare was in itself ungrammatical, perplexed and obscure'.[21] The Romantics, particularly Coleridge, estimated Shakespeare on a scale worthy of the poet,[22] and they could do this because of the affinity that they felt with his poetic ambitions. Coleridge indicated the crucial position of imagery in the poet's art. The image may not be detached from the poet's work or personality. They are not tacked on, but

19. C. Day Lewis: *op. cit.*, p. 54.
20. Dryden: *Preface to Shakespeare* (London, 1679).
21. Johnson: *Preface to Shakespeare* (London, 1765).
22. 'Few English critics before Coleridge had praised Shakespeare ungrudgingly and sympathetically, and none of these with a critical genius worthy of his subject'—Thomas M. Rayson; *Coleridge's Shakespearean Criticism* (Constable & Co., 1930), Vol. I, p. xvii, Introduction.

'become proofs of original genius only as far as they are modified by a predominant passion';[23] they must play an integral part in the poem. The Augustan image is subsidiary to the main theme, is used to point a comparison, and its object never overlooked. The Romantic image builds its own thought, and its means are not discursive or logical, but intuitive; the point of the comparison is not stated, or even formally implied. The Romantic poem is infinitely ambitious. Here is Wordsworth:

> My heart leaps up when I behold
> A rainbow in the sky.
> So was it when my life began:
> So is it now I am a man;
> So be it when I shall grow old,
> Or let me die:
> The Child is Father of the Man:
> And I could wish my days to be
> Bound each to each by natural piety.[24]

The stages from one experience to another are not pointed, and the link between the particular and the general is only implied. Wordsworth tries to give us an insight into his whole mental life, drawn from this particular experience. With this, we may compare Pope's:

> Come, then, the colours and the ground prepare!
> Dip in the rainbow, trick her off in air;
> Choose a firm cloud, before it fall, and in it
> Catch, ere she change, the Cynthia of this minute.[25]

The images here are pointed and useful; their function is pertinent, they are kept well under control, and do not create thoughts of themselves. The ambition of the poem is limited.

In the Victorian era, the image tried to serve the same function as it did for the Romantics. The Romantics had established a convention, and the Victorians tried to remain within it.

23. *Ibid.*, Vol. 2, No. 330.
24. W. Wordsworth's *Collected Poems* (Oxford, 1954), Vol. 1, p. 226.
25. A. Pope: 'To Martha Blount', lines 17–20, *Collected Works*, Vol. 3 (London, 1871).

Their verse treated of the same subjects, and they accepted the idea of the poem as a personal communication. But whereas the Romantics believed in the forces animating their poetry, the Victorians did not, so their Romanticism became a poetry of withdrawal, unresponsive to the world outside.[26] The Romantic tradition, according to some, found its true inheritors in the French Symbolists.[27] And then the French private 'symbole' became the English communicating 'image'. The 'symbole' is subjective, describing the poet's state of mind, and the 'image' purports to be objective, purely and precisely descriptive (of the external world). Whereas for the Symbolists, the 'image' was a means, for the Imagists, it was an end in itself.[28] T. E. Hulme (1886–1917), the leader of the Imagist School in England, attacked Romanticism, calling it 'spilt religion',[29] and saying that it was brought about by the 'perverted rhetoric of Rationalism'. But it has been stated[30] that

26. F. R. Leavis: *New Bearings in English Poetry* (Chatto and Windus, 1932), and W. Empson: *Seven Types of Ambiguity* (Peregrine Penguins, 1961), p. 20.

27. F. Kermode: *The Romantic Image* (Routledge & Kegan Paul, 1957), where the author upholds the view that Symbolism is a development of the introspection of Romanticism, creating its own symbols to record its private world; and *The Literary Symbol*, W. Y. Tindall (Indiana University Press, 1955), pp. 46, 47, for another support of this view. Also E. Wilson: *Axel's Castle* (Fontana, London, 1962), pp. 9–27.

28. See Rene Taupin: L'influence du Symbolisme Français sur la Poésie Américaine 1910–1920 (*Bibliothèque de la Revue de Littérature Comparée*, Tome 62, 1929), pp. 97, 98—'Pour beaucoup de symbolistes l'image n'était pas un aboutissement, mais un depart vers de lointains mystère. . . . Pour les imagistes, l'image doit être nette, pure, faite pour l'œil; le centre de la pensée du pœte. Elle ne doit pas s'effacer, mais au contraire se faire admirer dans toute sa netteté.'

29. T. E. Hulme: *Speculations* (ed. H. Read, London, 1924), p. 118.

30. F. Kermode: *op. cit.*, p. 121. See G. Hough: *Image and Experience* (Duckworth, 1960), p. 51, for the universally held view that Imagism derives from Symbolism.

Hulme and the Imagist movement returned to Romanticism with their assertion of the supremacy of the image. Hulme says that poetry uses means closed to prose, and that the means is the intuition: 'To deal with the intensive,[31] you must use intuition.'[32] His particular obsession was to get 'accurate, precise and definite description'.[33] Poetry must attain the concrete, and is better suited than prose for achieving this. The image is vital: 'Visual meanings can only be transferred by the new bowl of metaphor; prose is an old pot that lets them leak out. Images in verse are not mere decoration, but the very essence of an intuitive language.'[34] It seems that Hulme's sole purpose was to render visual images in words, to make description the purpose of literature.

Imagism as a literary movement could not last long, because such an ambition is partial; the image must be a means not an end. But the aims of the Imagist credo formulated in the anthology 'Some Imagists' (1915) had a great influence on literature in general, and are still exerting it. Its aims were: (1) to use the language of common speech, (2) to create new rhythms for new moods, (3) to allow freedom of subject, (4) to present a precise image, (5) to produce hard and clear poetry, and (6) to produce concentration of language and thought.[35] Such aims were embodied in the great new poetry of the twentieth century, in the work of T. S. Eliot and Ezra Pound, and it is the Imagist movement that exerted the most powerful influence over the new Hebrew poets of the twenties and thirties.

The modernist movement in Hebrew poetry, like Expressionism in Europe, was born of conscious iconoclasm. Expressionism is the blanket term[36] that we shall use to cover the

31. T. E. Hulme borrows this usage of 'intensive' and 'extensive' from H. Bergson. See Herbert Read's Introduction to *Speculations*.

32. T. E. Hulme: *op. cit.*, p. 139.

33. *Ibid.*, p. 132.

34. *Ibid.*, p. 135.

35. See Cassell's *Encyclopaedia of Literature* (1953), Vol. 1, on 'Imagism'.

36. See Ben-Or: *Toledot ha-sifrut ha 'ivrit bedorenu*, Vol. 1, p. 33, in

[continued overleaf

new directions in literature, following on the First World War and the Russian revolution. New instruments for literature were demanded in consonance with the violence and mechanism of the modern world. One of the main concerns was with the image in the way outlined above, and Imagism is a very important aspect of the new literature. It was the expressionistic use of imagery particularly that set off the neo-Hebrew writers from their predecessors and traditionally-inclined contemporaries.

Abraham Shlonsky was the leading spirit of the movement, and he gathered round himself a group of writers through the periodical *Ketuvim*, which he edited together with Eliezer Steinmann from 1926 to 1933.[37] At first, this was a platform for all leading Hebrew writers, including those of the 'Writers' Association'. But it was soon dominated by the modernists, and the traditionalists ceased to contribute. In 1933, there was an editorial split, and Shlonsky founded a new magazine *Turim*, and edited it for two years.

The new writing was thought by some to be uncreative. One of the older poets, Jacob Fichman (1881–1958), wrote that other literature could afford a destructive wave since their tradition was so strong, but that Hebrew literature could not: 'In a literature like ours that has not yet achieved Form, contempt for Form, and the modernistic caprices now current in other literatures are most dangerous.'[38] Shlonsky's work is characterised by images taken from contemporary mechanistic life, by the unusual conjunction of disparate images, by the concretisation of the abstract, and by the prevalence of metaphor over simile. His poetry is permeated by the violence of revolutionary Russian poetry, of Blok and Maiakovsky. It has the atmosphere of chaos engendered by the shattering events

which A. Ben-Or uses 'Expressionism' as the generic term, under which come the sub-headings 'Dadaism', 'Surrealism', 'Futurism' and 'Imagism'. See also Cassell's *Encyclopaedia of*

Literature, Vol. 1, 'Expressionism'

37. For information here, see Ben-Or: *op. cit.*, Vol. 1, p. 45.

38. See *Ha-tekufah 19* (1923), in an essay 'Form and Expression' (*Zurah u-vitui*).

of the previous years, and later adopts the pioneering ideology of the third *aliya*.

Other expressionistic traits of his are that he coined words, and wrote in irregular metre and rhyme. In one of his early poems, 'Sickness' (*Devai*),[39] written between 1922 and 1927, Shlonsky displays his early pessimism. The sickness of mankind can be cured neither by Religion (by the priest), nor by any particular economic set-up. All three stages of economic development have proved disastrous; the hunter is attacked by animals, the farmer cannot cope with the forces of nature, and industrial life is the worst of all. But Industry, in the person of Tubal Cain,[40] had inspired hope, and it is interesting to note the images Shlonsky deploys to express this: 'You have blown into us the breath of a steam engine. And thus we are, at full height, chimney pots on the face of the earth.'[41] The Biblical allusion is clear, the echoes are from 'and he blew into his nostrils the breath of life'.[42] But here the breath of life has become the breath of the steam engine, i.e. 'Life' has become petrified into the Machine. The surprise, contemporary imagery inviting other hallowed associations, is a common characteristic of modernist poetry. T. S. Eliot had already caused a great stir by speaking of the evening as 'spread out against the sky like a patient etherised upon a table'.[43] He transmitted his view of the contemporary atmosphere with phrases like 'Let us take the air in a tobacco trance.'[44] As for the concretisation of the abstract, and the mingling of them, W. H. Auden speaks in an early poem of 'the smells and furniture of the known world'.[45] Through this means, the poet

39. See *Collected Poems*, A. Shlonsky (*Ha-shomer hazair*, 1965), Vol. 1, p. 74.

40. A Biblical figure, Gen. 4:22— 'Tubal Cain, the forger of every cutting instrument of brass and iron.'

41. A. Shlonsky: *op. cit.*, p. 93.

42. Gen. 2:7.

43. T. S. Eliot: *ibid. Collected Poems 1909-1935* (London, 1936). 'The love song of J. Alfred Prufrock' (1917), lines 2 and 3.

44. *Ibid.*, *Portrait of a Lady* (1917).

45. W. H. Auden: *Collected Poetry* (Random House, 1945), *Kairos and Logos*.

tries to penetrate the world he lives in, to know it as a poet. It has been said of Eliot that he 'is as close to the contemporary world as could be'.[46] He has persuaded us of this by his careful use of the image, which reflects a sensitive spirit, living intently in his age.

One of the leading contributors to Shlonsky's second periodical *Turim* was Nathan Altermann, one of the major Hebrew imagists contemporaneous with, though ten years younger than, Shlonsky. He was a journalist, and wrote topical verse for a newspaper,[47] but even his more universal poetry has a gay, topical air, although his symbolism is not easily interpreted in the light of contemporary affairs.[48] Strongly under the influence of Shlonsky, he also leaned heavily on the surprise effects of his imagery.[49] Particularly strong in him is the inclination, already noticed in Shlonsky and the Imagists in general, to conjoin abstract with concrete. In his early poems,[50] he gives us his idiosyncratic view of Tel-Aviv, the new and rapidly growing urban centre of Palestine, and says of it, for example, that it is 'combed with light and rain'.[51] Sometimes, he uses an extended image, as in 'The Conflagration',[52] where he describes a fire in the city, and concentrates on one house to increase his effect, on the particular to vivify the general. In atmosphere, at least on the surface, Altermann differs radically from the early Shlonsky. In contrast to Shlonsky's aggressively unhappy urbanistic poetry,

46. F. R. Leavis: *op. cit.*, p. 78.

47. *Davar*. These were later published under the title of *Ha-tur hashevi'i*.

48. See D. Miron: *Arba' panim basifrut ha-'ivrit bat yamenu* (Tel-Aviv, 1962), pp. 18–22, on the poem 'Joy of the Poor'. But Ben-Or, *op. cit.*, p. 243, holds the more common view that it has a specific reference to Jewry under the Nazis.

49. Ben-Or: *op. cit.*, p. 241, claims that Altermann developed the image further than Shlonsky to attain the insight into the world beyond the superficial.

50. N. Altermann: *Kokhavim baḥuẓ*, his early verse written between 1931 and 1938 (Tel-Aviv, 1938).

51. *Ibid.*, p. 40.

52. *Ibid.* Ha-deleikah, pp. 27–9, in *Kokhavim baḥuẓ.*

Altermann's is positive and gay, an effect that he builds through rhythm as well as image. To Shlonsky, the city is a terrible blot, but Altermann revels in its gaiety and light.[53]

In Altermann's later verse, the image is replaced at the centre by a symbol or multiplicity of symbols, obscure but pregnant. But the image still illuminates, although, as has been pointed out, it is epigrammatic rather than specific.[54] Despite the macabre background of the poem, 'The Joy of the Poor',[55] the verse is apparently gay. The poet further develops the counterpoint of abstract with concrete: 'The shadow of death in its [the lightning's] light. Immortality in its coldness.'[56]

Leah Goldberg, of the generation of Altermann, also seeks the precise image, though her themes and rhythms are those traditional to poetry, and her verse is quiet and affectionate. Here, in a comparatively late work of hers, is a description of Autumn:

> Autumn, beautiful with apples, whose countenance glistens with a shy smile. As a girl's teeth between scarlet lips do the days glitter between the rising and setting [of the sun].[57]

It seems that the young contemporary Hebrew writers are making a belated return to the use of the image as exemplified by these Imagists. Yehudah Amihai, a young novelist, poet and story writer, counterpoints abstract with concrete in the manner now familiar. He speaks of the 'sun that burns thorns and thoughts'.[58] But in this instance, he seems to have no very good reason for doing so, as the image lacks surprise, power and point. Perhaps he is more successful when he says later:

---

53. E.g. *Ibid.*, p. 78.

54. D. Miron: *op. cit.*, p. 59.

55. *Ibid.*, p. 20. The motive of the dead addressing the living is already paramount in *Kokhavim baḥuẓ*.

56. N. Altermann: *Simḥat ʻaniyyim*

(Maḥbarot le-sifrut, Tel-Aviv, 4th edition, 1953), p. 13.

57. L. Goldberg: '*Al haperiḥah* (*Sifriyat poʻalim*, Tel-Aviv, 1948), p. 93.

58. See Y. Amihai: *Baruaḥ hanoraah hazot* (Tel-Aviv, 1961). A collection of stories, p. 7.

'You are like a torch that they left burning in the day.'[59] This
has a place in the context of the story, and does help to illuminate its character and situation.

The Imagery of Lamdan: Introduction

We have now to consider Lamdan's imagery and its importance
in his poetical work. We may remember that Lamdan was born
in 1900 in the Ukraine, the same year and the same place as
Shlonsky.[60] But he participated even more in the turbulent
events of his time. In 1917, after Kerensky had achieved power
and promulgated his liberal programme, Lamdan enthusias-
tically volunteered for the army in the war against Germany.[61]
But in the later ravages of the October revolution, his brother
was killed,[62] and he himself only escaped by a miracle. Under
the Bolsheviks, Russia retired from the war, and Lamdan made
his way to Palestine, arriving there in 1920, having witnessed
the disintegration of a society, and the particular devastation
wrought against the Jews.

　This is the background to Lamdan's first major poetic work
Masada, written in 1923-24, and the violence of the events
found a faithful echo in Lamdan's language. The form of the
poem is expressionistic,[63] and the language imagistic in the
extreme. Expressionist language is usually hysterical, and this
poem is no exception. But the hysteria here is kept well under
control. Although the images are spectacular and tremendous,
they do not appear ludicrous, and seem justified by the experiences that called them forth. We read on the first page of
the poem that 'the final banner of rebellion has been unfurled
there [in Palestine] and demands from Heaven and Earth, God
and Man: "Payments".'[64] Vast images are bandied about, but

59. *Ibid.*, p. 36.
60. For biographical details of these
　　two poets, see Ben-Or, *op. cit.*,
　　p. 222 (on Shlonsky), and p. 279
　　(on Lamdan).
61. As he says at the beginning of

Masada (*Sifriyat Devir La'am*),
　　p. 11, lines 4, etc.
62. See *ibid.*, lines 6, etc.
63. See above, Chapter 3, Section
　　'Form of the Poem'.
64. *Masada*, p. 11.

yet seem quite appropriate to the situation. Like expressionist literature in general, *Masada* reads like an apocalypse, in the consciousness that worlds are crumbling, and in the belief that mankind is standing at the threshold of 'the end'. *Masada* concludes on a cautionary optimistic note, but assured that if this attempt were to fail, there would be no further opportunities open to the people—'Here is the border. Further on, there are more borders.'[65]

The language of the poem echoes the language of the apocalyptic passages of the Bible. The 'last vision' (*aharit hazon*) in the final paragraphs of the poem is an adaptation of the Biblical 'end of days' (*aharit yamim*).[66] The footsteps of the end[67] that the protagonist of Nihilism awaits (see above on *Masada*) are associated with 'the feet of him that bringeth good tidings'.[68] Cultic terms are used to endow the pioneering project with a numinous air. The Palestinian workers are 'prophets prophesying redemption'.[69] In Palestine, Masada as the poet symbolically calls it, there is 'a Divine Presence dropping down atonement'.[70] Future possibilities are known as the 'curtain of future events',[71] echoing Isaiah's 'let us hear of the future events'.[72] Communism is spoken of imagistically as 'this red prayer shawl'.[73] In addition to traditionalist echoes, Lamdan can express violent distress through his use of modernistic imagery, thus: 'On tablets of rock, stubborn fingernails engrave the gospel of comfort.'[74] Here we find a successful super-imposition of the modern 'stubborn fingernails' and 'comfort' on the traditional 'tablets and 'gospel'. This image captures the obstinate and frantic attempts of people to seek peace in spite of all the odds against them. They do not do this with the proper implements, and they have to use their bare fingers. On the ancient code of Law (the metaphor is, of course,

65. *Ibid.*, p. 82.
66. See Gen. 49:1, Jes. 2:2, Jer. 23:20, Ez. 38:8, Hos. 3:5, Dan. 8:19 *et al.*
67. *Masada*, p. 18.
68. *Nahum* 2:1.
69. *Masada*, p. 12.
70. *Ibid.*, p. 12.
71. *Ibid.*, p. 12.
72. Jes. 41:22.
73. *Masada*, p. 13.
74. *Ibid*, p. 11.

taken from the tablets of stone on which Moses gave the ten
commandments, as well as applying to the 'rock' of the mountain Masada), they try to impose this new law of comfort, this
gospel (the metaphor is from the New Testament). But they
can expect to be hurt because they are scratching their fingers
on rock. The new Covenant that they are seeking will cost
them pain and suffering.

As we noted before when speaking of Shakespeare's imagery,[75] the image becomes far more effective if it is iterative,
i.e. recurring in different forms to create its own pattern and
mood. Shakespeare usually succeeded in making an image,
through all its metamorphoses and modifications, dominate a
play. In *Masada* we do not find a single dominant image, but
we do find a dominant mood, and we discover that this mood
is engendered by the consistent tone and type of imagery used.
The note is one of extremist, religious (though secularised)
hysteria, and apocalyptic urgency. We also find in later poems
of Lamdan an inner consistency of imagery within many
individual poems. In 'He who sows in the Darkness',[76] the
central image is of one sowing on unfruitful soil, and gains
particular potency by its association with the Biblical phrase—
'those who sow with tears shall reap in joy'.[77] The ironic contrast is pointed between the Biblical promise, and the Palestinian actuality. 'You shall not reap it'[78] (the stalk), the poet
assures the pioneer. The association is implied throughout the
poem. We also find in Lamdan's poetry that individual verses
retain a remarkable consistency through a thick cluster of
images. In the second verse of the introductory unnamed poem
to the first series of *Bema'aleh 'aqrabbim*, there are parallel echoes
throughout the whole verse. It runs:

Only its surface does the Heart plant—in shade or in sun,
In a lonely, silent corner or in the turbulent public places,

75. See above, p. 164 f.

76. See I. Lamdan: *Bema'aleh 'aqrab-
    bim* (Mossad Bialik), p. 11, the
    poem *Ha-zore'a ba-hashehah*.

77. See Ps. 126:5.

78. *Bema'aleh 'aqrabbim*, p. 12.

And see, even they have become entangled, have
                                          become a thick forest
In which silence, storm, and deep darkness reign by turn,
In which the roots are invisibly tied up with its soil,
And unearthly echoes stalk its secret places.[79]

Lamdan is saying here that the poet (the Heart) can express
only the surface, and must leave the depths untouched. But
even this expressible surface becomes complicated, like a forest
where the roots get entangled with the soil, and he can no
longer distinguish the roots (of what he can express, i.e. the
surface) from the soil (i.e. the inexpressible depths). Another
complication is the presence of matter that seems to have no
place in the poet's consciousness at all—the unearthly echoes.
Lamdan is telling us of the difficulties he experiences in writing
poetry. But notice the consistency of image, and the parallel
lines that run through the stanza. The central metaphor is pastoral—'the Heart plants', the surfaces have 'become entangled',
and are 'a thick forest', and 'the roots are invisibly tied up with
its soil'. 'Shade' and 'sun', themselves in opposition, are parallel
to 'a lonely, silent corner' and 'turbulent public places'. The
senses of sight and sound are employed, and their functions are
expressed by turn. The sound 'silence and storm' are followed
by sight 'deep darkness'. Then line five relates to sight, and
line six to sound.

Also to be noted in this verse is the freshness of the poet's
imagery. The Heart, biblically the seat of intelligence,[80] and
the modern seat of emotion, is the symbol of the poet, and the
poet surprisingly speaks of composition as planting. His surface
thoughts are like trees and become thick as a forest. and then
he can no longer distinguish between these surface thoughts
and what he does not even aspire to express; they are like roots
that are indistinguishable from the soil out of which they grow.
All these images are fresh, consistent, precise and illuminating.
We can understand Lamdan's problems more clearly through

79. *Ibid.*, p. 5.
80. E.g., see Prov. 10:13—'And a

staff for the back of a fool' (lit.
for one 'lacking heart').

this verse than if he had tried to express himself in non-metaphorical language, a task that would have involved clumsiness and unnecessary obscurity. Here we have depth communicated elegantly.

In the passage from *Masada* to *Bema'aleh 'aqrabbim*, a later collection of poems, eventually published in 1938, Lamdan has changed his tone considerably from his expressionist days. The main changes to be noted are (a) a return to formal metre and rhyme, and (b) a lowering and mellowing of the tone of his imagery. In most of the later poems, Lamdan deploys formal rhyme and metre, but even in those poems where the verse is free, there is none of the hysterical admonition that we observe in *Masada*, even where the theme is parallel. Sometimes, the pessimism is deeper and more assured; but we hear resignation on the part of the poet, not protest. Abram and Jacob, in two of the Biblical poems, do not want to accept the terrible fate of the Jewish people. But they do not rant, they resign themselves quietly. Abram 'kneels', 'and covers his face',[81] and Jacob just says that he wants to hear no more: 'I want to come no more. I do not want to hear.'[82] The destiny[83] of the Jewish people is spoken of in *Masada* as 'into our blood has the curse been poured, and it is the oil to the wick of our existence',[84] and in the poem 'The Covenant between the Pieces',[85] this destiny is a vulture, assuredly a terrible thing, but latent and evoking no reaction. In *Masada*, violent solutions were proposed at every point, and Zionism, the solution adopted by the poet, demanded positive fervour; in the Biblical poems, no positive course is recommended. *Masada* is committed to action, and *Bema'aleh 'aqrabbim* to passivity.

Lamdan could not properly be considered an Imagist. The Imagist movement considered the image as primary, and as creative in itself. For them, the image is the centrality of the

81. *Bema'aleh 'aqrabbim*, p. 15, line 23.
82. *Ibid.*, p. 18, line 19.
83. In Lamdan's sense *yi'ud*.

84. *Masada*, p. 13.

85. See *Bema'aleh 'aqrabbim*, p. 14. *Ha-brit ben ha-betarim.*

poem.[86] This characterisation would not fit Lamdan even in his most imagistic work. His image is always subsidiary; he does not hold it up as an object of delight as does the early Shlonsky: 'At our door does night crouch like an altar stone,'[87] or the early Altermann: 'And the house is old, and flames in its rags, and recites amongst the collapse of beams and wall.'[88] Lamdan's image is unselfconscious, and subdued to the context of the poem. To describe the fresh, optimistic appearance of the young pioneer, he says: 'your head is full of drops of dew'.[89] The image is pregnant with the association of love from 'Canticles',[90] and then serves the purpose of being associated with tears later on.[91] It does not step out of its context, and display itself for admiration. For Shlonsky, the image 'hears spectacles and sees them';[92] in other words, the image becomes suggester, and then creator. But for Lamdan, the image serves a purpose in a context; to illuminate his themes of struggle, destiny and poetry.[93]

The Imagery of *Masada*

We will now consider the imagery of *Masada* in detail. By comparison with the imagery of Lamdan's later poetry, certain differences will be observed in the tone of the verse. It is mainly through his use of imagery that Lamdan obtains his desperate, hysterical effects in *Masada* and his reflective effects in *Bema'aleh 'aqrabbim*. The themes of these disparate works demand different treatment, *Masada* dealing with national aspirations and universal ideologies, his later poetry being lyrical and personal. We will treat the imagery of *Masada*

86. See *Image and Experience* (London, 1960), pp. 12–13. Here Hough cites from Imagist tracts in which is affirmed that the sole aim of poetry is adequate description.

87. A. Shlonsky: *Collected Poems*, Vol. I, p. 13, line 1.

88. N. Altermann: *Kokhavim baḥuz*, p. 27.

89. *Masada*, p. 28.

90. Cant. 5:2.

91. *Masada*, p. 28, line 3.

92. *Ibid.* Quoted in Ben-Or: *op. cit.*, Vol. I, p. 221.

93. See *Bema'aleh 'aqrabbim*, p. 136.

systematically and chronologically, putting each image in its context, and estimating its effect on the context.

Masada begins with a description of the poet almost in despair after having suffered from the ravages of revolution and strife, but still determined[94] to salvage his human dignity. He says of himself, 'Whilst I, still fastening my crumbling soul with the last girders of courage, fled at midnight to the exile ship, to ascend to Masada. He fled to Masada[95] because 'the final banner of rebellion has been unfurled there'.[96] The constant use of the word 'final'[97] in the poem gives it its apocalyptic flavour. There is a feeling of 'the end of days', the climax of human history. And the poet demands 'payments', i.e. compensation, for all that his people have suffered.

We find that Masada is constantly spoken of as a wall (*ḥomah*). On page 12, we read of 'prophets wandering amongst the walls of Masada',[98] and we find that Masada is spoken of as 'a wall' thirty-two times in all.[99] This image, or symbol as it has probably become through repeated use,[100] could suggest peril, or preparedness for war, or isolation, or any combination of all three, since all these states are revealed in the poem. The wall can have further metaphorical usefulness as when the

94. *Masada*, p. 11.

95. I.e. Palestine, see above section on *Masada* for the significance of this symbol.

96. *Masada*, p. 11.

97. See above, Chapter 3, p. 50, 'Form of the poem'.

98. *Masada*, p. 12.

99. Pp. 12, 28, 29 (three times), 30, 31 (twice), 32, 37, 50 (four times), 57, 60 (twice), 61, 62, 63, 65, 66, 69, 70 (three times), 72 (twice), 74, 81 and 82.

100. It has been suggested that an image becomes a symbol used frequently. See René Wellek and Austin Warren: *Theory of Literature* (Jonathan Cape, London, 1949), pp. 193, 194.—'An image may be involved once as a metaphor, but if it persistently recurs, both as presentation and representation, it becomes a symbol, may even become part of a symbolic (or mythic) system.' And of the relation between images, metaphors and symbols, they say, 'The normal procedure is the turning of images into metaphors, and metaphors into symbols'—Note 12, p. 331.

immigrants speak of throwing themselves from it, i.e. committing suicide.[101] The 'wall' is already an image of defence in the Bible, e.g. Jer. 51:44.

We have already spoken above of the effects that Lamdan obtains by his use of religious or traditional terminology, applied in a modern and different context, and in the phrase just mentioned—'prophets wandering amongst the walls of Masada'—we observe the same technique. The pioneers and immigrants are spoken of with awe as 'prophets' and 'levitical sects'. They cry out 'To the victor' (*Lamenazeaḥ*), a psalm heading, and receive answer from the 'Morrow's echo'—*selah*, a psalmic full stop. The 'Divine Presence' (*Shekhinah*) is active in Masada, dropping atonements, and the same word is employed in a secularised sense (on page 69) as 'the genius of the people' (genius in the sense of spirit). The protagonist of nihilism speaks of Communism as 'a red prayer-shawl spread out—a new striped coat that the priests and prophets of the world have fashioned'.[102] The image is of the Communists trying to impose a new order on the world like a shawl, but the religious associations make the image more powerful. It is not just a shawl, but the traditional prayer-shawl of Orthodox Jews. The striped coat is what the favoured son Joseph received from Jacob his father,[103] probably as a sign that he would inherit the leadership of the family. The Communists are not here ordinary men, but 'priests' and 'prophets'. The nihilist wants to use this Communist front to hide his 'vengeful knife'. The word for knife used here is a comparatively rare one, the same word (*ma'achelet*) as is used in the chapter concerned with Abraham's proposed sacrifice of Isaac.[104] An image much in evidence is taken from the traditional prayer made on the termination of the Sabbath or festival, the *Havdalah*—'the dividing'—'to divide the holy from the profane'; 'the red curtain is lowered . . . to divide one campaign from another'.[105]

101. E.g., *Masada* p. 29: 'Then would I cast myself from the heights of the wall into the ravine.'

102. *Masada*, p. 15.

103. Gen. 37:3.

104. Gen. 22:6.

105. *Masada*, p. 15.

The poet's own words seem to support this apocalyptic vision, if they do not share this ideology. There is a description of the confusion and bloodshed that immediately preceded the poet's emigration, and the flames are for him also a *havdalah*—'the habitations of Israel burned (the hand of Fate had kindled a great red *havdalah* to divide Israel from the nations in the termination of the world).'[106] This is an ironic adaptation by Lamdan of the prayer on the 'termination' of the Sabbath. In that prayer, God is praised for dividing Israel from the nations,[107] but nothing is specifically stated there about the nature of this division. Lamdan here suggests a possibility, when he says that it was 'the habitation of Israel' particularly that were in flames. Characteristically, it is not God to whom this calamity is attributed, but 'the hand of Fate'. Instead of God dividing Israel off from the other nations for religious reasons, we have Fate dividing her off for reasons known only to Fate itself. The poet castigates the world for checking its 'preying nails by the light of the *havdalah*',[108] an image suggesting indifference to the suffering that 'the light', i.e. the ravages, represent. The image is taken from the custom of holding the fingernails up to the *havdalah* candle during this service, when the blessing for light is recited. Ironically, this blessing has become a curse.

The Nihilist protagonist again employs specifically religious terminology when he demands that the poet join in sacrificing to his God, 'the God of vengeance' (page 14)—'Come', he says, 'let us set an altar for him, and act as his priests in the temple.'[109] We do not find traditional beliefs, but we do find the terminology that once expressed them used in a different, and sometimes contrary, manner. The defeatist protagonist who has nothing positive to offer at all, categorises the others as 'those who seek solutions and conclusions',[110] that is, everyone who offers a solution at this stage is coveting an illusion. The phrase 'seekers of . . . conclusions' is an adaptation

106. *Masada*, p. 19.
107. See *Singer's Prayer Book*, 23rd edition (London, 1954), p. 216.
108. *Masada*, p. 21.
109. *Ibid.*, p. 14.
110. *Ibid.*, p. 17.

of the traditional 'calculators of conclusions', which is a term meaning those who work out when the Messiah will come. We find the expression in the Talmud: 'Blasted be the bones of those who calculate the end.'[111] The word 'end' (*kez*) appears frequently in an eschatological sense in the second part of the book of Daniel.[112] Of course, the end envisaged by this protagonist is not necessarily Messianic (in the traditional sense), but covers any proposed 'final solution' of the world's ills, whether it be Zionist, Communist, or violently nihilistic (anarchistic). He has despaired completely, and his sole impulse is to wait for the 'footsteps of the end'.[113]

'Fate' (*goral*) is, as has been stated, the responsible power in the universe in most of the poem. The violent nihilist says of Masada, i.e. the Zionist idea, that it is a 'snare' laid by Fate'[114] The resigned nihilist protagonist asserts that there is no escape from the evil of the world, which is controlled by Fate, there is no key to the lock. 'Why should you still seek the key to the lock of our heavy lot when there has never been such a key?'[115] But Determinism is not dominant throughout the poem. In the 'prayer' (page 68) the speaker addresses himself to God (*Elohim*), i.e. a power that can control Fate. Fate exists, but can be conquered if God will give strength and courage to the people.[116]

Lamdan describes the confusion of the revolutionary months by the use of imagery taken from the market place (page 20). This image suggests noise and tumult—everything is being offered cheaply. However it is not goods that are being sold, but ideologies—'flags of redemption'. The three protagonists, i.e. the three ideologies that the poet rejects, are there in the market place, the avenger blessing, the Communist blessing and cursing whilst 'weaving the dream of redemption', and the hopeless awaiting 'the last sole redeemer', which is death. Here the poet takes his leave in order to fulfil his Zionist dream. He uses

111. *Sanhedrin* 97:2.
112. Daniel 8:17, 9:15, 11:6, 27, 35, 12:4, 9, 12, 13.
113. Also a Messianic echo. See above, previous section.
114. *Masada*, p. 13.
115. *Ibid.*, p. 17.
116. *Ibid.*, p. 69.

the same imagery here as he did at the beginning of the section: 'binding my disintegrating soul, I fled . . .'. He goes to Masada, and places his 'disintegrating soul' there, as a piece of metal on an 'anvil' and asks to be beaten and moulded into shape.[117] He goes to Masada, despairing of the world he has left, but, 'drawn like a weary moth, deprived of day and sunlight to its cold consuming flame'.[118] He must resist the flame, and fasten himself to the bars of Masada's gates.[119]

The second section is set in Palestine, and we find that it is spoken of in terms of the familiar image of a bosom.[120] One of the settlers says: 'in the bosom of Masada shall I now bury my head'.[121] Masada is spoken of as a bosom again in 'And what shall you do for your thirsty fighters, poor mother [this addressed to Masada] when they bury their head in your bosom?'[122] This symbol is also used negatively for Masada, 'Spread out again, sailors of this anchorless people's boat, all the sails to the bosomless void.'[123] 'Bosom' is a traditional image of security.[124] Masada is required to serve the function of protective mother, and is blamed for not fulfilling it.

The image 'forest' represents confusion. We find the phrase,[125] 'In forests of confusion and darkness, the gold of our dreams has been despoiled'. Later the masses are spoken of as 'Forests of people'.[126] In *Bema'aleh 'aqrabbim* the complications that thought tends to are imaged as a 'thick forest'.[127] S. Shalom a contemporary poet, also describes those who have lost their way as wandering in forests.[128] The forests represent mental confusion, and obscure the desirable—'the beach'.[129]

117. *Ibid.*, p. 22.

118. Same image in *Bema'aleh 'aqrabbim*, p. 5.

119. *Masada*, p. 23.

120. E.g., A. Hameiri's poem on Abraham. *Anthology of Hameiri's poetry* (Schocken, Tel-Aviv, 1962), p. 1.

121. *Masada*, p. 27.

122. *Ibid.*, p. 53.

123. *Ibid.*, p. 49.

124. Particularly in the Hebrew Bible.

125. *Masada*, p. 32.

126. *Ibid.*, p. 80.

127. *Bema'aleh 'aqrabbim*, p. 5.

128. See S. Shalom: *Panim el Panim*, Mossad Bialik, 1941, p. 11.

129. *Ibid.*

Lamdan sometimes creates his effects by the iterative use of an image in a given passage. In the section 'From bonfires to bonfires' (page 38), 'bonfires' occur in every line but one, eleven times in all. Lamdan wants to show how bonfires have played such a significant part in Jewish history, though their function has, of course, changed. The essence of the change is summed up in the last stanza: 'Our fathers jumped into bonfires in deathful joy to become an enigma. Now around bonfires do children dance the dance of the solution',[130] the reference being to the Zionist solution. Iterative imagery is used again in the next two sections where the central image is that of the dance. This is the height of the optimistic section, and again the link between past and present is stressed. The fathers danced, and so do the sons, but whereas the fathers held the 'scroll of the Torah [Law]' the sons hold the 'burden of the age'. The second section is entitled 'Enthusiasm'. The Hebrew term for this, *hitlahavut*, is a technical word in Hasidic literature, meaning religious enthusiasm. Here, the enthusiasm is nationalistic. The terminology has been secularised. The rhythm of these passages is adapted to their mood and imagery, being quick and light.

Later in the poem, when the mood changes, the rhythm slows down, and though there is singing in the camp, it is of a different, mournful sort. Again, 'The chain' is mentioned, the link with the past! 'Thus did our fathers sing at the third Sabbath meal, grievingly. So do I sing in Masada.'[131] The pioneers are now the 'sorrowing violin in the joyous orchestra'.[132] Pessimism has taken over; the only answer the pioneers receive from the four winds is 'one unlimited sorrow'. This echoes the Biblical: 'I will empty out unlimited blessing for you',[133] but of course ironically, the blessing has become a curse.

Lamdan often uses the literary echo to point contrasts, and sometimes does it within a poem. At one point (p. 57) he begins the line with the phrase 'There are nights in Masada', the same

130. *Masada*, p. 39. 132. *Ibid.*
131. *Masada*, p. 51. 133. Malachi 3: 10.

opening phrase as he uses earlier (p. 37). But the mood has changed. In the earlier section the nights were 'heavy of breath with too much blood from too much strength flowing in their veins.'[134] But in the latter section, there are 'heavy nights of evil portent.'[135] We also have here a personification of despair, 'the face of one terrible guerilla . . . the face of open despair.'[136] The determination to resist this despair is expressed by the use of the word 'fist'—'Soon, the hands of bitter-souled, pain-swollen fighters will be clenched into a single fist.'[137] But the fist is useless—'fists are clenched in secret, and no one will raise them.'[138] This image has already been employed earlier in the poem, by the immigrants who have arrived desperate, and ready for anything—'The anguish of hatred shrinks us into one clenched fist which is brought down in all its fury on the skull of our Fate. Let either the fist or the accursed skull be dashed to pieces.'[139] The fist is a symbol of desperate determination, and of willingness to fight.

The images with which Lamdan ends the poem are again taken from traditional practices. He says 'We have finished the books of all the paths',[140] and then expresses the traditional formula used by Hebrew writers at the conclusion of a book, with a small alteration. The normal formula is—'Finished and completed, praise to God, creator of the world', but Lamdan says, 'Finished and completed, though we have no praise for God, creator of the world.'[141] Again, Lamdan uses a formula to contradict it. Here, he wants to assert his independence of God. He goes on to say, 'From now a new book of Genesis is opened on the wall',[142] that is, the wall of Masada. The Book of Genesis is the first book of the Bible, and so the first to be read in the yearly cycle, during which the whole Pentateuch has to be covered. But again, Lamdan turns this traditional image to his own use. It is his own book of Genesis that is to

134. *Masada*, p. 27.
135. *Ibid.*, p. 57.
136. *Ibid.*
137. *Ibid.*
138. *Ibid.*

139. *Ibid.*, p. 32.
140. *Ibid.*, p. 82.
141. *Ibid.*
142. *Ibid.*

be read. A new Zionist chapter is to be started. His closing words—'Be strong, be strong, and we shall be strengthened.'[143] This is the traditional formula that is recited in the synagogue when one of the 'five books' of Moses is completed. And this is Lamdan's sober message to his fellows on the completion of the poetic experience of Masada.

The Imagery of Bema'aleh 'Aqrabbim

Bema'aleh 'aqrabbim is a collection of six series of poems that often differ considerably in mood and treatment, so the tone of the imagery is naturally not completely uniform. But it is invariably more subdued than Masada. Only towards the end of the work, in his 'Prayer for Revenge',[144] written in 1943, when his subject demanded the same frantic treatment as that of Masada, does he veer towards his earlier hysteria. But even here his stanzas are all of the same length, his verse is metrical, and his language is less rhetorical than in Masada.

The introductory poem to the book has no title but sets the mood and states the theme of the book as a whole. He talks of his poetic potentialities and limitations and the impetus of his writing. His imagery is taken mainly from nature.[145] The heart, i.e. his poetry, 'plants'[146] in the sun or in the shade. His thoughts become a forest. The reader is spoken of as a casual rambler in this forest.[147] A single poem is 'a leaf rustling quietly from its stock at your [the reader's] feet.'[148] The ravages of the revolution ruined 'peaceful nests', tore up 'stems' (of trees), and trod flat 'the grass of dreams'. But the 'soul of a man', (again the poet) was hidden amongst the bushes, making poetry from the experience of the ravages. He, the 'forest of man', bore the 'rainy heavens . . . from the roots of the grass to the

143. *Ibid.*
144. *Bema'aleh 'aqrabbim*, p. 226. *Tephillat naqam.*
145. Parts of this poem have already been examined. See above, pp. 143–8.

146. *Bema'aleh 'aqrabbim*, p. 5. Two words are used here for planting. The words *shatal* and *nat'a*.
147. *Ibid.* 'If you happen to pass through my wood.'
148. *Ibid.*

tops of the branches.' Through these 'the petrification of an age passed like a mighty wounding comb'. It was Lamdan's task to record the experiences of the 'heart' and to raise a poetic monument to his suffering generation. Lamdan attempts to make an impression of the 'footprints' left by Fate[149] in this forest, and to give us his reactions.

Lamdan's next poem, 'He who Sows in the Darkness', also takes its central imagery from nature. Its impact lies in the irony of the sower who does not reap.[150] The sower is the pioneer of Palestine, and he will receive no personal reward. He receives no light—'no window blinks anywhere, the vistas nod no flash of light'.[151] The sower only sows because he has been 'terrified by the terror of Fate and Love'.[152] Lamdan counterpoints his traditional negative element—Fate—with the positive—love. The pioneers sow because they love the land, and also because they are driven to it by Fate. But, normally, one would not sow here 'unless he had thrown his flesh into the dim gullet of the morrow as an entrance fee'.[153] The sower is told not to cry out if he stumbles because 'there is no ear that hears'.[154] Either people are indifferent to his plight or God is indifferent. If the latter interpretation is correct, we may compare the plight and terminology to the desperate cry of the people to Isaiah in Bialik's poem *Davar*—'Even if we cry out and pray in the Darkness—whose ear would hear?'[155] In both cases, man is alone and can appeal to no greater power. The sower stumbles and falls, 'with a palmful of seed and tears'.[156] He has indeed sown in tears, but has not reaped in joy.

The next series of five poems are on traditional themes, four

149. *Ibid.*, p. 6. 'Here the heavy stamping of Fates has left its footprints.'

150. See above on this poem, Chapter 6, Section 'The Pioneer'.

151. *Bema'aleh 'aqrabbim*, p. 11. For use of 'window' as parallel symbol to light, compare in Bialik's poem 'Alone' (Levadi), the line 'When my heart longed for the "window" for the light.' Bialik: *op. cit.*, p. 147.

152. *Ibid.*, p. 11.

153. *Ibid.*

154. *Ibid.*, p. 12.

155. Bialik: *op. cit.*, p. 178, *Davar*.

156. *Bema'aleh 'aqrabbim*, p. 13.

with Biblical subject and one with Midrashic. In the first, 'The Covenant between the Pieces', Lamdan tries to recreate the awe of God's revelation to Abram and the promise of the land of Palestine, Abram is 'bathed in purple sunset, sparked by the light of the Future'.[157] Abram is prepared for the revelation, but is soon to be shocked by the appearance of the 'vulture' ('ayit) for the 'vulture' here becomes a symbol of his people's tragic fate: 'it is an eternal witness to the covenant between the pieces'.[158] The 'vulture' is taken from the Biblical source (Gen. 15:11), but only in this poem is it endowed with particular significance.[159] The people of Israel will not be in the land by themselves, the 'ayit will be there with them. The 'ayit and God are together, the positive element cannot be accepted without the negative.[160] Abram is subdued by the news. The last stanza echoes the first, but is contrasted by the weight of depression. Abram is not standing expectant,[161] but 'kneels and covers his face'.[162]

The same mood governs the next poem 'For the sun had set', where Jacob is the subject ,and he receives news of his people's chosenness. He is of course an unwilling recipient. He knows of God's love—but His love is a scaffold.[163] Jacob wants to be 'one strand amongst many, unwillingly spun.'[164] He wants to lead a simple life like anyone else, to eat 'bread and salt'; he does not want the 'wine with its sharp scent'. The darkness becomes a symbol of aweful Destiny, since God only speaks

157. *Ibid.*, p. 14.
158. *Ibid.*
159. Altermann also has recourse to the symbol of 'ayit in his *Simhat 'aniyyim* (4th ed., *Maḥbaroth le sifrut*, Tel-Aviv, 1953), p. 19, where the dead lover hovers round his beloved like a 'vulture' . . . The 'vulture' also appears in Avigdor Hameiri's poem on Abraham, see *Anthology of Hameiri's poetry, op. cit.*, p. 1.

But in neither of these poems is the word so significant, possessing the meaning of tragic fate.
160. *Bema'aleh 'aqrabbim*, p. 15.
161. *Ibid.*, in the first stanza, 'On the earth of vision stood Abram upright, impatiently expectant.'
162. *Ibid.* In the last stanza.
163. *Ibid.*, p. 16. 'I want to be dragged no further against my will to the scaffold of your love.'
164. *Ibid.*, p. 17.

to him in the dark.[165] At first, we read 'he has fenced me round with darkness', and then later, when apparently God wants to speak to him again, 'everything round me is dark'. But Jacob does not want to hear the message—'Let there be light, raise up your sun, O God. I want to come no more, I do not want to hear.'[166]

The second Jacob poem, 'And Jacob awoke', presents the gay, carefree life that Jacob aspired to—'A song for the heart, a sight for the eye, stones of rest, a crust in hunger, and in thirst a jug of water, vistas for longings, the shelter of a tent in storm.'[167] But this was not to be because 'the large, demanding eye of God has set its ambush for me'.[168] Thus, the landscape is no longer 'a nest of happiness', it has become 'a gate to heaven' —the reference is to Jacob's dream—(Gen. 28:12) where 'a ladder was erected on the ground, and its top reached out heavenwards'. He can no longer be happy with his human lot, he must aspire to the supernatural. The 'terrible one' tells him— 'Cease to grovel in the earth! Rise, ascend to the stars!'[169] Now Jacob will receive no more simple comfort—'No more will rocky couches be tender to my back',[170] because 'I go out from here, prisoner of subjugating Destiny, and bound by the word of God.'[171]

Jonah in 'Jonah flees from his God', also tries to escape his 'commanding Destiny'. Here Lamdan bases himself on the Biblical book, where Jonah does indeed attempt to avoid fulfilling God's command (Jonah 1:3) to prophesy to Nineveh. The moral of the Biblical book seems to be that people, or at least the prophets, cannot escape their duty to God. Lamdan adapts this belief to a modern setting, where God has become 'Fate' (goral). 'There is but one way by which a man is brought to his Fate, and there are seventy-seven by which he may flee, though not escape.'[172] Jonah had also believed that he could

165. Lamdan takes this idea from the Midrash on the Biblical passage. See p. 118 f.
166. Bema'aleh 'aqrabbim, p. 18.
167. Ibid., p. 21.

168. Ibid., p. 20.
169. Ibid.
170. Ibid., p. 22.
171. Ibid.
172. Ibid., p. 23.

lead a simple life, be 'just a person, with no yoke, with no double world or life'.[173] The double life is the duty he owes both to man and God, to be 'between God and man, between earth and Heaven, and a constant target for the arrows of both together'.[174] He also wants 'a headstone', symbol of the care-free, happy life, as was, so thinks the poet, Jacob's 'head-stone' (Gen. 28:11). But he must remain 'the servant of God and His truth, bound to the train of His splendour, who is dragged in the dust of the earth'.[175] Note the ironic interplay here of 'train of his splendour' and 'dust of the earth', the sublime juxtaposed with the common and suffering.

The message of these four poems is identical, that the modern Jew has a special covenant with God or 'Fate' that involves suffering, but that cannot be escaped. In the last poem of the series, the subject is the Midrashic Honi, and the theme is the forgotten and unrecognised pioneer, who 'wanders around as if in a foreign country' although he was 'faithful to it [the country] as a dog to its master'. But now 'you [Honi] keep to the sides, go by the way like a thief, careful of step, who fears to be seen and heard'.[176] Honi's prayer[177] was successful but the beneficiaries are ungrateful—'The distant heavens accepted your prayer. But the close earth killed every echo of it.'[178] Honi seeks grace to die.[179]

In his next series, 'A Twofold Image', Lamdan presents the conflict he feels between the private and public worlds, be-tween 'the landscape of childhood' and the 'yoke' and 'debt' that the world places upon him. It is this public image that Lamdan has adopted, and his poet's child world is for him his *alter ego*—so the first poem of the series bears the title 'Ballad of my other self'. He yearns for this other world, 'would sail to the invisible from the shore of solutions',[180] the solutions being

173. *Ibid.*

174. *Ibid.*, p. 24.

175. *Ibid.*, p. 26.

176. *Ibid.*, p. 27.

177. Based on the legend of Honi,

the circle-maker. See Chapter 4, section 'The Pioneer'.

178. *Bema'aleh 'aqrabbim*, p. 29.

179. The phrase is taken directly from the Midrash.

180. *Bema'aleh 'aqrabbim*, p. 33.

political and practical. This other world is 'a hidden nowhere,
a nameless legend', like 'a distant dream, both good and bad',[181]
and it entices—'it knocks on my door'. But 'it is too late', the
miracle won't occur again 'because I have murdered my love'.
Temptation must not be yielded to, because 'there is a duty
for which a man will do himself ill even for that which he so
loves'.[182]

In the following poem, 'The Poet', the temptation is imaged
by children playing outside. They bring light—'and in the
thick stillness, a single brightness was opened'. The outside
'extends around him, and the world is placed bound like
a question-mark'.[183] He 'stretches out his hand as if to gather
in from the vistas and bring back all that he had sent away'.[184]
He is here undecided—'he does not know himself'. In the
poem 'The absent one' we see that he is afraid of himself
and breaks his mirror. He has been 'like a stranger' in his own
eyes. He now no longer knows his own identity. When they
ask 'Who is that?' his thoughts are 'perhaps it is I, or he, or
you'. And he continues his flight from himself in his next
poem, 'On the threshold'. But he wants to return, 'he wants to
see his heart, to take it into his hands, and to feel that from now
it is entirely with him'.[185] He returns to himself and knocks on
the door, but does not dare to enter. He remains on the
threshold.[186] So he comes back in the last poem of the series,
'Ballad of an anonymous stumbler', after having been away 'to
find again the landscape of childhood' 'in which there was
nothing certain and concrete, nothing of the presence and
reality of the present'.[187] He could not get there because 'the
paths thither were spoiled, and there was no exit or entrance'.[188]
We see now that this world had been destroyed—'From the
tears of terror-stricken children, its destruction was reflected.'[189]

181. *Ibid.*, pp. 33, 34
182. *Ibid.*, p. 35.
183. *Ibid.*, p. 36.
184. *Ibid.*, p. 37.
185. *Ibid.*, p. 40.

186. *Ibid.* 'So he sank on the
      threshold of himself', p. 41.
187. *Ibid.*, p. 42.
188. *Ibid.*
189. *Ibid.*, p. 43.

The children have lost their faith. Now he must 'mourn' the death of a legend'.[190]

The third series of poems concerns his return visit to the Ukraine after twelve years, and the decline of Jewish civilisation that he witnessed. It is a 'sad homeland'. Its 'destruction is exposed beyond hiding or cover'.[191] From the depression he witnesses, from Fate—the only escape is poetry.[192] He witnesses 'bald courtyards', 'windows stopped with rags and paper', 'a door creaking on its hinge' (page 58). His conclusion is that 'the whole world is a scaffold for us'.[193] The 'House of Hillel' is a symbol of the generous, happy world, and the 'House of Shammai' its opposite.[194] As a child, he sympathised with Hillel but now that he is older, and has seen what the world has in store, he tends to Shammai's school of thought. At his departure, he asserts that 'all fruit and every nest hang trembling over nothing.'[195]

His fourth series of poems, 'Amongst my People', continues the same mournful tone—'Where the hand touches, it draws back in pain, where the foot treads, it is pierced to the bone.'[196] He says that if it were not for Gamzu's[197] philosophy, he would kill himself—he 'would get a rope and find a hook for it'.[198] For 'there is nothing new on our path, there is no change, beneath the heaven of one Fate is everything drawn onward'.[199] Man suffers anyway, but the Jew suffers particularly—'You have piled on the burden of a family sorrow . . . [and we are] in your world like a two-humped camel.'[200]

190. *Ibid.*, p. 44.
191. *Ibid.*, p. 47.
192. *Ibid.*, p. 53.
193. *Ibid.*, p. 60; compare Bialik's poem . . . *Al hasheḥitah, op. cit.*, p. 153.
194. Hillel and Shammai were two Tannaists (rabbis living at the time of the Mishnah) and were the founders of two schools of thought with relation to Jewish law. On the whole, Hillel was lenient, and Shammai strict.
195. *Bema'aleh 'aqrabbim*, p. 87.
196. *Ibid.*, p. 99.
197. Known as 'Gamzu' because, faced with disaster, he would always say: *Gam zu letovah*, 'This is also for the best.'
198. *Bema'aleh 'aqrabbim*, p. 101.
199. *Ibid.*, p. 120.
200. *Ibid.*, p. 123.

The fifth series, 'From Here Onwards', begins with a hymn to the lyric which is praised for acting as a refuge to suffering man.[201] But beyond that, sorrow is still dominant: 'Sodden sorrow stuck her palm into me from behind.'[202] The poet persists, though, in seeking the poetic past—'I want to go far and seek the hind of legend.'[203] He persists in believing that he will one day arrive at 'the nest of dreams and loving-kindness'.[204] He believes that 'not all the dreams are finished' (page 169). Surely it is the truth of the legend that once 'stirred the distant flute of childhood' (page 185). It is 'the flute of childhood' that is our last hope in disappointment: 'I hear your note from camps of weeping.'[205]

In the sixth series here, 'From the Book of Days', a collection of poems written between 1938 and 1943, Lamdan reaches his most desperate note so far. But on a different theme, his concern is, as in the poem 'Honi', that future generations will not appreciate what his own pioneering generation has done, that they 'stripped themselves of their last coat to make a banner calling to the future from an angry landscape'.[206] This is more the tone of *Masada* especially recalled by his use of the word 'last'. But the most important thing about this stanza is the paradox asserted in the first two lines, that they believed without a God.[207] This faith with no God is also characteristic of Bialik.[208] Lamdan here reverts to his *Masada* theme, to his

201. See above, Chapter 6, Sections 'Two faces of the poet', and 'The function of poetry and its limitations', also Note 93. Compare also S. Shalom's similar treatment of this longing at the beginning of *Panim el Panim*, where the poet also goes to seek his youth which has the purity of legend, p. 16.

202. *Bema'aleh 'aqrabbim*, p. 137.

203. *Ibid.*, p. 145.

204. *Ibid.*, p. 162.

205. *Ibid.*, p. 186.

206. *Ibid.*, p. 196.

207. *Ibid.* About the generation with no God in the skies that believed with desperation and furious self deprivation.

208. See Kurzweil: *Bialik ve-Tschernichowsky* (Shocken, 1961), p. 26, on the poem 'City of Slaughter'. 'This is the gospel of despair, the prophecy of nihilism, a message with no sender, the duty of modern man who is called in his duty without faith in the source of duty.'

desperate Zionists, who returned to their ancient land without believing that it was given to them by a Supernatural Power in the first place. As the scene darkens, and the poet becomes more aware of what is happening in the world, particularly to his people, he prays for revenge, identifying himself unconsciously with the revengeful protagonist in *Masada*. He does not pray that his enemies should die, however, because death is too mild (page 228), but that they should live—'Give them life, God of vengeance and retribution through which they should receive double what they have wrought to Israel.'[209] Lamdan concludes with a blessing to his people. He can no longer talk of 'debts' or 'accounts', but only of love[210]

* * *

The image always plays a central part in determining the mood of Lamdan's poetry. As the poet deals with key themes, so these key themes are indicated by the appropriate and illuminating word—the image. Lamdan has defined for himself a particular area of poetry, and has treated it uniquely through the medium of images. These images, within the limited purview of the poet's range of interest, are the abiding hallmark of Lamdan's poetry, and guarantee him an important place in modern Hebrew letters. Isaac Lamdan is the poet of the tragic and heroic Jewish Fate in the arena of world history.

209. *Bemaʻaleh ʻaqrabbim*, p. 228.
210. P. 232. 'In the face of these ravages can they [the nations] put before you accounts of credit and debit? No accounts, O my people. Now I feel nothing for you, but love, only love.' See Chapter 6, 'The Holocaust'.

POEMS IN TRANSLATION

MASADA

A Fugitive

1. *I was told*

One Autumn night, on a restless couch far from our ravaged home, my mother died:

In her eyes, a last tear glistened as she whispered me a dying blessing. Before I went to campaigns on distant, foreign fields, with my army kit pressing on my shoulder . . .

On Ukrainian paths, dotted with graves, and swollen with pain,
My sad-eyed, pure-hearted brother fell dead, to be buried in a heathen grave.
Only father remained fast to the doorpost wallowing in the ashes of destruction,
And over the profaned name of God,[1] he tearfully murmured a prayer.
Whilst I, still fastening my crumbling soul with the last girders of courage,
Fled, at midnight to the exile ship, to ascend to Masada.

I was told

The final banner of rebellion has been unfurled there, and demands from Heaven and Earth, God and Man: 'Payments'.

Stubborn nails grind the gospel of comfort on tablets of rock;
Against the hostile Fate of generations, an antagonistic breast is bared with a roar:
'Enough! You or I! Here will the battle decide the final judgement!'

I was told:

There are prophets wandering amongst the walls of Masada, prophesying redemption,

1. *Mezuzah*—doorpost. Parchment on which is inscribed Deuteronomy 6:4-9 and 11:13-21, fastened to Jewish doorposts in obedience to the commands in those passages.

And in the tents of the tabernacle, amongst the ramparts, Levitical sects are singing *la menazeaḥ*.[2]

With tomorrow's echo answering *amen, selah*.[3]

There the young priests extend merciful arms from the top of the wall to the orphaned and depressed night sky.

And pray for the restoration of its impaired moon . . .

I was told:

The Divine Presence,[4] dropping atonements, has descended on the heads of the warriors,

And through the curtain of the future, the large eye of Dawn is watching and caring for Masada.

2. *The God of Vengeance*

A friend encountered me in my flight. He called to me in the darkness: Masada is a fiction. A new snare laid by Fate in its scorn for the last remnant;

Into our blood has the curse been poured, and it is oil to the wick of our existence, without which the wick will not burn, even in Masada. . . .

Where will you flee to now, when the shadow of dread is tied unto you as the head is tied to the shoulders, and sucks its darkness from you?

How can you leave behind you the tight fists of graves, that, in their fury, have congealed against the extended tongue, whirling about between the furthest horizons?

Who will avenge the blood of brothers and sisters, of fathers and sons, that has been imbibed like wine by the earth, and not spewed out by that whore?

There is no way, none, so roars even dumb and empty space.

---

2. Psalmic chapter heading, meaning, according to interpretation here accepted: 'To the victor'.

3. 'Selah' is a psalmic full stop, 'amen' implies consent.

4. 'Divine Presence' is a translation of the Hebrew *shekhinah*, the Rabbinic term for the 'presence of God'.

Continents, seas and heavens have conspired against the few of us, and all the gods and devils have signed. With our blood they have signed.

To one God should the eye of Israel be lifted to extermination: the God of vengeance.

Come friend, let us faithfully serve the One that will gather us in.

A heavy night has descended on the world—come, let us strangle the sun of the morrow whilst it is yet in the swaddling clothes of its twilight, that it be not appeased with fresh mornings!

The world has gone off course—let us pour confusion into its blood, that it reel and stagger like a drunkard, and never again find its course!

Let us enmesh the net of its path, until, lost and powerless, it falls wounded and weary, and aches like us, like us!

Here is spread out a red prayer-shawl—a new striped coat that the priests and prophets of the world have fashioned for the festival of its happiness, for the morrow.

Come, let us wrap ourselves in this red shawl, and secrete the knife of revenge beneath it.

> The shawl is broad and large, let us wrap ourselves and the
> world in it,
> Let us wrap it, embrace it with love, with love, and as we
> embrace it—
> Let us stick the knife into its stomach, swollen of over-
> indulgence in our flesh, that the embryo of its happiness
> drown in its blood, whilst still in the womb of space!

The God of vengeance—One is He who covers us with his wings, when our tired heads are bared of all shadow and protection.

> Come, let us set an altar for Him, and act as His priests in
> the Temple—
> This is the task of every lad in Judah amongst the last rem-
> nant!

So raise not your eyes to the lie that shines bright from afar, and misleads. Do not go! Masada is a falsehood!

3. *The Red Screen*

As I was fleeing, a second friend called to me: Halt, where goest thou, O fugitive?

A lie is Masada, invented by the despairing and confused who have no strength to hold the oars, and to row in the stormy night to the shores of the morning that await the ravaged boat of man.

What darkness? Night has fallen to cover the corpse of the old world.

What murkiness? The free knight of the morrow is pushing the spears of its lightning into the dragon of yesterday, shaking the earth with final, thunderous roars.

Oh, despairers. too weak to raise the cup of the world with a cry, with the merriment of redemptive battles, and with festive feasts—

Because our blood is full![5]

But if our blood is full, has it ceased to be a cup of sorrow that expects faithful hands to pour the healing draught into it?

And why should you weep for the slaughtered and for Jacob's flock that is much bereaved?

This last tribute let us pay to Molech, let us cover this border duty before we pass on, cross-armed, with an afflicted and sick world to the atoning kingdom of redemption. . . .

See how the red curtain is lowered on to the great stage of events to divide one campaign from another;

Be strong, friend, until the curtain be raised and the storm abate with the appearance of the last campaign that the actors of the future have prepared;

Then shall the sceptre of the new kingdom silence the crazed masses, and kneel with a victory cry on the threshold of its new world.

Come, friend, let us ascend to the platform behind the red curtain, and weave with all the weavers of the future a final campaign of redemption!

You have dreamy eyes, and a heart sensitive to human agony, so why do your eyes bear their dream, and your heart its faith

5. I.e. because we have suffered so.

to sow them on the fallowness of Masada, upon rocks of a ruined fortress?

Masada will not arise, will not stand amongst the storm of great battles,

And there will be no revival for the piteous camp of the hopeless there!

But when the red curtain is raised over the stage of great events even Masada will kneel at the sight of the last campaign, and break off its rusty armour to place it at the feet of the regnant morrow!

Then where will you raise your eyes, O fugitive? A lie is Masada!

4. *To the Last Redeemer*

A third friend whispered to me as I was fleeing (stumbling he knelt at the pathside):

Masada? You would go to Masada? It is the same to me whether you go, or fall here near me on the pathside.

There is but one Fate for those guided by the light of fantastic lies,

And for those who, like me, shut-eyed, with open ears, lie awaiting the footsteps of the end . . .

Where is the last redeemer? He is wandering in the dense forests of generations, and has delayed until now, until now . . .

Woe to the pathfinders in Israel, to those who seek Solutions and Conclusions—and know not that we were created to be only a riddle of delight for the world when the evil spirit alights on it out of boredom and lustful satiety!

And why should you still seek the key to the lock of our heavy lot when there has never been such a key, and when we have always been a sealed lock to all keys,

A target for the files and saws of lockbreakers, night murderers and thieves . . .

And why should you still seek mercy on all the crossroads? How could the world pity you?

What would the crazed tyrant do without the clowning beggar in its temples to dance and sing before it, to ring the bells of its dome, and display its entertaining magic?

Oh, call the last redeemer to snatch the toy from its hands, and its soul would swell without it through lack of interest and idleness!

See how it dons a new, red veil on its contorted and withered countenance—it would hold a new carnival in its temples to drive the desolation from its midst.

And why are you also, O daughter of Israel, lured to the terrible carnival, why do you accept the love of the enticing male, the bearer of the red veil, kneel at his feet, saying: 'Lie with me tonight, my red prince, and I shall be a faithful wife to you forever at morning' . . .

Do you not know whose face is hiding beneath the veil? It is your afflictor of yore! Do you not recognise him?

He will take you to his bed at night, whilst his heart is brimming with red wine, but in the morning, not as a faithful wife, not even as a mistress, but as a despised and afflicted maidservant shall he throw you out of his court, and incite the camp of his ravenous dogs against you . . .

Where is the last redeemer? Ah, why do his footsteps delay still?

Why do the false prophets still stand on the high places, and prophesy redemption, redemption, redemption, and still call to go to go, to go?

Cast down the frauds from their platform, and stop up their mouths!

As there is but one sun in the firmament, so there is but one Fate for Israel, a fixed planet amongst the heavenly bodies whose course cannot be altered!

Masada? Woe to those who believe that the planets will change their course!

It is the same to me whether you ascend,[6] or fall by me on the pathside.

There is one lot for both of us. Come, friend, and lie here by my side, and let us await together the footsteps of the end.

Perhaps it will come quickly, since it has delayed up till now, until now . . .

6. I.e. emigrate to Israel. The noun is *aliya* in Hebrew—ascension.

5. *On the Way*

The darkness of my way was lit up: the habitations of Israel
burned—

The hand of Fate had kindled a great red *havdalah!*⁷ to divide
Israel from the nations in the termination of worlds.

Cries rose to the heights, and the mocking tongues of the pyre
were stretched towards them in answer . . .

A choir of throats emitted a roar: 'O save.' And tens of thousands
of bow-knives laid on the violins of necks answered with a melody.

(Go out, go out, show yourself, O conductor of the bloody sym-
phony! The poets of the morrow will sing you odes, and the
historians of the world will bind your head with bay leaves and
wreathes of victory and redemption!)

They have blessed the sacrifice: 'Here is the red shawl, here
is the new coat of many colours—wear it well, wear it well, O
world!'

A command has been given: Lower, lower the red curtain before
the great hour comes, before the last campaign.

Revels, revels, revels—the red mask has gone to meet the carnival
of a night of horrors (a nightmare carnival)—'before morning
comes, before morning redeems', says the man donning the red
veil.

*   *   *

Great was the confusion in the markets of redemption. All their
merchandise was brought out for sale.

And the buyers flowed in camps, from the adulterous Shehem ben
Hamor to the least of thieves. . . . Buy, buy trinkets cheaply, jewels
—flags of redemption!

Take, buy, for beauty, for grace, as a treasure! (Yea, O my God:
'For grace, as a special treasure!')

And as for you, Judas Iscariot, where are you?

Why should you become like one of these small traders that deal
in Messiahs, flags and kingdoms?

7. The traditional prayer recited on the termination of the Sabbath.

Ascend and sell the top of the world for thirty prutah[8] (not shekel!) to Azazel![9]

And throw the thirty prutah to the heavens in return for their favour and goodwill towards us from then till now!

And afterwards, with the last roar of chaos, proclaim the end of the sale, and the riot of the markets!

★　　　★　　　★

They proclaimed 'redemption!' They cried 'deprivation!' 'Orgies,' they laughed. They wept 'deliverance!'

The *havdalah* was burning, and they chanted the morning service: 'Rise, rejuvenate thyself . . .'

May your crazy spirit be blasted, old, withered world. Why do you still check your preying nails by the light of the *havdalah*?[10]

Oh, suffering, distracted man, ache, ache eternally without mercy of God, for you have despised my agony!

★　　　★　　　★

Great was the tumult in the markets of the redemption.

One friend joined the tumult, wrapped in the red shawl, with a knife buried beneath, in the service of the God of vengeance . . .

(Woe to me, O woe, for I shall surely bless Him! . . .)

A second justified the sacrificial judgement, and behind the red screen wove the dream of redemption, awaiting the wonders of the last campaign . . .

(Woe to me, that I must bless Him, and curse Him! . . .)

A third was taken by the roadside, with closed eyes. Only his ears were open awaiting the beats of the end—the final, the only redeemer . . .

(Woe to me that I can neither bless Him nor curse Him! . . .)

Whilst I, at midnight, amongst the tumult of the markets, still

8. The smallest coin.
9. The Biblical word for damnation, though perhaps the Biblical concept is more concrete than the modern.

10. It is customary during the *havdalah* prayer for the person reciting the prayer to hold his nails up to the light of a candle that is lit for the purpose.

binding my disintegrating soul with last girders of courage, fled to the exile boat, and ascended to Masada.

6. *At the Entrance*

Open thy gates, O Masada, and let me, the fugitive, enter!

At thy feet, I place my disintegrating soul—place it on the anvil of thy rocks and beat it out, shape it and beat it out anew!

For where more can I take this my weary, stumbling body when all the shells of rest have fallen from it?

The graces of the world have disappeared!

The circle of the earth has become a gallows for my neck, and its expanse is the palm of the hangman that, strangling, closes on me with the fingers of its ways.

Here I am, all of me, before you, a fugitive:

In my bosom, swollen with sicknesses, the God of Israel has inserted a severed head; its blood has touched mine . . .

On my image have the sharp nails of disbelief engraved convulsion and a tattoo of enmity towards everyone, everyone, everyone . . .

In my brain are flags of blood unfurled for the storm of terror that blows from the four winds of heaven, and the scorching tongues of the *auto-da-fe* lick my wounds . . .

And over everything: chaos, chaos, chaos—no people, no land, no God, and no man.

Well do I know that a ready refuge is this chaos for a fugitive like me.

Like a weary moth, deprived of day and sunlight, am I drawn to its cold, consuming flame—

Deliver! I shall close my eyes that they be not drawn to this terrible refuge, and that they be not attracted to its flame.—I pin myself entirely to the bars of your gates:

Open them, Masada, and I, the fugitive, shall come!

To the Wall

1. *From the Gallows*

Who ascends here, and steps in the silence?

One who fell, one who escaped execution. My eyes had already started from their sockets, my tongue was already extended with a curse to everything—when I slipped out.

Now shall I bury my head in the bosom of Masada, and ask: what shall I do with the end of the rope that still pinches at my neck? . . .

2. *A Tender Sacrifice*

And who are you who ascend here joyously with your head full of dew spots?

They are not dew spots but tears that good parents shed on the head of their only child, when he went away.

Mother sobbed, and father wept: Where are you going whilst you are yet tender, oh, so tender?

But I hardened my heart: What of it? A tender offering would be welcomed!

So I went. And so joyously do I ascend, and though my head be full of tears, I am happy and satisfied.

I know that my parents weep bitterly there into their trembling palms, and I love them, love them so . . .

But the legend of Masada is so beautiful, and the wondrous wall attracts so.

If only my father and mother knew the legend they would not weep so for their only child, who has gone towards it! . . .

3. *A Remnant*

And who are you, ascending with heavy dumb steps?

A remnant. I alone was left on the day of a great slaughter without father or mother, brothers or sisters.

An empty barrel in a courtyard corner pitied me, and I was in it as a baby in the womb of a trembling mother—and was left.

For days on end, I wept and pleaded in the bosom of Fate: It is through your finger that I have remained—answer me then why?

Is it to bear the disgrace of the world and of humanity, and to pillory it for generations—

Leave me alone! The world will not be abashed by this disgrace, it is accounted a virtue in it, and an honour!

And if you have left me to find atonement—answer me, O Fate, where is it?

And it happened that whilst I was so pleading, a secret voice answering me; 'In Masada!'

I hearkened to the voice, and came.

Dumbly do my steps lead me to the wall, dumbly as all steps in which fear of the future is moulded . . .

High, high is the wall of Masada, therefore does the ravine that crouches at its feet go deep . . .

And should this voice have cheated me—then would I cast myself from the heights of the wall into the ravine that there be no record of the remnant, and nothing remain!

4. *The Hands of Israel*

And who are you, ascending with outspread hands?

They are not my hands! They are the hands of Israel, clutching everything, though everything slips from their grasp.

Like empty pails are they suspended over the full wells of the world . . .

Oh, these hands, the first to raise the flags of every gospel, and the last to receive comfort—

At last are they raised towards Masada to embrace!

I implore you to grasp the wall of Masada, to grasp it unceasingly. If not, may these hands from which everything drops be cut off!

5. *The Caravan of First-Fruits*

With song and marching drums, loaded with all good things, do we ascend to the wall.

We bring handfuls of hearts, and the gold of dreams. In full jugs of youth, do we carry joyful blood and first clusters of life in baskets of love,

Everything is an offering for the battle, and a dedication to Masada!

Open, O wall, the gates of your empty stores, and let the purity of our lives be stocked in them for the years of battle.

For still are the fields of Masada desolate and smitten by drought, and who knows how long the battle will last, and how long more the days of siege will continue?

Until the years of plenty come, until the rains fall in their season, and dew drips nightly on the open earth;

Until the sickle of victory reap the blessing of the fields in safety— receive the first-fruits of our lives, provision for thy hungry fighters, and the springs of our youth for thy thirsty ones! [Addressed to Masada—L.I.Y.]

6. *The Caravan of the Needy*

We, needy and barefoot, ascend to the wall.

On all the poles fixed in the crossroads, we have hung our cloaks as flags, announcing freedom.

In festive processions, far over there, are the flags waved, and we, naked, are forsaken on the crossroads . . .

In forests of confusion and darkness the gold of our dreams has been despoiled, and our despoilers offer it for the price of a drink in every public house.

So our hands are empty, and we come without gift-offering.

But despise not, Masada, the procession of the needy! We still have one treasure: the defiance that follows despair—the jewel of all hopeless, and friend of the oppressed:

If this is still ours, and we are still yours, O Masada,—why should we be in dread of battle, and how could we be treacherous?

When everything was taken from us, our love too was stolen, and its name vaunted on every brothel. How could we be sparing or sin without love? . . .

The anguish of hatred shrinks us into one clenched fist that is brought down in all its fury on the skull of our Fate,—

Let either the fist or the accursed skull be dashed to pieces!

7. *To the Sun*

Sun, sun, sun. And the earth is an open book of light: read every stone in it, every shrub, nothing is shut up in it, nothing is hidden from the light of the sun.

Woe to him who still hides a dark secret; the sun shall stick all the nails of its rays into him, will uproot his dark secret that, like a torn and plucked feather, it be swept into the light!

For the roar of light is raised round about, and it stirs everything dark from its depths.

Even mountains roar upwards: 'Split us, yea split us, O sun, and expose our dark interior!'

And as for me here, what is to become of me?

In my blood do distant winter nights still howl, and

the complaining psalmic melody of my father murmurs in it;

The sinking of Sabbath rest brings tears to my eyes, and coals of destruction glimmer in them;

On my shoulders is the black cloak of sorrow in which I went out to seek the last remaining stars on orphan nights.

Like a lost desert wolf do I send a lonely howl into the night: hunger, hunger, hunger!

And who here in Masada will take in a forlorn wolf who has fled from Winter nights and deserts to a sun that is still strange to him, so strange?

Gather me in, O sun, and place your yoke on my neck that is still probing the night with a howl of hunger!

Night Bonfires

1. *There are Nights*

There are nights in Masada that crouch heavy-breathed from too much blood, from surplus power flowing in their veins.

Then the earth has a tremor and live, flaming breath at the touch of soles of feet that walk on it.

The heavens are so near, high, but also so near. Every raised head touches them, every lifted hand knocks them . . .

As scattered silver crowns, the rocks round glow white; soon a secret hand will gather them in one by one, and place them here on every head . . .

For many are the princes that have come from afar, from wandering and straying, as ill-dressed, charity-seeking paupers: now the nights of the fatherland will anoint them once more, will restore them to their original splendour.

These nights, there are no weary in the camp. No one stumbles thirsty for rest when the air infuses strength, pouring joy into the limbs.

A wondrous roar—extra power—goes from the chest to the throat; there is a scorching fire in the arms, and a flame of strength in the soles of the feet.

At such a time are night bonfires raised on to the wall, and round them the children of Masada go out with flaming dances.

2. From Bonfires to Bonfires

Bonfires, like eternal avenues, are planted on all of Israel's paths, bonfires—the marks of every path that ascends to Masada . . .

From bonfires did our orphan-cry 'Hear O Israel' go out, and was hung as a shaming earring on the uncircumcised of the world . . .

From bonfires did the script of our burnt scrolls fly up: at the light of bonfires, let us now gather up the letters that have flown away . . .

On nights of terror did bonfires illuminate the dream of Masada from afar; by bonfires let us now illuminate its realisation, near at hand . . .

Bonfires on Masada's wall are great lamps for the souls of the habitations of Israel raised in bonfires.

Into bonfires did our fathers jump with deathful joy to become an enigma; around bonfires now do children dance the dance of the solution.

3. *The Chain of Dances*

The chain is still not broken, the chain still continues, from father to child, from bonfire to bonfire, the chain still continues . . .

The chain is still not broken, the chain still continues, from nights of Simḥat Torah[11] to nights of Simḥat Masada; the chain still continues . . .

Thus danced our fathers; one hand on a neighbour's shoulder, the other holding a scroll of the Law—a people's burden is raised with love—thus danced our fathers . . .

So let us dance; one hand gripping the circle, the second clutching the load of a generation, a great, heavy book of sorrow—so let us dance . . .

When our fathers danced, they closed their eyes firmly, and wells of joy were opened. Their feet were light, so light, and their eyes closed when they danced . . .

Then did our ancestors know that they were dancing on the abyss; that if they were to open their eyes, wells of joy would be stopped up, the chain would crumble into the deep. Our ancestors knew then . . .

Thus let us dance too, with our eyes closed. Thus shall we continue the chain with closed eyes, lest it be snapped and disintegrate. Thus let us dance too . . .

Thus let us continue the chain; the chain is still not snapped. Where does it lead, whither ascend? Onward, onward, onward, onward. Let us not enquire, nor let us ask. Thus let us continue the chain! . . .

4. *Enthusiasm*

A dance was struck up on Masada in spite of everything! East, West, North, South in the dance.

The Masada-dance is sparked, and burns—clear the way, Fate of generations, be wary!

11. A religious festival in the Jewish calendar, when the conclusion of the yearly cycle of readings from the Pentateuch is celebrated. The two words *simḥat torah* mean literally 'the joy of the Law [Torah]'.

The fire of our feet ignites stones, burns them. Where there are rocks, may they be diverted and ground! ....

You are low, O heavens, for our heads. Come down, lie flat like carpets here at our feet!

Surely we have grown big and tall! When the dance is sparked off—with our heads do we smite the firmament as with a drum!

Smiting, smiting our heads against the skies—thunder is emitted! Thus the dance of Masada is heard in the ears of the world!

A chant for the dance of the solution: 'Let the "no" to Fate dare!' Mountains, mountains, bow your heads, and answer 'Amen!'

Yesterdays are smitten at our feet, they bend the knee. Oh to-morrows, prepare a gift, build up the way!

Make the suns drums, and the stars cymbals! Thus is the victory of Masada foretold beneath the heavens!

Bend, O world, your bald head to our redeeming dance. God with us in the circle will sing: 'Israel!'[12]

5. Encouragement

Who is kneeling? Who has fallen? A tired brother? Why do you groan, child of Masada? What ails you? Are you in pain?

Arise! Who is twisting there at your feet? The limping yesterday? No matter! Rise, break its neck, cast it to the bonfires, and return a free, lightfooted man to swing into the dances!

Again stumbling feet are carried—no matter! Weep not for fractured[13] yesterdays; we have the morrow!

Bolster the leg, strengthen the knee, round and round increasingly!

No matter! Does a crying mouth open the heart? Close your sobbing mouth! No regrets for what is passed, no regrets at all!

Does enticing sorrow whisper supplication? Does persuasive sorrow depress the head? No matter! Our chain shall bind it well, and choke it, that it be tempest tossed in our dance!

12. The literal meaning of 'Israel' is possibly 'he who fights with God', vid. Gen. 32:29, for the origin of the name according to the Biblical tradition. This is the interpretation of the word that the poet accepts here.

13. Lit. 'broken of neck'.

Days weep on our necks: 'Where shall we go? Where is our recompense?'

No matter! Draw, O days, without asking. If you have been presented as lacking all—Masada is the reward!

Bolster the leg, strengthen the knee, round and round increasingly!

Ascend, chain of the dance! Never again shall Masada fall! Does the leg stumble? Let us ascend! The son of Yair[14] shall again appear. He is not dead, not dead! . . .

If the age-old Fate derides: 'In vain!' we will pluck out Its inciting tongue! And in spite of itself, the derisive negation, defeated, shall nod its head: 'Indeed, indeed. Amen!'

Outside the Camp

1. Sober Awakening

Fate has anointed us kings over nights of wandering. So with the setting of the restful sun and the end of the kingdom, let us ignite a new vision of hunger amongst foreign, fertile fields until we are again called to reign on another night of confusion.

It is the last watch for the night of wanderings in the world. Soon the invisible scissor blades will yawn open, and then close with a mocking creak on the chain of our dance . . .

Ah, kings for a moment, I already see the hand lying in wait to remove the crowns of night from our heads,

I already hear from our depths the howls of the end, already do rudderless boats wait in all the seas—

And why does the camp still kneel to the God of the dry land, and still pour out all the juice of its life at His feet?

He will not gather us in! When our heads are bared of the nightly

14. Eliezer ben Yair was commander of the Zealots in Masada. See H. Graetz: *History of the Jews* (Philadelphia, 1891), Vol. 2, p. 316.

crowns—spread once more, O sailors of this anchorless people's boat, all the sails to the bosomless void, for thus were we commanded . . .

Ended is the night of wanderings. Peoples go out to their work for a long day of sunshine, whilst we, the desolate of the world, go our way;

To be raised anchorless over all the seven seas, awaiting the night of wandering to anoint us anew, and so *ad infinitum*. Thus says the sobered one.

2. *The Dislocated One Walks*

Who sent me here, and told me not to look back? Who ordered me: 'Go, dislocate yourself on Masada's wall as a sign and a symbol!'

But whatever the sign or the symbol, this weighty vision is poured into me like boiled lead:

No one expects a sign, and no one awaits a symbol in all the house of Israel!

For bread will the hungry cry out, and the smitten for small mercies; those that are satisfied and quiet request nothing, and those fired by the last vision ascend to Masada's wall—for dislocation.

Oh, let me deliver a bitter lament for all those dislocated here who are unable to weep for themselves, for there is no one amongst those that walk below who weeps for them.

There is no eye that waters when their corpses flow with drops of blood, and the people's hand does not extend a golden bottle for the drips . . .

Ah Masada, if I have not been dislocated too on the heights of your wall—I do walk about dislocated, and meander on your paths!

Only now do I know what is the sign and what the symbol, and for whom:

For all who abandon their lives on the wall I am a sign of 'no more exit' and a symbol of unchangeable Fate!

Thus says the dislocated walking around on your [Masada's] earth outside the camp.

3. *Messengers of Sorrow*

Why, O brother, have you gone out of the camp to sing sorrow-fully? Thus did our fathers sing at the third Sabbath meal,[15] griev-ingly.

Like them do even I sing in Masada, outside the camp. We, only we, know the great sorrow of the void, and in the depths we bear its coil that has been weaving the webs of Autumn on every bud-ding Spring field since we went . . .

Therefore were we like an old bigot, hated and sowing tremors when we walked about amongst child nations yearning for delight;

The heavy shadow that we cast on their play-mornings frightens them, for it is the shadow of the sorrow of the beginning and the end in history itself.

How could we now be like them playing their battle games on stormed dungheaps and in transient puddles of time?

There has been but one way for us from the beginning; to be the messengers of sorrow on the face of the earth, to expose it to the eyes of God and idols with a rebuke:

'See how you are all too poor and small to render it atonement!'

We come to the last 'third Sabbath meal', and on every full table, at every merry, festival banquet, we are the sorrowing violin in the joyous orchestra.

Never amongst the nations' cries has been swallowed our rebel-lious voice:

'Hear O Israel, the Lord is our God, the Lord is One!'

And with orphaned howl, on echo answers from the four winds: 'One insatiable grief!'

4. *In the Ḥamsin*[16]

On the ways outside the camp did the heat wave hit me.

From the flame of the East wind in the shadow of a bush on the way I came, though there is no shelter in the shade.

15. The third main meal of the Sabbath is the evening meal, which is an occasion for hymn singing round the table.

16. Hot desert wind.

I let my head droop hopelessly, and I know: here, even shade melts in the heatwave, here God also forgot to encamp.

On the head of one orphaned of kindness like me did the bush sink, and I heard its complaint: 'How great is my shame, O God, and how hard is the pain; for you have given me shade, but there is no shelter in it for the weary . . .'

The distant murmur of pine-forests caresses my ear.

The ark of youth floats on the cool waters of the *Ikvah*[17] amongst the shady reeds—leave me, visions of yesterday! Why have you set on me?

From your flourishing earth I have pulled out all my roots, and if a heatwave should shrivel them here—let them shrivel!

To you I shall no more call in distress, and I shall no more plant them in your earth!

Your sun on my back has been a yellow badge of shame for me, and I am come hither to shoulder the burden of that other sun, though it be a curse—

Bear it as well, bear it, O my aching back! I am too proud an Israelite to seek another refuge or deliverance!

*   *   *

How little divine grace caresses you, O Masada, you who are pushed between sea and desert; what will you do for your thirsty fighters, poor mother, when they bury their heads in your bosom, the last that they have . . .

I am suspended in dumb thirst around your neck, but I will not press you for I know your torments . . .

I know all . . . why do you still thrust out your breast to me, when it is parched?

*   *   *

And why did Hagar weep for Ishmael when he was thirsty, and water failed the flask?

She need not have wept—Ishmael grew up, and became a wild man learned in the desert.

17. Name of a river in the Ukraine.

His bow now threatens great expanses, and heavy with plans, he rocks about and sings out on the humps of his camels—

Where is Sarah who should be weeping for her son Isaac, whose total possessions are cast here on the dread of the wilderness?

Reveal yourself, oh, reveal yourself, angel of God, show the well, reveal the shade to the fugitives of trance-like fury, whom the heat-wave has greeted at their shelter, and whom the thirst has smitten!

Reveal yourself! There is no more any mother to raise her voice to weep and call to you!

It was not Hagar's son who was cast under the orphaned shrub in the desert of refuge.—

Here thirstily does Isaac faint—the seed of Abraham and Sarah!

When Bonfires Die

1. *There are Nights*

There are nights in Masada, heavy nights of evil portent.

Like black, heavy-winged birds they descend on to the wall to darken the ramparts of the battle, to close the way to the fighters that they might fall limp-handed, and no more remember the sun of the morrow . . .

A tear, heavy, large, and invisible, is suspended in the air; something moves and makes it tremble—that it falls down like a stone.

A sob restrains itself in the darkness. Touch the stone, and it cries out; a bush, and it weeps . . .

Bonfires that have been raised die down, and hands are so weary. No one adds a bough to the fire, and no one rises to light it.

The heroes of day—each man individual and alone, sink down wearily, and from black wells of night silently drink anguish.

Anguish, anguish—these nights, the children of Masada see the face of one terrible guerilla (whose name is not brought to the lips whilst hand draws the bow, whilst the eyes grope forward)—the face of open despair.

On nights such as these, the heavens of Masada are tensed like drumskins. Soon the hands of bitter-souled, pain-swollen fighters will be clenched into a single fist, which is banged again and again on the heavens—and their spirit will swell, the spirit of a silent, cheating drum!

But tired are the hands, fists are clenched in secret, and no one will raise them.

By the dying camp-fires, heroes stumble, kneel, and murmur their sorrow in the gloom:

2. *Weeping*

And I said that there was no Autumn in Masada, that the sun is constantly warm.

But even today, the scent of casting leaves still comes to my nostrils, and the tremor of Autumn passes through all my body . . .

Now heavy night has descended upon us as well, and I am cold, so cold!

The Autumn storm approaches; I feel its breath on my face, and I, as a lamb when it smells a storm, am pressed to the stones of the wall, and weep.

—I press my aching head with clenched fists, and weep.

—In my dream, a mother, old and forsaken, stoops over me and weeps.

—Nightly does a childless father appear to me, but he tells me nothing. I plead: 'Say something to me, Father', but he remains silent, and weeps, weeps, weeps . . .

—As an unwanted object does the empty cup of my youth roll at my feet. I have poured faithfully all its wine on the rocks of Masada.

Now, nothing remains for me, and I am distressed, so distressed that I weep in secret . . .

—As a fading flower do I now nightly lower my head, and realise how great are my affliction and torment when the bonfires die.

Like bonfires do we die out, and where does our light go? For whom and for what does it come alight? And who wanted it?

Ah, as God was absent from accepting the offering of our lives, and the sacrifice of youth and love when we raised the bonfires, so does He now not listen to our weepy plaints as the bonfires die.

Everyone weeps, everyone. Woe that I weep about everything, and about you all.—Listen, Masada weeps too. Do you hear?

Surely Masada weeps too, and how should she not? All of us, with thirsty arms, are suspended about her neck, and seek motherly pity, protection and deliverance—and she knows that she can give nothing, that she can deliver no more!

She cannot deliver that consumed by the curse of generations; she cannot deliver that which Fate has commanded not to deliver.

3. *And they Murmured*

Then why did we leave everything to ascend to the wall?

Even if I knew, it would be all the same to me. I am too tired! I can no longer stand on the wall facing the battle. I am too tired!

'Why? Why?' I won't even ask. I knew the way from the beginning: to the scaffold! But I went towards it because this has always been our way—

As for me, I have been cheated by my light, path-thirsty feet. Ah, these feet that love to wander, to be caressed by the grass on every path, to be covered with the dust of every byway, to go on and on without knowing where to and why—how did they lead me to Masada?

Now I cannot rise, my feet stumble, the desire to walk still caresses them; but they can walk no further—there is no way out of Masada . . .

I remember scenes of yesterday: on soft carpets of forgetfulness I rolled as a young foal rolls on grass beds in the Spring.

Why did I come to wallow in Masada nights in the ashes of dying bonfires?

I remember the nest of the motherland, upholstered with ancestral love. Day and night dropped balm on it. Gay mornings used to greet me when I rose, and laughing Springs would extend their arms to me.

So what was the bad dream that uprooted me, and dragged me here?

I remember the dream: holy martyrs, brothers and sisters, all of them gathered round me, the living, with a plea: 'Atone, O remnant, atone for our blood!'

I come to atone. Now I know that there is no atonement, none. Neither shall Masada atone. Where can I now take the plea of my martyrs?

I remember nothing, and do not want to remember. I only know that which is now with us.

On our heads rides the mocking scorn of the morrow; I know him—it is he who puts the veil of today on his face, and acts as our guide, that we follow him and believe him . . .

Masada—the end of all Israel's ways, dwells on the sides of chaos. He who is careful not to ascend thereto is delivered from the terror of chaos . . .

Woe to him who ascends to the top of the wall, and weary, stumbling, peeps over the side! . . .

I have peeped, and quaver at the sight—ah, Masada, what do you offer, what can you offer to these my arms that grapple with nothingness?

Masada, surrounded by mountains, dwells on mountains and amongst mountains.

One who looks to himself will walk on the straight, then will his foot be light, his step firm and unstumbling . . .

Here stand mountains round about, congealed and silent. They are eternal witnesses, ever intelligent, seeing everything always, hearing everything always, and knowing how vain the toil of the climbers has always been.

What and who am I but a tender, stumbling creature, that I should bend my head and incline a poor shoulder to everlasting suffering, that I should bolster my knees to aspire, prepare the battle, and dream of victory before these ever-intelligent, whose glance knows everything? . . .

Today, at evening time, the canvas of our tent reddened at the light of the setting sun, and were contorted with the wind like wounded wings.

I trembled at the sight, which was like a dreadful vision in my eyes: By the light of the decline, on the height of the wall, the last eagles of the people flutter with the rustle of wounded wings—

4. Bereavement

I said that my people sent me, and that I bore everything for my sender.

Now I know that there is no one who waits down below for the announcement of victory that is to come from here, from above.

No one has cast the burden of his Fate on the scales of battle that are suspended on the necks of a few despairing people.

No one would know if we were to fall here, as no one would know if we were to triumph . . .

—There is no one to substitute for the weary and stumbling amongst us; when one falls, there is none to take his place;

It is because they have forgotten us down below, it is because the people have scattered to their tents, and forgotten their fighters.

Is the people scattered? And when was it assembled to ascend? Who invented this story, that we believe?

Now with my very eyes do I see the mists of invention rise and evaporate.

Whither may I now raise my eyes that see this?

Do you know that many slip away into hidden places in the darkness, and secretly descend from the wall . . .

Whither? Whither? All ways outside of Masada are but one way for the Israelite, on all of them does he flash void eyes towards heaven and earth, and weary of wandering does he twist a thirsty tongue like a mad dog, and howl at all the suns and moons without knowing why . . .

—Again have they turned the boats of their voyaging towards all the coasts, and the admirals in all the seas look out and inspect;

Again are the flags of exile spread to the four winds, and the Satans of wandering mock our brothers the mariners, and divert them from the single course that ascends to Masada . . .

—Daily do I look out from the heights of the wall, and see boats coming to Masada beach. Are they not our brothers in the boats? Are they not coming to us?

—They are our brothers, they are coming to us. But oh woe, they are pedlars!

They have heard that there is a crisis in Masada, that there is a battle, and they have come here as camp followers to store the spoil of the battle . . .

All the left-overs of food that were lost when we ascended, all the pieces of golden shields that roll down from the breasts of those that fall on the wall—are gathered in their hands,

And for money in deceitful scales, they sell everything . . . but if the battle should prove too tough, they would hasten to their boats, and sail to lands of safety . . .

And with the subsidence of the storm of battle would they come again. Again would they set up their markets down below . . .

My God, my God, God of Masada, God of the few aspiring men who bear the last prey in the great famine of generations,—should we fight for them?

Is it to them that we want to bring the tidings of victory?

Last night, old Abtalion[18] appeared to me in a dream. I knelt at his feet and asked him: 'You seer of Masada who have raised us to battle, and trained our hands to bear the shield and draw the bow. You who have always dropped the comfort of your tasks on our wounds, saying:

The oppressed genius[19] of the people awaits the reward of your work. The bald, wandering head of the people longs for the crown of redemption, and you shall crown it!

'Look—pedlars, our flesh and blood, come to Masada, spread out in camps at the foot of the wall (they would not dream of aspiring to its peak for their fear of battle, and do not even desire victory), as previously they came only as camp followers, and it is all the same to them whom the camp belongs to, and where it goes.

Is it their head that longs for the crown of redemption? Did you not err, seer of Masada, in your vision?'

Abtalion listened closely, and whispered in answer:

'Do not ask, and do not enquire, my son. You redeem yourself, and say to your friends: let each man redeem himself in the battle, for you are the vanguard[19] of the people, and your head is its head . . .'

A tear glistened in his eyes, and great sorrow stood darkly on his glance, and I knew that it was as hard for him as for all of us here . . .

And in my dream I saw the wallower;[20] I asked him: 'What is the burden of your words to us?

You, Nazarite of Masada, who have strengthened with your sorrow and contempt, for your hatred was love, and your anger—comfort;

You, who taught us to lick our wounds in order to cure them and mercilessly bared every bereavement and our great failure[21] that we

18. A. D. Gordon. See Chapter 3, Section 'Gordon, Brenner and Trumpeldor'.

19. Heb. *shekhinah.*

20. J. H. Brenner, the novelist and publicist. See Chapter 3, Section

'Gordon, Brenner and Trumpeldor.'

21. Reference to Brenner's novel: 'Bereavement and Failure'— *Shekhol ve-khishalon.*

might see them and know them as one knows the face of an enemy in the battle . . .

You who have abandoned your blood as does every child of Masada who is on the wall—

See, our tongue is dry already from so much licking of wounds, and great is the bereavement, too great to be seen and known . . .

And what is the aftermath of vision? Have we really dreamed a true dream, and are the ashes of our dying bonfires its solution?'

He answered me not a word, but his dumb reply was: 'I know that I have not wallowed all my life for nothing. To wallow, to wallow!' . . .

—You spoke, O brothers, of pedlars coming and spreading out at the foot of the wall.

And I know how many, so many amongst us as well on the wall, were like pedlars and misers just like them,

That we should watch every ounce of life that gets lost as we ascend; every passing day we should count as coins at a time of distress, and quake at every hour that goes up in the fire of battle.

—Do not speak wildly, brother, of our brothers, children of Masada, if they ache and sin in their pain, which is great.

Great is their pain, and who can tell if it will not become greater, grow, and become more righteous than this distant charity for which they sin?

Daily I consider them, I look and see how strong is their affliction, and how great is their pain.

As tender, upright trees have they set up their tops here, but under the iron of Masada's heavens on the brass of her earth, they daily decline and wilt,

As Autumn leaves drop from their twigs day after day, and no one knows whither the winds lift them, if there is still sap in the roots, if they may bring another branch to flower . . .

If the dumb rocks knew how many hearts fall here as sapless fruit from live, wilting trees that no one picks up—

Then would they stretch out their arms to glean and gather them, and to bemoan them pitifully . . .

5. *The Supplicator*

By the light of dying bonfires, a shadow raised itself: one rose. Without speaking, he lay as all the camp murmured, and listened, only listened.

Comforting? Encouraging? There was no word in his mouth. To murmur sorrowfully with them all—the heart would not allow . . .

Great mercy is sought when the bonfires die; a tear yet unshed lies heavy, and crouches like a stone on the well of mercy.

It is not shed in despairing sorrow, it does not flow in vain comfort. Only the steady hand of prayer unrolls the load . . .

One kneels, crawls, goes out of the camp. He goes far, looks back: no one sees him. (Let no one see him whilst he sheds tears of prayer.)

He is pressed to the breast of one of the rocks, buries his face in it, and kneels in prayer.

6. *The Prayer*

As for those who escaped execution in a foreign land, and ascended to the wall—make firm their step, O God, that they totter not, that they fall not, for they still stumble and are weary!

For those whose suns in the seven heavens of the world are dark—order, O God, a kindness of the last Masada sun, for if this also darkens for them—where else would they go, or make for?

To those who have left the swaddling clothes of the flags of seventy nations, and come naked, give, O God, one cloak that will warm them, that will cover their tremor-stricken nakedness . . .

To those whose mothers' milk on their lips is not yet dry, and on whose cheeks still flutters the warm caress of a father's hand—relieve, O God, their orphanhood,

Be a father and guardian to them, sustain the strength of their tender arm to hold the heavy, pressing shield.

Soften the hard rocks of Masada at their heads when they weary! To those who sowed here with a tear the seed of a soul and of dreams—let them not be struck by the hail of sorrow, or dried up by sudden heatwaves.

Command, O God, many comforting rains, that dew should fructify them by night until they blossom into a harvest of compensation!

To those who from their wallowing ascended to the wall, the ashes of destruction on their head and sacks of mourning on their loins to derive comfort in the battle of Masada—bolster their spirit, O God, bolster their spirit when comfort delays!

To those whose people's Presence[22] has loaded the enigma of their Fate on their shoulder, to bring it to solutions, to lead it to the gates of the exit—

Grant power, God, grant courage to carry off and bear this heavy thing to the border that the sick Presence saw in Its last vision! . . .

So weary, so weary are the children of Masada, deep is the suffering of the few.

Those who have been tried in many battles, and have bared their breast to every arrow—have not yet been tried in one battle, this drawn-out and obstinate battle on but one piece of land—

Support their spirit, O God, and let not the flames of their rebellion that they have brought with them to the wall like holy Sabbath candles in the twilight of worlds, die out.

When night falls on the wall—do not let the bonfires flicker! From dark horizons, loneliness rises and threatens.

Doubt stalks amongst the ramparts, and whispers its message in every ear, and the ears of the weary are extended, and absorb the whisper . . .

Memories of yesterday enfeeble hands, and make upright heads that were always stretched towards them droop behind them with fatigue.

Vain dreams bring terror and confusion to the fighters, and the

22. Heb. *shekhinah*.

sickle of sorrow reaps amongst the campaigns, and many are those that fall.

Is it a little thing, God, that the battle should consume—why do these also impose so on Masada, and upon its warriors?

Why should all the stars be extinguished when the bonfire dies out on the wall except for one star—the mocking planet of Israel—

It is seven times brighter in the nightmarish light, sowing terror, fixing its rays in the breaches of the wall, and giving light outwards, to chaos, ah, again and again to chaos . . .

Till when will the wasted hand of the people grapple with blind fingers on the enclosures of salvation?

Oh God, look, it is stretched out, and on its palm is the last dream that it has drawn up from nights of wandering: 'MASADA!'

This dream and its interpretation have been entrusted in the hands of a few people on the wall.

If this time as well, O God, you have no mercy, and do not accept the dream with favour, and even now do not turn to the sacrifices of its interpreters—

God, guard Masada!

7. After the Prayer

The crags of rock absorb the last tears. The supplicator raises his head, and it is as if the nightly heavens are not as black as before the prayer—the heart is lightened. Security brightens his face:

Whilst prayer pours down—there is an ear that hears, and the eye of the supplicator does not cry into a sealed flask.

For who has bridged the abyss, and gathered all of us here, and stuck us, kindled with one flame like candles, into one lamp of light: Masada?

Wait, O heart, wait, there is a great, merciful Father. He has not called us from the depths unto chaos—Masada will not fail!

The supplicator stands erect. With a cry of 'To the victor', he steps confidently to the camp. And in the camp, over dying bonfires, stumbling heroes still bemoan their sorrow.

8. *Into the Abyss*

Did you see? Today, in the midst of battle, someone cast himself from the top of the wall into the abyss . . . too weary to bear, exhausted.

—Today? Tomorrow and the next day as well will many cast themselves from the wall. For no more as in ambush—but openly does despair stalk the camp, and many are its corpses amongst the corpses of battle.

—Erect of head does complaint stalk amongst us, there is no tent that it skips over. It carries away its prey from us, and casts it into into the abyss . . .

—And I know that no complaint crosses the lips of those that fall from the wall. They are silent, and as dumb people, they open not their mouths.

But deep, deep is their silence.

—Since death crouches on its enclosure . . . they are silent, and their silence is dreadful.

One of them was lying amongst us here; he buried his head in the ground, listened to our talk, listened, but said nothing . . .

Then I saw him slip away from the camp. This was but what this terrible silence had become, and he slipped away to drop its fruit into the abyss . . .

Ah, who knows if all of us here, one by one, will not slip away to the abyss . . .

9. *Revelation*

Look ye, something stands out there in the darkness. One erect, quick of step, approaches us from outside the camp.

I can also hear the sound of song: 'To the victor, to the victor' . . . It must be that the one walking is singing.

'To the victor' . . . how sweet is the voice and how comforting. Thus did Father sing Psalm tunes on Sabbath mornings, when I listened with frustrated longing . . .

No! Thus did they sing there when the rebellion was raised, and when flags were unfurled . . . thus sang I too when I ascended to the wall . . .

And thus we know not how to sing any more as we stumble here, as bonfires die out . . .

—At the sound of this song, my fainting heart moves, and my tired body quakes: rise up, rise up and out to battle . . . in spite of everything, again to battle . . .

And in spite of everything . . . yes, I know: That same unseen great man who told us to ascend will not let us descend.

He calls: 'Ascend, ascend!' But I am tired . . . have no strength . . . cannot . . . and yet, in spite of myself, answer: 'Amen!'

I am also true to that same calling answerer. I? I and not I, someone else in me, one bold, obstinate, blind, answers . . .

Look, suddenly illuminated, the dying bonfires move, and an unseen hand again binds crowns of flame to them.

And by their light, above the mountains, the mountains of Masada, a figure appears. And the figure has an afflicted smile, a comforting look, and the majesty of might . . .

Who watches so? Who smiles? Who is this wondrous person? It is Joseph Galilee![23]

Not Yet

1. A Havdalah (division)

With the termination of tranquillity, with the disappearance of the Sabbaths, we come now to Masada with havdalah cup in our hands, in which there is a remnant of our ancient wine, the last preserved.

23. Joseph of Gamela was a Galilean Zealot leader in the war against Rome. He was the last remaining leader. See Graetz: op. cit., pp. 289–90. Also Josephus: The Jewish War (London, 1959), pp.

214, 218. Here he is a symbol for the modern Zionist leader, Joseph Trumpeldor (1874–1920). See Chapter 3, Section 'Gordon, Brenner and Trumpeldor'.

Poison is mixed in this remnant, the poison of the mocking ways that we have passed through until our arrival at Masada.

Poison is mixed in our wine, it is like floating, rising oil that a seeing, discerning eye would recognise . . .

The *havdalah* cup is in our hands; let us learn to distinguish between the remnant of wine and the poison mixed therein, that we sip them not together!

The hand of Fate, happy to embarrass, crouches constantly behind us—let us not forget!

Thus did our ancestors when they made *havdalah* at the termination of rest; with a pure hand, they would shade their eyes, and inspect the cup:

Well could they examine the purity of the wine. Let us do likewise when we divide in Masada! Let us not forget! Let us smite foreheads on rocks, smiting until blood squirt out:

The blood of divorcement to forget, the blood of the covenant to remember!

2. *Towards the Future*

Bleakly do forests of people stand, storm-swept at the light of the sun, with a tremor of confusion and suspicion do they still tremble at every wind.

Songful rest does not peal out. There is no confidence in the quiet . . .

Distant spots of the horizon still anger the eye of a generation yearning for relaxing sleep:

Clouds rise bearing in their bosom a new tempest . . . the hand of Fate eager for play tires for a moment, and the wheel of events turns lazily:

But whose ear is attentive will hear dreadful tremors from the deep: the hand of Fate stretches, tenses its muscles, exercises its strength in hidden places to grasp the wheel again more firmly, and to swivel it at blinding pace, and with grinding madness . . .

As for you, Masada, how have you anticipated the day of fury that will come again? How have you strengthened the breaches in the wall for this new earth tremor?

ISAAC LAMDAN

VIEW OF MASADA

You have no fleet on the sea, and fearful fingers of cannons are not extended to the four winds from the lattices of your wall—

The eyes of visionaries and dreamers look through them, and seek eternal paths . . . on your purple heavens, no aeroplanes roar with the roar of birds of prey to cast your dread upon the enemies, and partisans do not crouch in the crevices of your rocks for passers-by.

As they are, shieldless are the breasts of your few fighters bared, and protruded to the danger.

We do not yet know if there is such a great and mighty hand of kindness that can direct your bold ones who step on the banks of the abyss into battle—

Oh, where is the Joshua of the generation who might order the orb of the world: 'Be still!' or the hand of Fate: 'Wait!' until Masada be firm, until victory come!

Appoint, Masada, guards on the wall, and scouts at the four corners, know every rising cloud there on the horizon;

See every smoking dust column on the distant paths, learn every sign, and listen for every distant tremor;

Then at the count bring all your supporters to be alert for the future!

3. *In the Beginning*

We have not yet seen the end of the vision, but our eyes are already opened for the revelation of a great dread:

'This is the frontier; from here onwards there are no more frontiers, and behind—to no single exit do all paths lead.'

We have finished the books of all the paths; experience, heavy with years, reads out in tears and blood, and we follow with a signature:

'Finished!' (Finished, finished and completed, though not 'finished and completed with praise to God, creator of the world.'[24] We have no praise for God, creator of the world)—

As from now, a new book of Genesis is opened on the wall.

24. Traditional subscription to Hebrew book in mediaeval times.

And as did our fathers on finishing the book of the Law [the Torah] before starting it again, let us roar with a new and last roar of the beginning![25]

Be strong, be strong, and we shall be strengthened!

25. The first book of the Pentateuch is known in Hebrew as *Bereshit*, which means 'in the beginning'.

BEMA'ALEH 'AQRABBIM

FOUR BIBLICAL POEMS

The Covenant between the Pieces

'And it came to pass that the sun set, and there was thick dark-ness, and behold an oven of smoky fire, and a torch of fire that passed between these cuts. On that day did the Lord cut with Abram a covenant' . . . (Genesis 15).

Bathed in the purple sunset, sparked by the light of the future,
Abram stands against the horizon—fire kisses fire.
It is not tranquillity but a secret terror and fateful expectation
That the evening silence casts. The sign flickers and rises.
Like a large, lone torch raised in a magic hand,
Abram, erect, impatiently watches on the hearth of vision.

Like a lifted screen was the enclosed horizon suddenly torn open,
And Abram's eye wandered through the engulfing cloud,
As to a magnet, vista upon vista is drawn to it,
And scene upon scene sink into its pupil.
'Not all at once, O my God! The sign is too strong, too heavy!
Wherever I look I see; I am alone between my pieces.'

'You are not alone, Abram! Look, three of us wander there.
Within the cloud: I, you and this—see how it encircles and
examines' . . .
'The vulture ['ayit]! Great God, why is it again between us?'
'It is a witness, an eternal witness to the covenant between the
pieces!'
'I have already driven it from here, and it flies tremblingly away!'
'Wherever the blood of the pieces is spilled—there will it return,
and again descend!'

'And on whose pieces, O my God, will it descend into the distant
future?'
'On your pieces again, Abram, always on your pieces, always!
Wherever your sacrifice is bound, to whatever you attach your
yearning—
There will the black of wing cast the shadow of terror.'
'O God of Abram, cutter of the covenant, are You my God?'
'I shall always be revealed to you at night and in thick darkness.'

'And so always unceasingly are the vulture and God to be
together?
The two of you constantly on one side, and I—on the other, alone?
Is it for this that You have called me, O God, to regard my future,
Is it with this that I will always accompany those that follow its
seasons?
Is this the covenant that You have cut with me? And is this all
of it?'
'This is the covenant, Abram! Rise, go out and bear its yoke!'

'And this land that You have given me for myself and my seed,
is it also
For You and for the vulture, pieces for the both of you?'
No answer. Voicelessly, the hearth of twilight smoulders.
Only the flapping wing scratches, scratches threateningly in the
silence—
And a shadow on the pieces . . . 'Enough, close the window of
scenes!
Show me nothing else, my God, I do not want to see!'

Bathed in the purple sunset sparked by the light of the morrow,
Abram bows against the horizon—fire licks fire.
It is not tranquillity but an everlasting terror and dread of the
future
That the evening silence pours. The sign of Fate is cut round
about.
Like a large, lone torch dropped from a magic hand,
Abram kneels on the hearth of vision, and covers his face.—

For the Sun had set

'And Jacob went out . . . and came upon a place and lodged there, for the sun had set.' For the sun had set—he extinguished the sun.* It teaches that the Holy-One-blessed-be-He made the orb of the sun set before its time, in order to speak in confidence to Jacob our patriarch. It is like the friend of the king who occasionally comes to him. The king would say: 'Extinguish the lights, put out the lamps, for I would speak with my friend in confidence.' (From the Midrash Agada.)

Where am I? Terrible is my lover, he has fenced me round with
                                                                darkness,
There is no heavenly light, there is not even an earthly lamp.
                                                                Woe!
This must mean that You once again have a loving message for
                                                                me,
And that it is too terrible to be heard by anyone but me,
And is too precious to be exposed to the light of the everyday sun,
So You once again heap loneliness and darkness upon me.

It must mean that You again call me into Your confidence,
Your very respected, exalted and divine confidence.
Therefore have You extinguished everything, to cover up my
                                                        exits and my entrances,
That is why Your hands spread out a nightmarish web at my feet,
And encircling night sets up the division of its fears
That we be not seen as we converse secretly—

See how the smallest of marks is blotted off my path!
No lamp flickers there; there is not the faintest spark from a
                                                                lattice.
You have torn me from the heart of the world, from all its many
                                                        various colours,

* Play on the likeness in sound of
  the two Hebrew expressions to
  give these two meanings.

That I should be for You by myself, and only with You, with
                                                    You!
Leave me alone! I want to be dragged no further against my will
To the scaffold of Your love, O my lover and seducer!

As one unique, appointed person am I called to You,
And as I come, I have no countenance and no sound spot.
I am like the worm of the earth, a trampling place for unclean
                                                    paws,
Rejected of men, despised of the world, and devastated of
                                                    appearance.
'Jacob, Jacob!'—No, I do not want to come to hear.
And to be, once more, despised by man, though loved by God.

If there is a matter You have for me, a precious and great, loving
                                                    matter—
Spread it out at my feet like a grassy, Spring carpet,
Raise it to my head like a flaming lily of dawn,
With all the sounds of the universe, let it play in all men's ears.
Fit in it Your stars by night, and Your sun—by day,
And let the butterflies of Your word play in it innocently!

But no—please none of Your love, and none of its torments!
None of Your love, if in all the fullness of its stores
There is no crumb of kindness or any glimmer of light,
If night constantly sows in it loneliness and bereavement,
If its touch—is the sting of a nettle, and strangulation its embrace.
And beneath the weight of faithfulness to it, I am brought very
                                                    low!

If this is love, then hate me, Friend of my soul!
Leave me to join the community of the small.
I would cross the paths of life unheedingly like them all,
Subject to the toil of the day, and free for the relaxation of the
                                                    night,
One strand amongst many, unwittingly spun
In the texture, both dark and bright, of man and the universe.

Leave me, and let bread with salt taste pleasant, O God,
Let the waters of the earth from earthenware jugs be sweet to me,
And let me be not struck dizzy by the strong and bitter wine of
God,
Let not my restful sleep be disturbed by a mocking dream
Of untilled heavenly corn, of magical corn, unsown
With the tear of toil and hope upon black soil!

(Oh that otherworldly wine! I smell its sharp scent—
To the sewers and filth does the intoxicant cast me,
Abandoning [me] as a target for stones of hatred, and to the cry
of arrogance.
Oh, dream of heavenly corn, lying mirage!
Empty-handed does it send me away, empty-handed does it set
me
At foreign gates, hungry and constantly begging!)

Again have You besieged me. Everything round me is dark.
This sign comes back again and again . . . woe,
Again am I called to You for a loving talk—
Leave me alone! Let there be light! Raise up Your sun, O God!
I want to come no more, I do not want to hear!

And Jacob Awoke

'And Jacob awoke from his sleep, and said: Surely the Lord is in
this place, and I did not know. And he was afraid, and said: How
terrible is this place. This must be the house of God, and this the
gate of Heaven' (Gen. 28:16, 17).

Joyful and light of step did I leave the house of my father.
My youth cheered my path from pace to pace
At heartbeat rhythm, and wreathed round above my head
Was the distant firmament in bright purple.

As the lambs of my father in the plain of Beersheba and its
         meadows
Did the clouds, bright with faith, accompany me from a broad
         height.
Every shadow blessed my arrival, the vista burnt me sweet-
         smelling incense,
And I knew that I would see my happy birthplace wherever I
         turned.

The day poured its good wine into me, poured it with singing
And at eventide, my body sank to rest, heavy with restful drink—
Like a heavy, full jug when it is lowered with a sure hand
Slowly and surely from a sturdy shoulder.

And the stone at my head was as tender to me as sheep's wool
Before the shearing, and night, like a secure tent,
Took me into its silence, so that once again into the hands of the
         ways
He should hand me at dawn, descending from the crags.

With a prayer of thanks: 'How pleasant you are, O world, how
         beautiful you are to me!'
And with an expectant smile: 'The good of the morrow is still
         plentiful!'
I fell asleep until the dream, and after it—
God was standing over me so exalted and terrifying.

Now that I am awake, I know: I was not here alone
With the joy of the sight of my eyes, with my expectation of the
         future,—
The large, demanding eye of God has set its ambush for me here.
It (I do not know why) watches my step.

And this landscape that yesterday fondled me with its kind ways,
Is, alas, no more a nest of happiness for mankind—
It is a gate to Heaven, a ladder to their terrifying angels,
A trap set by God for me, and a far-ranging ambush.

And this landscape has been given to me, not as pasture is
given
To innocent looking sheep, not as bread for the consumer.
When I clutch the bosom of my earth—I am reminded with
trembling:
It is a gate of Heaven, a ladder to the unseen!'—

And when I rejoice at the stalk of the field, and moisten the clods
here
With the sweat of labour, with tears, and the libation of my
hopes—
As upon his prey, does the Awful one descend immediately
upon me:
'Cease to grovel in the earth! Rise, ascend to the stars!'

(The stars! Last night, everything in me was quiet and slept
As they twinkled to me, so quiet and good,
And I said: These distant things demand nothing . . .
But now I fear, I understand: this is not the case—)

I fear you, O ladder of God! Constantly ascending and descend-
ing,
And always, unceasingly in this great hollow of a sling
Between Heaven and Earth, to be slung from here to there,
To be rejected by both, and to bear the yoke of both!—

Is it for this that I went out? Is it for this that every path
Lured me, and called me? Oh God, steeped in mysteries,
You promised me great things—and they are very frightening,
And Your generous promise casts terror into me!

I fear You, my great benefactor, I fear You, O aweful Presence!
I sought a human inheritance: a song for the heart, a sight for
the eye,
Stones of rest, a crust in hunger, and in thirst—a jug of water,
Vistas for longings, the shelter of a tent in storm.

It was to seek love that I left the tents of my father in the South
For Padan Aram, but I have not yet found it—
Though I espied the light of its face from the light of the sky's
                                                             face
And felt its touch in every bush and clod here.

But now the heavens have grown heavy of a sudden over my
                                                             head,
The earth scorches my feet, burns them painfully,
Every path and track in it bites the heel like a serpent!
I awoke stiffened with great matters, but bent, afraid and
                                                        orphaned—

No more will rocky couches be tender to my back.
The way does not cause its countenance to shine upon me, nor
                                         the morrow—its horizon,
To the tribulations of the future I go out from here
Prisoner of subjugating Destiny, and bound by the word of God.

Jonah flees from his God

'And Jonah arose to flee to Tarshish from before the Lord . . .
and the Lord cast a great wind into the sea, and there was a great
storm . . .' (Jonah 1:3, 4).

You have found me, O my God. Between the sea and the sky
                           has Your tempest caught up with me.
Alas, I did not ask: 'Can a man flee his shadow, or can a tree
Tell its roots: Let go of me, my children of darkness,
That I, the stock, alone and without you, may wander far off!'—
Now I know: there is but one way by which a man is brought to
                                                        his Fate,
And there are seventy-seven by which he may flee—though not
                                                         escape.

I thought: A man may lie down and sleep in the recesses of a boat,
And not be the son of Amitai,* who is too weary to sustain his
truth,
Not Jonah, whose burden burns inside him like a fiery coal,
And whose vision walks over him terrifyingly like a howling
flock of jackals—
But just a person with no yoke, with no double world or life,
A bundle of dust and ashes, living restfully on a floating cradle of
waves,
A person, never bothered, regarding people and nations
As one regards the stars, whose course never changes.
But now Your tempest has caught me! And I know not which is
angrier,
My heart, held in Your palm, or this sea raging in its fury
To assault the boat, because it has offered refuge to a man,
Who, from the womb, was destined to be without refuge.

Oh my God, God of my heart, my persecutor, why do You
impose so upon me?
Answer me, what have I taken with me that would be lacking
when I flee?
Why do You seek occasion of me? Is the key of the whole universe concealed with me?

Will the sun not rise and set in its time without me,
And will the world's sounds be silenced when I am silent?**
Will the earth cease its produce, and the trees not bear their fruit
If I do not bear my burden?
Why do You pursue me? From every wave does Your voice roar
to me:
'Return and prophesy, Jonah, return, and proclaim my word as
yours!'

* Play on the Hebrew 'emet' meaning 'truth'.
** I.e. do not prophesy.

No, I shall return no more, O my God! I swear that I shall speak
                                                        no more!
I shall flee! Though I know that my pursuer and persecutor is
                                                        inside me!
I shall go far from my continent, not wanting any more to be
                                                        a mediator
Between God and man, between Earth and Heaven
And a constant target for the arrows of both together!
I no longer want to be slung constantly between the two of them
                                                        as in a sling
Without knowing which of them I belong to, and what I am
                                                        doing with them,
That I get neither the corn of the land, nor the choice fruits of
                                                        Heaven!

I no more wish to be an unwanted thing on your earth,
On the earth from which I was taken, on the earth that I have
                                                        loved.
Release me! If I am contemptible in Your eyes when I walk with
                                                        You contrariwise
Who am I that there should be a storm through me? And what
                                                        can my presumption be worth
That you stir the depths of the sea and the humming army of its
                                                        waves for this?
And if I am very dear to You—Why do You not let me go free,
                                                        O my God,
Without Your yoke that bends my life and draws it with its
                                                        weight
To the terrifying depths?
I shall not continue to be what I have been since Your hand
                                                        rested on me!
And if I am mourned, and it is said: 'Vision has been closed up
                                                        from Jonah,
The spirit of God has left Ben Amitai!' Would that this were so,
                                                        it would not matter!
As for those who would mourn me thus—did they not only
                                                        yesterday

When I bore my word to them, send the tongue of their scorn
                                                against me:
'What babbles that man, drunk with speech, that he works his
                                        lips so arduously?'
As I despise their mockery, so is their mercy a foul thing to me,
                                        and an abomination!
And as for Nineveh—it is to be entirely my worry? Let it sin as
                                                it pleases!
As I tasted not of the wine of its sins, and thirsty and empty with
                                                hunger
I would wander in it when its evil table was so full—
So not a crust will touch my lips from the bread of its righteous-
                                                ness!
I know its righteousness! As a horse intent on the race goes back
That it can increase its dash and the rate of its locomotion seven
                                                times,
So does Nineveh cease to sin, in order to add two sins on the
                                                morrow
For every single sin of yesterday.
Let Nineveh sin, let it live, rejoice, and also perish for its sins!
Is this not its fate? Has it not been destined for this?
I am tired of being a vain mark and an ineffective stumbling
                                                block
To an immovable, eternal law!

I swear that I shall not go back, O my God! Is there nowhere
                                amongst the crannies of Your world?
A retreat and a refuge for me as well, as there are cities of refuge
For every murderer?
Why should You withhold sanctuary from a man who has mur-
                                        dered his peace of mind,
And thrown its pieces to others who have not sought it?
Is there not a corner, O my God, where I could, like the tree of
                                        a field, suckle
Your light above in silence, and the darkness of Your earth below,
Where I could bend my head with the changing times at the
                                wind of your torrents?

Is there not amongst the stones of Your fields a headstone, on
                                                          which
I could put my head at eventide, to the echo of the paces of
                                                departing day,
That I might sleep without the terrors of dreams, and without
                                the dread of a vision of the future?
Let me flee there, to a landscape where I know nothing
Besides the kindness of the transient, and the pick of the grape
                                gleanings of its vintage.
Oh, cease from me! Every rising wave, like a titanic arm,
Exalts itself against me in its wrath, in order to grasp me, and
                                                          turn me back.
But I have decided of myself: I shall return no more, O my God!

Rise, O storm, and swell, wrap me round and cast me to the
                                                          depths
Like a discarded, trampled stone, as an anonymous mariner is
                                                          destroyed!
Let waves finish me in their anger, let the great deep swallow me—
That I should no more be Jonah-ben-Amitai in the land,
Servant of God and His truth, bound to the train of His splendour,
Who is dragged in the dust of the earth.

LIKE A TEMPLE-LAMP

Like a temple-lamp does my body stand before you in the night,
My two embracing arms—two reeds!
Love and desire,
From one lamp-pedestal both rise,
And one is my soul that pours into the oil for the light.[1]
And one are you who kindle both
As one.
Still there is much oil for the light in my soul—
My reeds are full.
And in your kindling hand how great still is the fire!
Night! Draw the curtain[2] over your temple entrance.[3]
The two of us within your sanctuary are acting the priest.[4]

*　　*　　*

This is a previously unpublished poem,[*] and the only love-poem that Lamdan ever wrote. But the technique with which we have become familiar in Lamdan's poetry is still in use. Language from a sacred or ritual context is transferred to another—in this case, to the act of love, and thus makes of this act a sacrament.

The poem immediately establishes the situation in a ritual context, both in the title and in the first words. The body is compared

1. The imagery is taken from Exodus 35:14, as is much of the imagery of this poem.
2. This 'curtain' is a ritual object covering the holy ark.
3. The image is adapted from Exodus 15:15—where the 'door of the tabernacle' is spoken of.
4. The phrase in Isaiah 61:10 probably means 'put on a priestly turban', but it is probable that

Lamdan did not understand or use it here in this sense. The Isaiah passage speaks of a bride and bridegroom adorning themselves, thus giving the reference added point in this love scene.

* This poem is now seeing the light for the first time, with the kind permission of Lamdan's widow, who has the manuscript.

to a temple lamp. The apparent dualism of the personality represented by the two arms, and the two elements of love and desire,
derive from one source—'from one lamp-pedestal', and from one
soul. They are also kindled/inflamed by one person—'and one are
you who kindle both as one'. There may be two forms of expression
—but they are still, ultimately, a unity.

Still much oil/fuel remains in the ritual lamp, and still much fire
remains to be kindled within the beloved. Night is invoked—night
is the traditional setting of the act of love—and requested to draw its
curtain over the temple entrance. It is as if they are performing a
secret holy ceremony. The act of love is transformed and trans-
muted.

LAMDAN'S MANUSCRIPT OF THE POEM
'LIKE A TEMPLE-LAMP'. See page 247.

BIBLIOGRAPHY

(Works referred to in the course of this study)

Agnon, S. J., *Oreaḥ natah la-lun* (Jerusalem, 1950)

Ahad Ha'am (Asher Ginsberg), *Writings* (Tel-Aviv, 1947)

Altermann, N., *Kokhavim ba-ḥuẓ* (Tel-Aviv, 1938)

Altermann, N., *Simḥat 'aniyyim* (Tel-Aviv 1953, 4th ed.)

Amihai, Y., *Ba-ruaḥ ha-noraah ha-zot* (Tel-Aviv, 1961)

Aristotle, *Poetics* (O.U.P. 10th reprint, London, 1959)

Auden, W. H., *Collected Poetry* (London, 1945)

Band, A., *Nostalgia and Nightmare* (California, 1968)

Bedell Stanford, W., *Greek Metaphor* (Oxford, 1936)

Beer-Hoffmann, B., 'Halom Ya'akov' in collection of plays *Yisrael ve-yi'udo* (Tel-Aviv, 1954)

Bein, A., *Toledot ha-hityashevut ha-ẓiyyonit* (Tel-Aviv, 1945)

Bein, A., *The Return to the Soil* (Trans. of above by Israel Schen, Jerusalem, 1952)

Ben-Or, A., *Toledot ha-sifrut ha-ivrit bedorenu* (Tel-Aviv, 1954), Vol. 1

Benshalom, B., *Hebrew Literature between Two World Wars* (Jerusalem, 1953)

Berdichevsky, M. J., *Collected Essays* (Tel-Aviv, 1952)

Bialik, H. N., *Devarim she-be'al peh* (Tel-Aviv, 1937), Vol. 2

Bialik, H. N., *Poems* (Tel-Aviv, 1944)

Bodkin, M., *Archetypal Patterns in Poetry* (London, 1935)

Brenner, J. H., *Collected Works* (Tel-Aviv, 1928), Vol. 7

Brenner, J. H., *Selected Works* (ed. Poznanski, Tel-Aviv, 1953), Vol. 1

Brown, S. J., *The World of Imagery* (London, 1927)

Cassell, *Encyclopaedia of Literature* (London, 1953)

Clemen, W. H., *The Development of Shakespeare's Imagery* (London, 1951)

Cohen, I., *Le-shirato shel Shlonsky* (in *Moznayim*, Vol. 5, p. 561, Tel-Aviv, 1937)

Day-Lewis, C., *The Poetic Image* (London, 1946)

Dryden, J., *Selected Poems* (London, 1926)

Dryden, J., *Preface to Shakespeare* (London, 1679)

Dujardin, E., *Mallarmé* (Paris, 1936)

Elbogen, I., *A Century of Jewish Life* (Philadelphia, 1946)

Eliot, T. S., *Collected Poems, 1909–1935* (London, 1936)

Empson, W., *Seven Types of Ambiguity* (Peregrine Penguins, 1961)

Florinsky, M. T., *Russia, a History and an Interpretation* (New York, 1958), Vol. 2

Garton, H. F., *Modern German Drama* (London, 1959)

Goldberg, L., *Pegishah 'im meshorer* (Tel-Aviv, 1952)

Goldberg, L., *'Al haperihah* (Tel-Aviv, 1948)

Gordon, A. D., *Writings* (Jerusalem, 1952), Vol. 1

Gordon, Y. L., *Writings* (Tel-Aviv, 1953)

Graetz, H., *History of the Jews* (Philadelphia, 1891), Vol. 2

Greenberg, U. Z., *Kelapei tish'im ve-tish'ah* (Tel-Aviv, 1928)

Greenberg, U. Z., *Sefer ha-kitrug ve-ha-emunah* (Tel-Aviv, 1937)

Greenberg, U. Z., *Ha-bagrut ha'olah* (Tel-Aviv, 1926)

Halkin, S., *Modern Hebrew Literature: Trends and Values* (New York, 1950)

Halpern, Y., *Ha-mahapekhah ha-yehudit* (Tel-Aviv, 1961), 2 vols.

Hameiri, A., *Anthology of Poetry* (Tel-Aviv, 1962)

Hazan, L. and Palar, Y., *Divre yemei ha-ziyyonut* (Jerusalem, 1951)

Hazaz, H., *Avanim rotehot* (Tel-Aviv, 1946)

Hazaz, H., *Sippurim nivharim* (Tel-Aviv, 1952)

Heller, J., *The Zionist Idea* (London, 1947)

Hough, G., *Image and Experience* (London, 1960)

Hulme, T. E., *Speculations* (London, 1924)

Johnson, S., *Preface to Shakespeare* (London, 1765)

Josephus, *The Jewish War* (ed. G. A. Williamson, Penguin Books, 1959)

Jung, C. G., *Contributions to Analytical Psychology* (Bristol, 1928)

Kermode, F., *The Romantic Image* (London, 1957)

Ketuvim (per.), *Steinmann and Shlonsky* (ed.) (Issue 27.11.27, No 59, Tel-Aviv)

Kurzweil, B., *Massekhet ha-roman* (Tel-Aviv, 1953)

Kurzweil, B., *Sifruteinu ha-hadashah-hemshekh o mahapekhah* (Tel-Aviv, 1959)

Kurzweil, B., *Bialik ve-Tschernichowsky* (Tel-Aviv, 1961)

Kurzweil, B., *Hatoda'ah ha-historit be-shirei Lamdan* (in *Molad*, Issue 19, Tel-Aviv)

Lamdan, I., *Masada* (10th ed., Tel-Aviv, 1961)

Lamdan, I., *Ba-ritmah ha-meshuleshet* (Berlin, Tel-Aviv, 1930)

Lamdan, I., *Bema'aleh 'aqrabbim* (Tel-Aviv, 1944)

Lamdan, I. (ed.), *Gilyonot* (monthly—Tel-Aviv, 1934)

Leavis, F. R., *New Bearings in English Poetry* (London, 1932)

Lestchinsky, J., 'Jewish Migrations 1840–1946', in *The Jews* ed. Finklestein (Philadelphia, 1949) Vol. 4

Milton, J., *Poetical Works* (London, 1874), Vol. 2

Miron, D., *Arba' panim ba-sifrut ha-'ivrit bat yamenu* (Tel-Aviv, 1962)

Muller, M., *Three Lectures on the Science of Language* (London, 1891)

Murray (ed.), *New English Dictionary* (Oxford, 1883)

Patai, R., *Israel between East and West* (Philadelphia, 1955)

Penueli, S. Y., *Demuyot besifruteinu ha-ḥadashah* (Tel-Aviv, 1946)

Penueli, S. Y., *Ḥuliyoth basifrut ha-'ivrit ha-ḥadashah* (Tel-Aviv, 1953)

Pope, A., *Collected Works* (London, 1871), Vol. 3

Poznanski, M. (ed.), *Meḥayyei Joseph Trumpeldor* (Tel-Aviv, 1945)

Rayson, T. M., *Coleridge's Shakespearean Criticism* (London, 1930)

Richards, I. A., *The Principles of Literary Criticism* (London, 1930)

Rodker, J., *The Future of Futurism* (London, 1926)

Roth, C. (ed.), *Standard Jewish Encyclopaedia* (Jerusalem, 1958)

Rottenstreich, N., *Ha-maḥashavah ha-yehudit ba-'et ha-ḥadashah* (Tel-Aviv, 1952), Vol. 1

Sdan, D., *Dyokan*, essay in *Molad* (Tel-Aviv, 1954, Issue 7)

Shaanan (ed.), *Millon ha-sifrut ha-ḥadashah* (Tel-Aviv, 1954)

Shalom, S., *Panim el panim* (Jerusalem, 1941)

Shimoni, D., *Idylls* (Jerusalem, 1957)

Shlonsky, A., *Yalkut Eshel*—a prose anthology (Tel-Aviv, 1960)

Shlonsky, A., *Collected Poems* (Tel-Aviv, 1965), 2 vols.

Shmueli, M., *Ha-ẓiyyonut u-tenu'at ha-'avodah* (Tel-Aviv, 1942), Vol. 2

Silberschlag, E., *Saul Tschernichowsky* (East and West Library, London, 1968)

Sonne, A. (Ben-Yitzhak), *Poems* (Jerusalem, 1957)

Spurgeon, C., *Shakespeare's Iterative Imagery* (London, 1931)

Sturgeon, C., *Shakespeare's Imagery and what it tells us* (London, 1939)

Stein, L., *The Balfour Declaration* (London, 1961)

Steinmann, E., *Be-sha'ar ha-vikkuaḥ* (Tel-Aviv, 1933)

Taupin, R., *L'influence du Symbolisme Français sur la Poésie Américaine 1910–1920* (Paris, 1929)

Tschernichowsky, S., *Poems* (Tel-Aviv, 1968)

Tindall, W. Y., *The Literary Symbol* (Indiana University Press, 1955)

Umen, S., *The World of Isaac Lamdan* (Philosophical Library, New York, 1961)

Vogel, D., *Collected Poems* (edited and introduced by D. Pagis, Tel-Aviv, 1966)

Weizmann, C., *Trial and Error* (Bristol, 1949)

Wellek, R., and Warren, A., *Theory of Literature* (London, 1949)

Wilson, E., *Axel's Castle* (Fontana pub., London, 1962)

Wordsworth, W., *Collected Poems* (Oxford, 1954), Vol. 1

Zemorah, L., *Sifrut 'al parashat dorot* (Tel-Aviv, 1949), Vol. 2

INDEX